TRADE
WAR

TRADE WAR

GREED, POWER, AND INDUSTRIAL POLICY ON OPPOSITE SIDES OF THE PACIFIC

STEVEN SCHLOSSSTEIN

CONGDON & WEED, INC.

NEW YORK

Copyright © 1984 by Steven Schlossstein

Library of Congress Cataloging in Publication Data

Schlossstein, Steven.
Trade war.

Bibliography: p.
Includes index.
1. United States—Commerce. 2. Japan—Commerce.
3. Industry and state—United States. 4. Industry and state—Japan. I. Title.
HF3031.S37   1984   382'.3'0973   83-24081
ISBN 0-86553-104-8
ISBN 0-312-92824-6 (St. Martin's Press)

Published by Congdon & Weed, Inc.
298 Fifth Avenue, New York, N.Y. 10001
Distributed by St. Martin's Press
175 Fifth Avenue, New York, N.Y. 10010
Published simultaneously in Canada by Methuen Publications
2330 Midland Avenue, Agincourt, Ontario M1S 1P7

All Rights Reserved
Printed in the United States of America
Designed by Irving Perkins
First Edition

FOR
MARTHA, MY MISTRESS,
AND
MASHIKO, MY MUSE

Foreign trade is a war in which each party seeks to extract wealth from the other.

—Honda Rimei, Tokugawa philosopher, 1744–1821

Free trade is the hypocrisy of the export interest, the clever device of the climber who kicks the ladder away when he has attained the summit of greatness.

—Charles P. Kindleberger, *The World in Depression, 1929–1939*, 1973

Eighty years ago, Japan was compelled to open her doors to Europe and America. Small-scale industries of Japan could not stand the competition of Western goods which were produced with superior machinery. Consequently, they all ceased to exist. That is history.

Japan was then told that free trade was a means whereby the common welfare of mankind was promoted. By discarding industries which did not suit her and by concentrating on those best suited to her, she has now attained that stage where some of her industries are superior to those of the old industrial countries. But as soon as Japan begins competing with them, she is condemned in the name of humanity.

—Asahi Isoshi, *The Secret of Japan's Trade Expansion*, 1934

CONTENTS

PART IV:
INDUSTRIAL POLICY. (WHAT?)
INDUSTRIAL POLICY. (LOUDER, I CAN'T HEAR YOU.)
INDUSTRIAL POLICY!

PART I

THE SEEDS OF WAR

CHAPTER I

THOSE LITTLE YELLOW PEOPLE

Soothed out of the depths of sleep by your Sony Slumber-Magic clock radio, you pad into the kitchen and switch on the Sanyo coffee machine, which automatically grinds the beans, brews the coffee, and keeps it hot until you're ready to drink it.

Then you toss a few orange quarters into the Panasonic food processor and tap an electronic touchplate that instantly commands the machine to make juice. Or maybe you have a Cuisinart. It doesn't matter, it's also Made in Japan.

You glance at your Seiko quartz wristwatch. Got to get moving, or else the traffic will be unbearable. You switch on your small kitchen TV, the Pioneer Mini, to catch five minutes of sports and weather while you down your breakfast. Then you set the Toshiba telephone answering machine to take any calls that come in while you're at work.

Back upstairs, you wrestle out of your pajamas and into your shirt, made of the finest batiste cotton. You glance at the label. Japan.

Your Honda starts instantly. It should. Its quality is unsurpassable. You back out of the garage and head downtown. As you wait for an opening onto the freeway, you watch the cars stream by.

Datsun. Chevy. Mustang. Peugeot. *Toyota.* BMW. Buick. Chrysler. *Mazda.*

And then it hits you.

One out of every five cars is Japanese.

As you listen to the news on the car radio, one item attracts your attention. Former Vice President Walter Mondale, front-running candidate for the 1984 Democratic presidential nomination, is addressing a group of unemployed autoworkers. There's a lot of chanting and angry noise in the background. You turn up the volume as you slow down to let a trailer truck go by.

Mondale's familiar voice is at the microphone now. "We have got to get tough," he says, "and I mean really tough. If you try to sell an American car in Japan, you better have the United States Army with you when they land on the docks."

3

The union loves it. They roar their approval. Lots of potential votes in Detroit.

"We've been running up the white flag," Mondale shouts over the boisterous crowd, "when we should be running up the American flag. What do we want our kids to do, sweep up around the Japanese computers and spend a lifetime serving McDonald hamburgers?"

The crowd goes nuts. Democrats and union workers go together hand in glove, but Democrats and *unemployed* union workers are as thick as flies and honey.

You change the station.

"The United States intends to file a full-court press to open Japanese markets to a broad range of American goods," a new voice reports. "Senator Jack Danforth, Republican of Missouri, says the root of the problem is that American markets are generally open, those of Japan generally closed tight to imports. What's needed is a clear policy, and tough minded."

On the third station you try, Michigan Democratic Representative John Dingell is being interviewed. He quotes the latest trade statistics: a $50 billion deficit worldwide for the United States in its merchandise trade account, and nearly $20 billion of that is attributable directly to Japan.

"There's only one reason our automobile industry is hurting," the Michigan Democrat says. "Those little yellow people."

You snap off the radio in disgust. *What's going on here?* you wonder. Japanese products have helped me fight inflation, improve my standard of living, and redefine the meaning of quality. Yet my politicians are bringing back memories of Pearl Harbor.

Why?

Shades of the Past

This is a book about trade.

A whole generation of Americans grew up in an era when the United States was the biggest kid on the block: the largest GNP in the world, the highest per capita consumption, the strongest currency, the best technology, the richest in natural resources, the most food, the most churches, the most country clubs, the most everything.

During that time, in the immediate postwar years and continuing through most of the 1960s, America could do anything. Launch an artificial satellite, create the wealthiest society in history, put a man on the moon, make the world safe for freedom and democracy.

The terms bilateral trade deficit and double-digit inflation and devalued currency were as foreign to this generation of Americans as outdoor toilets, breadlines, and Smoot-Hawley. Consequently, our businessmen got used to winning rather easily, and you don't have to go back very far to remember the fears of our European friends as American capital came streaming onto the Continent, bringing cornflakes to the Old World.

It was a time when no matter what we did or failed to do brought us growth, wealth, and success.

In today's vernacular, we were number one. There wasn't another team in the world that could even come close. How could they? Their players were mostly dead, their playing fields destroyed, their coaches old and tired. It was a perfect setup. We made the rules and said, in effect, you only have to run half as far and score a third as many points and we'll tie one arm behind our backs to give you a sporting chance.

American companies made so much money during this period that American management techniques were studied to find out how we did it. Europeans flocked to the Harvard Business School to learn the case study method. Armies of Japanese businessmen swarmed through American steel plants and automobile factories and machine tool companies to pick our brains.

We could do nothing wrong.

Or could we?

Exports as an Indicator of International Industrial Competitiveness

This is also a book about Japan and how the Japanese have outpaced us with competitive exports in world markets. And why.

"Neither has Japanese ambition been content with those fields of industrial activity, where natural advantages counterbalanced the lack of experience, organization and capital," the learned English scholar Basil Hall Chamberlain wrote in 1895. "Doubtless, Japan is passing from the agricultural into the industrial stage, and she may look forward to a bright future, with China's huge market at her gates. Nevertheless, so far as our own mills and factories are concerned, we see little reason for alarm at the prospect of competition in this quarter."

Well, Dr. Chamberlain was wrong in 1895, just as Representative Dingell was wrong in 1982. In fact, few saw reason for alarm at the prospect of competition from the Japanese until their Hondas and Sonys and cold-rolled steel started displacing our Chevys and Zeniths and

Pittsburgh's finest. Even then, America's basic response has been to find ways to keep Japanese products out of our market rather than find ways to make our own goods more competitive.

Until 1970, in fifty years of foreign trade, America had never run a merchandise trade deficit. Since 1973, our cumulative deficit has reached over $300 billion. In 1982, our merchandise trade deficit with Japan alone was more than $20 billion.

A merchandise trade deficit means you import more than you export—you buy more than you sell. Which means somebody else is getting all that money, not us.

One reason is that we are not very export-minded. It is easier for us to sell to Chicago than to Japan. We export only about 6 percent of our GNP in merchandise trade. The Japanese export about 12 percent. The Germans export about 23 percent. Perhaps that's why the Germans speak more languages than we do.

To encourage American companies to export more, Congress passed the Export Trading Company Act in 1982. If Japanese trading companies were successful, Congress figured, American trading companies could be so, too. But Japanese trading companies—those billion-dollar international brokers, with names like Mitsubishi and Mitsui, who intermediate practically everything from iron ore and grain to heavy-duty earth-moving equipment and high-speed letter-quality printers—have been around for over a hundred years. So nothing much happened, despite the new law. Trading companies, also prevalent in Europe, are another foreign concept to us.

Since 1953, American export growth has been only about 6 percent a year, whereas total free-world trade has expanded at a rate of over 7 percent a year. Total manufactured goods exports have grown even faster, at a rate of 7.8 percent a year, but the United States hasn't kept pace. We creep along at a rate of around 5 percent. That's a rate you want for mortgages, not for manufactured goods exports.

Merchandise trade is to manufactured goods trade as corn and molasses are to Datsuns and Mazdas.

The primary reason our merchandise trade has been growing faster than our manufactured goods trade is because we sell a lot of wheat and soybeans. Especially to the Japanese, who are our number one customer.

The primary reason foreign manufactured goods trade has been growing faster than our manufactured goods trade is because their products are more competitive than ours and frequently better. Especially those of the Japanese.

In 1955, America had a global market share of manufactured goods

PRINCIPAL PRODUCT EXPORTS, UNITED STATES, 1982
($ million, CIF basis)

CATEGORY	AMOUNT	% OF TOTAL	% TO JAPAN
Food & Live Animals	23,953	11	16
Grains & Cereals	14,746	7	14
Crude Materials	19,248	9	21
Soybeans	6,240	3	17
Machinery & Transp. Equip.	87,148	41	5
Machinery	59,324	28	5
Special Purpose	13,024	6	5
Transport Equip.	27,823	13	4
Aircraft	13,725	6	7
Total These Categories	130,349	61	9
Total Merchandise Exports	212,275	100	10

SOURCE: U.S. Department of Commerce, Bureau of the Census, Foreign Trade Division, *Highlights of U.S. Export and Import Trade*, December 1982.

exports of over 25 percent. Not a lot of foreign competition back in those days. We were number one.

By 1980, our total market share had dropped to 15 percent. Who was eating our lunch?

You guessed it. The Japanese. Their share of this pie had increased from 3.4 percent to over 11 percent in the same period. Nor had the Europeans done too badly, having jacked up their share from 26 percent to 36 percent.

Well, so what, you say. We're a service economy now, with over 70 percent of our GNP in hamburgers and health care. The reason those other countries still export so much is they haven't reached the post-industrial stage of development yet.

Economies grow and mature, just as human beings do. They have an infant phase, called agriculture. Then they go through adolescence, or the industrial stage. Then they reach maturity and become post-industrial economies, symbolized by the McDonald arch.

Postindustrial economies don't make cars and television sets and steel anymore, they make hamburgers and silicon chips and shampoo. And they buy their cars and TVs and steel from industrial economies, like Germany and Japan.

PRINCIPAL PRODUCT EXPORTS, JAPAN, 1982
($ million, FOB basis)

CATEGORY	AMOUNT	% OF TOTAL	% TO UNITED STATES
Manufactured Goods	**31,100**	22	24
Iron & Steel	15,645	11	25
Machinery & Transp. Equip.	**78,069**	56	35
Non-Elec. Machinery	20,317	15	63
Elec. Machinery	19,718	14	47
Transport Equip.	38,033	27	38
Cars	18,015	13	55
Misc. Manufactured Goods	**18,723**	13	19
Scientific/Medical	4,842	3	9
Cameras & Lenses	1,388	1	53
Audio & Video Equip.	6,163	4	78
Total These Categories	**127,892**	91	30
Total Merchandise Exports	**138,831**	100	29

SOURCE: Government of Japan, Ministry of Finance, 1982
Statistics.

But even though America is in its postindustrial senescence, manufactured goods exports still account for 11.3 percent of our manufacturing employment and over 18 percent of the net output of our manufacturing sector. At latest count, 1.2 million jobs in manufacturing were directly related to exports. Another 1 million Americans produce components and spare parts for exports, and *another* 1.3 million supply materials and services for exports.

So we have 3.5 million people in this country whose jobs depend on exports. And it could be more if we were as serious about selling to Japan as we are to Chicago. The Wharton Business School at the University of Pennsylvania has estimated that a million new jobs would be created for every $15 billion increase in our manufactured goods exports.

Why have our exports lagged so badly in comparison with other countries?

Our politicians would have us believe it's not our fault. It's the Japanese who keep our products out of their market by cunning Oriental devices known as nontariff barriers, infant-industry protection, and product-certification standards. After all, we run a trade surplus with Western Europe, so the Europeans don't keep our products out. And we have traditionally run a global surplus in services, so we must be doing something right.

But the answer is not that simple. It's not only because we are not export-minded, but because our productivity growth has been the most languid of any industrial country in the postwar era, our product quality has not kept pace with our competitors, our technological advances have slowed, our currency has behaved like a patient in intensive care, our research and development expenditures as a percentage of GNP have dropped, and because we're more interested in money than we are in market share. We can scarcely compete anymore in our own domestic market, let alone Japan's.

So our politicians respond by trying to protect our beleaguered industries. Over the years, the International Trade Commission has been petitioned for import-injury relief from, among others, footwear, mushrooms, bicycle tires and tubes, motorcycles, automobiles, steel, honey, fresh-cut flowers, asparagus, slide fasteners, and bolts, nuts, and large screws of iron or steel.

"It's not our fault," is the traditional response. "Keep the cheap foreign goods out." In the old days, we used tariffs and quotas and cumbersome customs clearance procedures. GATT—the General Agreement on Tariffs and Trade—has changed all that. Today, we use orderly marketing agreements and voluntary export restraints and complex duties to countervail predatory dumping charges.

So what ever happened to free trade?

The Legacy of Smoot-Hawley

Otto von Bismarck knew what free trade was all about. He said free trade is the weapon of the dominant economy anxious to prevent others from following in its path.

Dr. Kindleberger refined this. Charles Kindleberger is a well-known international economist from MIT who is to international economics what Tom Landry is to professional football.

"Free trade is protection for the established exporter," he once wrote. "Most tariffs are not to shield an infant in youthful and adolescent years, but to defend an adult one approaching senescence. The vested interests are usually industries which are beginning to lose out to competition from imports."

We have lots of industries that are losing out to competition from imports. You read about them every day in the newspaper, under such headlines as "Widening Trade Gap." Or you hear about them on TV as another auto plant or steel factory is shut down.

Many years ago, Dr. Kindleberger established a link between Smoot-Hawley and breadlines.

Smoot-Hawley is not a word that automatically jogs the memory like Stutz Bearcat or Nixon-Agnew. Smoot-Hawley was *the* tariff act of 1930. There was no General Agreement on Tariffs and Trade in those days, so when cheap foreign imports threatened American economic well-being, Congress got right to work.

At the time, our farmers were threatened, not our manufacturers. Italian olive oil and Spanish wine and Portuguese Madeira and Greek olives were flooding into the country. Congress decided our farmers needed some temporary protection, so it passed the Smoot-Hawley Tariff Act of 1930, which raised tariffs on olive oil and wine and Madeira and olives and just about everything else.

Because once the protectionist bandwagon started rolling, everybody wanted to jump aboard. What was good for the farmers might also help the chemical companies, our congressmen thought, so they jacked up tariffs on imported resins. And what was good for the chemical companies might also help the textile industry, so they raised tariffs on imported yarns. A thousand economists petitioned President Hoover not to sign the bill, saying other countries wouldn't buy from us if they couldn't sell to us. But he signed anyway. Congress had the votes.

The economists, for once, were right. Foreign governments weren't about to take this lying down. They retaliated. Rome, for example, slapped unheard-of duties on American automobile imports, which put GM, Ford, and Chrysler out of business in Italy by November 1930.

The vicious cycle was underway. Foreign trade shrank like unsanforized underwear every year for the next eight years. Breadlines were the result.

But it's not Italian olive oil anymore, it's Japanese automobiles. And it's not Spanish wine, it's Japanese steel. And it's not Greek olives, it's Japanese semiconductor chips.

So Candidate Mondale gets a roar from the autoworkers, and Senator Danforth wants to put a full-court press on the Japanese, and Representative Dingell would like to slap those little yellow people around.

Worried, I called Dr. Kindleberger. The spectre of a contemporary Smoot-Hawley bill was just too frightening.

"Easy," he said. "In economics, things equal to the same thing are equal to each other. In politics, appearances count a great deal."

Were the chances of more protectionist legislation strong?

"Frankly, I'm scared," he said. "I used to think the risk of another major deflation was maybe fifty-fifty. Now I'm up to about fifty-two and a half."

A equals B equals...

Something Dr. Kindleberger said reminded me of those basic econometric equations, the ones with the Greek letters turned on their sides. But this was a simple equation: things equal to the same thing are equal to each other.

$$Y = A + B$$

Simple enough. Now all we have to do is define A and B.

$$A = C + I$$
$$B = X - M$$
So $$Y = (C + I) + (X - M)$$

Fine. Except what do all those letters mean?

If C stands for consumption, and I is investment, and X is exports, and M is imports, and Y is our national income, then the economists say our national income equals consumption plus investment plus exports minus imports.

If both A and B go up, then our national income goes up.

If A (consumption plus investment) goes up and B (exports minus imports) goes down, then A has to rise faster for our national income to go up.

But B is going down.

Why is B going down? Because, for one thing, our merchandise trade imports are increasing faster than our merchandise trade exports.

Is A (consumption plus investment) rising faster? If it is not, then our national income must be decreasing.

It's all M's fault. We're simply buying more than we're selling.

Because things equal to the same thing are equal to each other, we can also write this equation another way.

$$B = Y - A$$
Or $$(X - M) = Y - (C + I)$$

Exports less imports equals national income minus consumption and investment. So if B is a negative number, then $(Y - A)$ must be a negative number. Which is the economist's way of saying that merchandise trade deficits are a drag on our national income. All those dollars flying to Tokyo to pay for cars and to Riyadh to pay for oil.

The classical economists had it easy. There was this free-trade model based on the principle of comparative advantage, which the British economist David Ricardo established back in the early nineteenth century. He said each country will tend to export those products the comparative costs of which are cheaper at home than abroad. And import those products the comparative costs of which are lower abroad than at home.

So if the Japanese make Toyotas cheaper than we make Chevys, we will buy Toyotas and the Japanese will buy...Toyotas.

Oops.

Well, two more economists came along from Sweden, Eli Heckscher and Bertil Ohlin, and they revised the theory in the 1930s to state that comparative cost differences are based on differences in "factor endowments." Each country tends to have a comparative advantage in, and to export, those goods requiring in their production the factor in relative *greatest* supply in that country, and to have a comparative disadvantage in, and to import, those goods requiring in their production the factor in relative *scarcest* supply in that country.

Factor endowments are things like land, labor, and capital.

America had lots of capital, and Japan had lots of labor. So America should tend to *export* capital goods, thought Heckscher and Ohlin, and Japan should tend to *import* capital goods. Well?

Japan exports Toyotas and imports...*wheat*?

It took another economist to figure out what was going on. Wassily Leontief of Harvard sat down in the early 1950s to test the Heckscher-Ohlin theory. Through his input-output tables, he determined the capital and labor requirements for a given bundle of our exports and imports. Assuming that the United States was a capital-abundant country, he reasoned, Heckscher-Ohlin would predict that its exports would tend to be relatively capital intensive and its imports labor intensive.

The results of Leontief's study indicated the reverse.

America exported labor-intensive goods and imported capital-intensive goods. Which is why we sell wheat and corn and soybeans to the Japanese, and buy Toyotas and Canons and Sony video tape recorders from them.

What's wrong with that, you ask?

Nothing, except that it's the traditional pattern of an underdeveloped country to supply natural resources and raw materials to an advanced industrial economy, only in this case, America is fulfilling the role of the underdeveloped country. And that's partly why our politicians are upset. They aren't happy seeing the United States as an Indonesia or a Brazil. It's the Japanese who are supposed to be underdeveloped. Also, wheat and corn and soybeans are not subject to learning curve product cost reductions, like manufactured goods; they are what the economists call price and exchange-rate inelastic: people have to eat, regardless.

But what our politicians don't realize is that America is no longer such a rich country. And Japan is no longer so poor. Much of our wealth has been transferred to the Japanese through the medium of exports and imports. *Their* exports and *our* imports.

"The root of the problem lies deeper," wrote the editors of the *Harvard Business Review* in a recent book called *Survival Strategies for American Industry*. "Where American industry has fallen short is in the strategic determination—and the ability— to make excellence in manufacturing a primary competitive weapon. As we all have too good reason to know, domestic producers of tires, cameras, motorcycles, televisions, radios, machine tools, autos and a host of other products, have suddenly found themselves faced with shrinking market shares and aggressive foreign competitors with a knack for turning out goods at low cost and high levels of quality."

It's even worse than that. Nearly half of all U.S. manufactured goods exports simply go to foreign affiliates of American companies. And Japanese trading companies alone account for 10 percent of all American merchandise exports, including manufactured goods, worldwide. Japanese cars now have a 20 percent share of the American market, and Japanese steel has a 10 percent share of the American market, and the Japanese make half of all the TV sets in the world.

The Japanese save more than we do, and they invest more than we do, and they sell more aggressively in world markets than we do. And for various reasons that we shall consider, they regard foreign trade as the commercial equivalent of war.

Well, we don't regard foreign trade the same way as we do our national defense.

So a central theme of this book is not that we are in danger of having a trade war. We have already been fighting one. Only the Japanese realize it, and we don't.

CHAPTER 2

DOWNSIZING THE AMERICAN DREAM

When the patient is sick and in the hospital, you don't go stomping around in the corridor.

—Amaya Naohiro, former MITI Vice
Minister for International Affairs,
quoting an old Japanese proverb

Automobiles were not the first shot fired in the trade war between Japan and the United States. Textiles were, back in the 1950s, when the spectre of dollar blouses flooding into our market from Japan made American textile industry executives see red.

So a trade war has been raging between the two countries for nearly twenty-five years. Textiles was just the first battle. Color television sets came next. Steel was third. And *then* autos.

Everything in the American auto industry was in good shape until a small group of oil-exporting countries got together in the late 1960s and gave Uncle Sam a smart kick in the shins. Oil was selling at a little more than $2 a barrel (that's forty-two gallons); America had a network of interstate highways that, if laid end to end, would take you to the moon and back; and Detroit's famous two-ton, eight-cylinder gas guzzlers were getting, oh, maybe twelve miles a gallon. Who needed more when gasoline was only 39.9?

But the oil exporters wanted a bigger cut of the oil revenues, the royalties, and a little more power to deal with the Seven Sisters, who had pretty much dominated the international oil industry in the postwar years, so they formed themselves a new fraternity. They called it the Organization of Petroleum Exporting Countries, or OPEC* for short. As they wanted to be strong, the group modeled itself after another fraternity that had achieved good things for its members—the Texas Railroad Commission.

*See p. 261 for a list of the various acronyms and abbreviations used throughout.

Until the Arabs got power hungry, few paid much attention to the small-car market. Volkswagen was the dominant name throughout the 1950s and 1960s with its popular Beetle model, and VW owners proudly thumbed their noses at the big Detroit buggies.

As recently as 1965, the total U.S. market share for imported cars was only 6.1 percent. The Japanese market share was only 0.2 percent. That year, three out of four cars sold in America had eight cylinders, weighed more than two tons, and used lots of gas.

Because our energy policies encouraged driving, we were paying only 39.9 a gallon, whereas the Europeans and the Japanese were paying approximately three times more for theirs. A gallon of gasoline in Tokyo in the late 1960s cost well over $1. When you don't have your own oil, you tend not to waste it. And to harbor your supply, you tax it and develop light, four-cylinder, fuel-efficient cars. Japan imports nearly all its oil. Like 99 percent.

By 1971, as foreign imports into the American market took a 15 percent share, the Japanese reputation for quality and dependability began to grow. The Japanese gathered up over 6 percent of the total market that year, and Detroit reintroduced four-cylinder machines into their product mix to slap away those pesky flies. Remember the Pintos and Novas? In fact, 7 percent of Detroit's production in 1971 consisted of compact cars. But by then, over 80 percent of Detroit's models had those huge eight-cylinder engines. The American compacts stole not from the eights but from the sixes.

For a very simple reason. The big eight-cylinder cars were Detroit's cash cows. As one Detroit executive put it at the time, "Shrinking the size of cars came hard, because it implied cutting back on the most profitable models."

But there was a second reason Detroit cited for not building a smaller car sooner. "The public didn't want it."

Now when Detroit automobile executives talk about "the public," they usually mean Bloomfield Hills, a rich suburb outside Detroit where the executives all live. Joseph Kraft once described it well in one of those long *New Yorker* articles. "The auto industry is not in close touch with the city (Detroit) or with the people who live there," he wrote. "It is not in touch with the people who live in other cities. The industry talks to the industry."

So when a Detroit executive says the public didn't want a small car in 1971, you have to wonder who he was talking to.

The president of General Motors was even more precise: "The challenge of foreign imports...reached its peak in 1959."

But one out of every six people in America was buying small cars in 1971, not including the few that Detroit made, and nearly half of them were buying Japanese cars. If the handwriting was on the wall across the country, why wasn't it being read in Bloomfield Hills?

Because the industry talks to the industry.

In 1973, the figures were almost identical. The foreign import market share slipped slightly to 14.6 percent, and the total Japanese share was 6.7 percent. Now, 81.5 percent of Detroit's production consisted of those giant eight-cylinder gas guzzlers. What a year! New auto registrations reached a postwar peak as 11,350,000 people bought new cars.

But 1973 was the beginning of the end.

On October 15, OPEC put restrictions on oil exports to the United States; by Thanksgiving, a new phrase had entered the American vernacular: gas lines. By January 1974, the price of a forty-two-gallon barrel of crude oil had quadrupled to $11.65, and although OPEC removed its export limits in May, it was clear what had happened. The era of cheap oil was gone.

Or was it? In 1975, foreign imports surged to over 18 percent of the market, with the Japanese accounting for more than half of them. Still, 72.6 percent of Detroit's production continued to be heavy cars. But the green flag was out.

By 1977, the real price of oil had declined in the absence of OPEC price escalations and foreign imports had stabilized at around 18 percent of the market. The Japanese share now stood at 12.9 percent as they pushed their smaller, more fuel-efficient cars aggressively, and for the first time in years, Americans began to see some technological innovations: transverse-mounted engines and front-wheel drive. The last technological innovation from Detroit had been automatic transmission in the 1930s.

But in January 1979, gas lines reappeared as Ayatollah Khomeini deposed the Shah of Iran and cut off oil shipments to the American devils. This time, even Bloomfield Hills sat up and took notice. By the end of the year, foreign imports had taken 23.9 percent of the U.S. market; 16.6 percent was Japan's. General Motors had gotten its act together, too. The X-car materialized and helped Detroit boost production of four-cylinder cars to nearly 20 percent of their total, but not without cutting into the cash cows, which dropped to 59 percent of production.

By 1980, all the pieces were in place for another battle in the trade war. Foreign imports took 26.7 percent of the market, and the Japanese share had ballooned to 21.3 percent. The Japanese now had *80 percent* of the foreign-car market in the United States. And as Detroit's production slipped to just over eight million vehicles in 1980, Japan overtook the United States as the world's leading automaker. They built over eleven million cars that year.

All the milk from those eight-cylinder cash cows suddenly turned to blood. Detroit was hemorrhaging. Although General Motors was still in relatively good shape after strong years in the mid-1970s, following its introduction of the X-car, Ford and Chrysler were not. The only money Ford was making came from its foreign operations, and Chrysler was seeking a federal bailout. The Big Three lost $4 billion in 1980.

In May of that year, the United Auto Workers, who by then had seen their union membership drop by over 300,000 workers to a new low of 1.25 million, joined forces with Ford and Chrysler in petitioning the International Trade Commission for relief from injury sustained by the growing surge of Japanese imports into the American market. It was clear to them that Tokyo was to blame, not Bloomfield Hills.

President Carter, running for reelection in November, tried to pressure the ITC into a quick decision. Fifty U.S. senators signed a letter to the commissioners recommending their decision be made before the manadatory six-month period expired. There were more votes in Detroit than in Tokyo.

In November, after the election was over and Ronald Reagan was the new American leader, the ITC ruled three to two that "Japanese automobile imports were not causing serious injury to the American automobile industry. The economic downturn and shift in consumer tastes to smaller, fuel-efficient cars were greater causes of the troubles plaguing Detroit."

Commissioner Paula Stern summed up the majority decision: "After the two great oil crises of the last seven years and the perceived quality deficiencies of the domestic autos, the U.S. market changed significantly, and imports were in a position to benefit. We should not blame the messenger for the bad news."

The Cracker Jack Company agreed. Right after the ITC decision was announced, they put five coupons good for Mazda station wagons into their boxes of candied popcorn as a Super Toy Surprise Campaign. But convenient scapegoats, like sacred cash cows, die hard.

DOT Says Current Difficulties of Auto Industry Pose Security Threat

Statistics for the American automobile industry are hard to put into perspective, but some of the following numbers may at least suggest what's at stake.

In 1980, Detroit accounted for 8 percent of manufacturing (what economists call nonresidential, nonfarm) employment, or 15 percent of total manufacturing employment including parts and service. In that year, our automobile industry took 57 percent of the total synthetic rubber output in this country, 53 percent of total malleable iron production, 45 percent of all oil, 29 percent of all flat glass produced, 22 percent of all steel, 20 percent of all machine tools, 15 percent of all aluminum, 15 percent of the consumer's household budget, 12 percent of all copper, and 3 percent of all electronics production.

By 1980, Japan's trade surplus with the United States was nearly $8 billion in autos alone.

In 1949, there were 49,000 car dealers in America. By 1980, only 22,000 were left.

The UAW organized in 1935, brought GM to its knees in 1937 and Ford and Chrysler four years later. It reached its peak in 1974 with over 1.5 million members. By 1982, union membership had dropped to less than 1 million.

The U.S. Department of Transportation estimated in 1980 that the switch to small, front-wheel drive production in the United States would require $70 billion in new capital investment by the Big Three between 1980 and 1985. In the prior decade, a total of $50 billion had been invested in the automobile industry worldwide.

The DOT also estimated that 45,000 industrial robots, those steel-collar workers, were employed worldwide in 1980, 80 percent in Japan. Each robot had an eight-year useful life, cost $4.80 an hour to operate, worked sixteen hours a day, replaced two human welders, and would eliminate 20 percent of direct labor costs by 1985. Message to Bloomfield Hills: a lot of human welders weren't coming back to work.

In 1977, the hourly compensation cost for an American autoworker averaged $11.45, just under half of which was for fringes: vacation, sick leave, medical benefits, and pension. Japanese autoworkers made $4.82 an hour, of which about 15 percent was for fringes.

By 1982, the American autoworker had become what former MITI Vice Minister Amaya Naohiro called America's labor aristocrat: he made $19.65 an hour, of which two thirds now went toward fringes. Wages in the U.S. auto industry were at a 50 percent premium over the general industry average, and some unemployed autoworkers who had signed up for retraining programs in other industries simply quit when they learned how little they would be making compared to their former wage scales. That same year, the Japanese were getting paid $7.24 an hour, of which 17 percent now went toward fringes.

In 1970, American carmakers had about 200 models for sale. By 1980, they were making 370 different models. And over a third of these were still the large cars.

Union absenteeism in the American auto industry averaged 3 percent in the 1950s and doubled to 6 percent in the 1980s, peaking at *15 percent* on days preceding weekends or holidays. According to a 1981 Harvard Business School study on the industry in transition, "Disciplinary problems were partially responsible for the American auto industry's poor rate of productivity growth." Lordstown, Ohio, became synonymous with Blue-Collar Blues. Beer cans got welded onto the chassis of certain cars, and our labor aristocrats worked with their heads in clouds of marijuana and hashish. The word went around fast: don't buy a car made on Friday or Monday.

The American automobile industry was indeed sick. Economists call this phenomenon "declining international industrial competitiveness," and it had nothing whatsoever to do with trade. Washington complained that Japan kept Detroit's large cars out of their market by means of various tariff and nontariff barriers. But Detroit couldn't even sell its monsters in our domestic market, let alone overseas.

The day of the small car had arrived.

"What's Mine Is Mine, and What's Yours Is Half Mine"

How had the Japanese done it?

Quintessentially American, the automobile industry is like the cowboy. Americans perfected the internal combustion engine. We invented the assembly line. We put cars into mass production and made them available at reasonable prices to the average consumer. Our industry dominates employment figures across the board. Consequently, we get upset when somebody shoots us out of the saddle.

Professor William J. Abernathy of Harvard University, a specialist in auto industry problems, testified before a Senate subcommittee in January 1981 on the seriousness of the patient's disease. His testimony summarized the advantages that the Japanese had taken away from their American competitors over the years.

By 1980, no Japanese plant was older than fourteen years. They had made continued investment in state-of-the-art equipment, emphasizing higher and higher productivity. They enjoyed a $1200 to $1800 landed cost advantage over comparable domestic U.S. cars, offering a limited number of styles and models in the subcompact sector. Domestic shipping distances for spare parts rarely exceeded one hundred miles.

"Centralization of production enabled the Japanese to capture economies of scale and learning curve experience," Dr. Abernathy said, "while downplaying shipping and inventory costs." The Japanese industry used eight thousand supplier firms, fifty of which controlled 60 percent of the market, and most belonged to a major automobile "family." (In 1872, when Japan's first trade commission went abroad to survey foreign techniques, they returned with the view that close-knit groups would be more effective than adversarial units, so they pushed the family concept of industrial organization.)

The Japanese actively solicited technological licenses in the United States and Europe, buying over a thousand by 1980. Small-parts companies acted as subcontractors and delivered components to larger firms, who incorporated them into subassemblies and sent them on to the final assemblers. There was strong emphasis on price competitiveness and quality: there were no inspections of subassemblies at the plant. If problems developed, then the automaker would send a team to the supplier to work them out. Advanced components technology got a big shot in the arm, and plant and process inventories were kept trim. For example, inventories of heaters and radiators were kept to one hour. The U.S. average was eight days.

In 1977, Toyota received 460,000 quality control suggestions from its workers, of which 86 percent were adopted by the company—an average of 10 per employee. Shop workers were able to stop the assembly line and look for defects under self-check and quick-inspection programs. Their straight wages were perhaps 20 percent above the national average (compared with over 50 percent for their American counterparts); by 1980, their total compensation was about half that of their American competitors. Half their wages were paid in the form of straight salary, the other half in semiannual bonuses of two to five months' salary linked to productivity and performance.

Between 1965 and 1975, Japan's overall production of automobiles *tripled*, but direct employment increased by only half. Company unions, affiliated with the National Automakers Union but strongly loyal to their principal employer, emphasized cooperation and harmony over the antagonism and confrontation that had characterized union-management relations in America from inception. Absenteeism averaged less than 1 percent, the Japanese autoworkers welcomed productivity-enhancing technological change to preserve long-term employment, and they followed the old Confucian tradition of socializing together to strengthen the corporate "family."

In short, Japan's strategy was to have more economically efficient capacity in place than its foreign rivals. The Japanese knew the automobile market was global.

By the early 1980s, more American specialists were coming around to share Tokyo's view. During the three-year period 1980–1982, nearly *one hundred* separate reports were commissioned on the American automobile industry, its international industrial competitiveness, and its position in world trade—from an MIT report titled "The Financial Restructuring of the World Auto Industry" to a lengthy paper prepared by the Committee on Technology and International Economic and Trade Issues of the National Academy of Engineering called "The Competitive Status of the U.S. Auto Industry: A Study of the Influences of Technology in Determining International Industrial Competitive Advantage."

Everybody wanted a report on the patient.

And they all reached pretty much the same conclusion the ITC had in November 1980: Japan was not to blame for the drop in industrial competitiveness of the American auto industry. High labor costs, fuel-inefficient engines, expensive inventories, an unwillingness to invest in state-of-the-art plant and equipment, and, above all, an inability to make a quality small car, all played a role.

Even GM's president James McDonald had to admit that their X-cars were plagued with uneven doors, shabby paint jobs, and other problems that did not match the quality standards of the Japanese. But what to do? Washington's best idea was a Band-Aid: all the patient really needed was a little tax and regulatory relief and he would be all right. But the ITC itself had estimated the cost of putting an American autoworker back on the assembly line through protective tariff increases at $100,000 per man per year!

So much for hard facts. Now for the political reality. The Japanese were perceived as causing massive unemployment in the American auto industry with severe ripple effects across those numerous industry sectors that depended on automobiles for their livelihood. Iron. Steel. Machine tools. Aluminum. Glass. And in politics, of course, perception is reality.

Never mind that Detroit tried to sell its big cars in the Japanese market with the steering wheel on the wrong side of the car. Never mind that all three major American automakers had capital tie-ups with several Japanese firms and sourced an increasing number of their own components in Japan because they couldn't meet quality standards or domestic demand from their own production facilities. And never mind that the Big Three had had the domestic market entirely to themselves throughout most of the postwar period.

Something had to be done.

Item: Unemployed autoworkers began to take matters into their own hands. Just outside Bloomfield Hills, one laid-off union employee grabbed his Winchester and took a few potshots at passing Toyotas.

Item: A group of union workers in Detroit organized a raffle, bought an old Datsun, and sold hits with a sledgehammer for a buck a smash.

Item: Representative Dingell of Michigan took to the microphone and accused "those little yellow people" of being responsible for the problems in our auto industry. Senator Gore of Tennessee grabbed another microphone and said those same little yellow people were putting two thousand unemployed citizens of his state back to work in the new Datsun truck factory at Smyrna.

So former Vice President Walter Mondale made his famous speech about sending the U.S. Army to Yokohama to help our beleaguered automakers sell their two-ton, eight-cylinder, wrong-sided monsters in Japan.

And Senator Jack Danforth called for a full-court press on the Japanese. The bilateral deficit was getting out of hand. Senators Danforth and Bentsen introduced legislation designed to restrict Japanese market share to a specific level, to send a strong "signal" to them. Secretary of Commerce Baldrige stated that the U.S. government wasn't going to sit idly by and watch Ford and Chrysler go under.

Despite the ITC ruling, in early spring 1981 the U.S. trade representative, Ambassador Bill Brock, hammered out an agreement with MITI whereby the Japanese "voluntarily" agreed to limit their automobile exports into the U.S. market to 1.68 million units a year, beginning April 1. These restrictions were called Voluntary Export Restraints, or VERs. They were to last no more than three years, through March 31, 1984, and were to be renewable annually.

The Japanese automakers were furious. Not only with the concept of VERs but also with MITI. Amaya Naohiro coached the MITI team and was Brock's counterpart during the negotiations.

Everybody learned something. The United States learned the hard way that the Japanese had not been responsible for Detroit's problems, but it was simply unacceptable politically for the Japanese market share to expand further. Their cars were all over the place, and too visible.

MITI learned they could no longer control their industry participants, as had been the case twenty-five years earlier. MITI never did have the kind of historical influence over its automakers that it had with the steel and chemical industries, and earlier forced mergers were successfully resisted by the auto people. MITI had to play hardball both with Brock *and* with the Japanese auto companies.

Nor could the Japanese automakers go stomping around the corridors when the patient was sick. But that didn't stop their asking how long the doctors thought it would take the patient to get well.

Three years, came the reply.

Three years?

Look, if it took Bloomfield Hills twenty years to realize the era of the small car had finally come, how long do you think it will take Detroit to start making them? *At least* three years.

So the Japanese reluctantly agreed. The 1.68 million figure was based on market share data for 1980. The Japanese had 21.3 percent of a 9.9 million new-car market that year, which should have entitled them to a 2.1 million ceiling. But the domestic market was declining, not expanding, and a compromise figure had to be reached, so the Japanese agreed to a 7.7 percent reduction in their 1980 share. But they insisted on, and got, percentage increases for the second and third years based on growth rates for the U.S. domestic-car market overall. As it turned out, these proved of no value. Sales by the domestic producers continued to plummet.

Even with a 1.68 million unit ceiling, the Japanese made out like bandits. For what happens in cases like this, when to all intents and purposes you have an export quota, even though it may euphemistically be called a Voluntary Export Restraint, is that the exporters level up. That is, they begin shipping more of the top-of-the-line cars with the higher sticker prices (such as Cressidas and Camrys) and fewer of the smaller, less expensive models, shifting their overall product mix but staying within the 1.68 million limit. MITI, playing referee, monitored intraquota levels among the producers.

Beyond giving the U.S. auto companies a three-year breathing space, during which time they would presumably regroup, retool, and make strides at becoming more competitive again, the VER was also designed to cut into the growing bilateral trade deficit between the two countries.

But look what happened.

In 1980, our bilateral merchandise trade deficit with Japan totalled $10.4 billion. In 1981, $15.8 billion. In 1982, $16.9 billion.

Ford's president Philip Caldwell summed up the Bloomfield Hills position: "This country cannot afford the continuing exploitation of our auto market by the Japanese." Caldwell's plan, which the UAW endorsed, was to roll the Japanese back to nine hundred thousand units a year for five years.

The Japanese automakers responded by arguing they were helping the American consumer fight inflation and high fuel prices. And they would be damned if the VER would be extended beyond March 31, 1984: three years was more than enough time for Detroit to regroup. Sure enough, by summer 1983, as the oil glut caused another drop in gasoline prices, the Big Three began making money again—on their large models, not on sales of smaller cars.

But damned, they were. On November 1, 1983, MITI and the USTR agreed to a one-year extension of the VER through March 31, 1985, expanded to 1.85 million units. Chrysler had opposed a short-term extension, arguing they still had not had time to retool. GM was silent;

its Toyota joint venture hung in the air, awaiting an antitrust ruling. And the Japanese automakers reluctantly realized it would not be smart to derail the U.S. economic recovery by flooding the American market with their cars after April 1. But as a quid pro quo, the Japanese this time insisted there would be no further renewals.

The voluntary restraint agreement had restricted Japanese auto imports without a quid pro quo from either the Big Three or the UAW. The effect of the VER, as the *New York Times* put it, was to place an inflationary sales tax increase on consumers.

In fact, the real loser was, indeed, American consumers. They were deprived of a greater number and selection of smaller, lighter, more fuel-efficient Japanese automobiles. But although consumers spend, and drive, and vote, they are seldom well organized.

And they are no match for Bloomfield Hills.

MITI's House Theorist

Amaya Naohiro entered the Ministry of Commerce and Industry, MITI's predecessor, in 1948, on graduation from Tokyo University. During his thirty-five-year MITI career, Mr. Amaya served as director of the important International Economic Affairs Department of the International Trade Policy Bureau and as director-general of the Agency for Natural Resources and Energy.

In 1962, as assistant chief of the General Affairs Section, he wrote the first of several internal papers that would lead to his becoming known as MITI's House Theorist. It was called "What Do the Times Require of Us?" and argued strongly in favor of "public-private cooperation," a policy line put forth by certain senior MITI officials that pushed further conversion of Japan's industrial structure from heavy industries to higher added-value, technology-intensive manufacturing. But some of his superiors thought the young Amaya was being too pushy, so they sent him overseas to the consulate in Sydney to cool down.

After he returned to Tokyo, in 1969, he wrote another position paper, "Basic Direction of the New International Trade and Industry Policy." This became known as "the second Amaya thesis." In it, he argued that the ministry should answer the public who were calling for less high-speed growth for growth's sake. Mr. Amaya felt Japan was already shifting from an industrial society to a postindustrial one and would, therefore, require changes in policy direction every bit as monumental as those away from an emphasis on heavy industries that had begun many years before.

This new transition would (1) emphasize robot-operated factories, (2) "verticalize" Japanese companies engaged in high-tech assembly operations, (3) revolutionize industrial technology, and, most important, (4) coax Japan into the emerging "knowledge-intensive" industries: aviation, computers, and space technology.

Early in 1980, Amaya was promoted to Vice Minister for International Affairs, a post directly under the Vice Minister, the highest position to which a career bureaucrat at MITI could aspire. He was also the coach of MITI's auto-negotiating team. Late in 1980, I met him for the first time.

We sat in his office at MITI together with two assistants who took copious notes. This is standard practice. There is probably a greater institutional memory within the Japanese government than anywhere else in the world. I began with an apology for my Japanese, as nearly five years had passed since I had lived in Tokyo. He laughed and said his English could also be better, which was a tactful (and very Japanese) thing to say. Mr. Amaya's English is fluent.

I mentioned ITC and the auto dispute.

Amaya divided the airspace in front of him into two imaginary blocks and explained U.S.-Japan relations before and after 1973. "The pre-oil shock era was the age of Pax Americana," he said. "The United States was easily able to provide the free world with six fundamentals."

He edged forward on his chair and ticked the six off on his fingers.

"One was values. It meant American democracy, the free-enterprise system, and, as a way of life, the American lifestyle of driving cars, having electric appliances, and drinking Coca-Cola.

"Two, security. America provided an umbrella for both Europe and Japan.

"Three, low-cost oil. The American oil majors gave the world an abundant supply of oil, at a low price, from its discovery until the Arabs organized OPEC.

"Four, food. You got us and the Europeans through a nightmare after the war with your ample food supplies.

"Five," he said, rolling the fingers of his right hand into a fist, "technology. What we know, and have applied in our steel, automobile, and electronics industries, we bought from America.

"And six," he said, a sole left finger propped in the air, "GATT, the IMF, the UN, the World Bank, and Bretton Woods. America provided the fundamental economic order for the free world and gave it both moral and financial support."

Mr. Amaya leaned back in his chair and ran a hand through his shock of snow-white hair. He was small even for a Japanese, with an angelic face that belied his fifty-three years. As he had been MITI's hit man for steel and autos, it was no wonder his hair was white.

"After the oil shock, all this changed," he continued. "The dollar declined, American values were shaken by the Vietnam War and by Watergate, the oil majors lost their pricing prerogatives, and American supremacy in technology sputtered to a halt. You could no longer provide these fundamentals. World economic institutions also lost some of their influence, and trade frictions took on a new look."

So how did that spawn the phenomenon known as Jap-bashing, I asked.

"What used to be disputes in labor-intensive industries, such as textiles, turned into disputes in technology-intensive industries, such as steel, consumer electronics, and automobiles. The earlier frictions were easier to resolve. But Americans began to see their own values and security threatened. High-technology industries represent the nucleus of a country. Frictions in these industries directly affect a nation's pride, unlike the disputes in labor-intensive industries years before."

I mentioned that Japan was a dirty word in Detroit now and that it was better not to be caught driving a Toyota around the streets of Bloomfield Hills. How did he perceive the problems of our auto industry?

"American industry and labor union leaders seek to stall Japanese exports of small cars because they fear that during the few years necessary for the American auto industry to tool up for small-car production, a substantial share of their market may be captured by Japanese automakers," he said. "The U.S. auto companies are still very powerful competitors, I think, and once they have retooled, we will find it tough to compete again. The Americans think the Japanese auto companies are stronger than they actually are, just as they perceive their economy to be stronger than it actually is."

What was Amaya's position on direct investment by Japanese companies in the U.S. market? Could Japan expect to go on exporting forever?

"Obviously not," he said, and then he smiled. Amaya has a very disarming smile. "The basic posture Japan should take in the future is to observe our own proverb: the strong walk on tiptoe. In mahjong, there is nothing wrong with one player winning every game. But he does so at the risk of being excluded from the game the next time around."

I mentioned some Americans had taken the view that young Japanese would no longer continue the hard work ethic of the past, that some softening was inevitable: five-day workweeks, four-week vacations. America's postindustrial problems could haunt the Japanese as they had us. Would the Japanese succumb to the pleasures of a leisure lifestyle?

"We may not work as hard in the future as we have in the past," he said, leaning forward and sipping his tea. "But I frankly doubt we will imitate your experience with leisure. It's all relative. I think it will not be difficult for us to maintain our edge in productivity growth because the future belongs more and more to automation. In additon, we face a rapidly diminishing work force ourselves, as our birthrate stabilizes and the number of young people out of the primary sector continues to decline. You realize that 80 percent of the industrial robots in the world are being used in Japan."

I nodded, feeling just a little depressed. My hunch was that even if we doubled the number of industrial robots in the United States over the next couple of years, Japanese robots would still work harder than ours.

On parting, Mr. Amaya gave me a copy of one of his recent papers, in Japanese. It was called "U.S.-Japan Trade Friction and Mercantilism: Militarist America and Mercantilist Japan." It dealt with America's proven supremacy in military weaponry and Japan's growing superiority in commercial technology.

After he retired from MITI in late 1982 to become an advisor to the ministry, that paper together with several of his other recent articles, such as "Japanese Logic and Western Logic: Rethinking Anti-Japanese Criticism" and "History of the U.S.-Japan Love-Hate Relationship: Killing the Protectionist Bug," were collected and published in Japanese under the general title *Japan, Inc.: Our Remaining Options.*

The House Theorist never lets up.

CHAPTER 3

THE MEN IN MAROON

It is much harder to nullify the results of an economic conquest than those of a military conquest.

—Takahashi Korekiyo, former Japanese Minister of Finance, 1936

Automobiles. Symbol of America's decline from a position of industrial supremacy in the 1950s and 1960s to one of relative weakness today. Outdated plant and equipment. Wage rates out of line with the rest of American industry. Management philosophies out of touch with reality. Unemployment nearing Depression-era levels.

Instead of taking a deep breath and looking systematically into our own problem areas, we turn to scapegoating and fingerpointing as a way out of our current dilemma. Because there are more Japanese products around to scapegoat and because the Japanese represent an Asian culture with a racial minority in this country, they are an easy mark.

So what has happened to the American fighting effort, the ability to innovate, new game plans, belt-tightening, the Frontier Spirit? And how did the Japanese come so far, so fast?

Discipline

"This can't be Japanese 101," I whispered to the young black-haired woman on my left as I squeezed into a small wooden chair. I glanced around at the dozen Japanese students listening and nodding to the professor's words, meaningless to me, a beginning language student in the University of Hawaii's graduate program in Asian Studies. "Got to be an advanced course."

She shook her head, her eyes never leaving the blackboard. "You're in the right room," she whispered back out of the corner of her mouth.

"Elementary Japanese." Opening her book, back to front, she showed me a page of meaningless *kanji*.

My chair squeaked as I shifted, and the professor's dark eyes fixed immediately on me.

"*Dai ichi peiji o yonde kudasaimasenka?*" he asked, walking toward me, gesturing with his chalk.

"Sorry...?" I asked in return, and glanced back nervously at the woman beside me for a hint, any hint, as to what I should say.

She covered a smile with her hand. "He said, would you mind reading the first page aloud?"

Taking her cue, I opened my book, and stared down at the maze of ideographs splashed across the page like iron filings on a magnet. Swallowing, I looked up.

The professor's eyes narrowed. "Won't you even try?" he asked, in English this time. His voice was a mixture of disbelief and scorn.

Try? I asked myself, glancing down at the book. Try what? The stuff was illegible.

Looking back up, I shook my head. Then I swallowed again. Reaching under the desk, I wiped my sweaty palms on my jeans.

The professor's eyes, cold and black and tunnel deep, burned with intensity. Neither of us smiled.

"Miss Sawada?"

The young girl on my left raised her book and recited the page effortlessly. "This is a tree. It is bamboo. Over there is a river. It is below the mountain. That is a rice field...."

The professor's eyes bored through me as he listened to Miss Sawada read from our elementary text. I returned his stare, unblinking. We sized each other up like two tomcats in an alleyway. It was a moment I would never forget.

The month was September, the beginning of another school term. The year was 1964. A few thousand advisors had been sent to Vietnam, scarcely back-page news. The St. Louis Cardinals, buoyed by the brilliant pitching of Bob Gibson, would face the Boston Red Sox in the World Series. And the Tokyo Olympiad had just launched Japan into the world's consciousness, their women's volleyball team winning a gold medal and the hearts of millions.

I sat through my first hour of intensive Japanese waiting desperately for the bell. It had to be the wrong class. Somehow the scheduling was screwed up. What was I doing in with a group of advanced placement kids, each matching stride with the prof?

He was erasing the blackboard as I approached his desk after class. "Professor...?"

"Kugimoto," he said, turning around to face me now. "Tokyo University." He pulled a cigarette from his pocket and lit it. Then he extended a hand. I shook it.

"Schlossstein," I squeaked. I cleared my throat. "May I ask if there's been a scheduling error?"

He inhaled a lungful of smoke and blew it out through his nose. "You're in the right class," he said. "Beginning Japanese." He smiled for the first time.

I swallowed again. "But these girls," I said. "How come—?"

"*Sansei*," he said. "Third-generation Japanese-American. They grew up with Japanese at home."

"And they're taking *elementary* Japanese?" I asked.

Professor Kugimoto nodded as he collected his papers. "Shall we go?"

We stepped out into the cool trade winds, heading for his office across campus.

"Language requirement," he continued. "They're undergraduates. That's why they take the intensive course."

"And you're gearing the pace to their ability level?" I asked, slowing my gait to match his shorter stride. "Christ, I'm the only round-eye in the class."

He stopped and took a final drag on his cigarette, flicking the remains behind him as he looked me in the eye. "That just means you'll have to work harder at the beginning," he said. "But you can do it, if your discipline matches your desire."

I shifted my books to my left hand and flexed my fingers. "Tomorrow's assignment?" I asked. "How about a hint, in English?"

He laughed. "Sorry," he said. "I'll give you the assignments on a sheet of paper so you can prepare. But the classroom discussion will be entirely in Japanese. For tomorrow, I want you to memorize the entire *hiragana* phonetic alphabet. We'll start with a written quiz."

I swallowed again. "All forty-six symbols?" I asked, frowning.

He nodded. "And for Wednesday, the whole *katakana* alphabet," he went on. "You have to know these before you start on the *kanji*."

"Right," I said. "I hadn't realized we'd complete all two thousand current-use characters by Christmas."

We laughed, together this time, spontaneously.

"I've seen your German scores," he said as he turned to head up the stairs to the white stucco building. "Remember, Japanese is just another foreign language. If you've mastered one, it gets easier the second time around."

I propped a foot on the first step and squinted up at him, shading my eyes from the bright sun. "I think that applies to other European languages," I said.

"But the discipline is the same." Kugimoto paused. "*Hiragana*," he repeated, his voice lower now. "Tomorrow." He disappeared inside.

Discipline. It was a concept that would take on a new meaning for me in the years to come.

Zama

It was one of those idyllic January mornings in Tokyo, the sun lazy and warm in a clear, windless sky. Not exactly shirtsleeve weather, but so springlike as to make an overcoat unnecessary.

I shot a glance at my watch as I stood in front of my hotel. It was just 7:30. Footsteps approached to my left.

"*Schlossstein-san desu ka!*"

"*Hai*," I said, turning to face a bowing form. I bowed in return.

"Tsukatani. Pleased to meet you." We exchanged name cards. "I will escort you to Zama."

The Zama plant of the Nissan Motor Co., Ltd., was perhaps the most visited automobile factory in the world. Streams of engineers, bankers, politicians, union officials, and just plain writers went to see it first-hand, principally to watch those famous industrial robots automatically spotwelding and assembling what the rest of the world still did by hand.

This was my third try in a year's time. So many people are whisked through the plant, from Southeast Asia to South Wales, that considerable advance planning is necessary. Tsukatani and I climbed into a small black Nissan sedan. It gleamed like marble. The driver eased the car into traffic, already heavy with morning commuters, and headed south, toward the Tomei expressway.

Tsukatani Takuro was a young member of Nissan's International Division. American-educated and with a doctorate in industrial engineering, his previous experience, unusual for a Japanese, included several years of statistical work for the European Community office in Tokyo. For a representative of corporate Japan, his hair was modishly long and swept back over his ears.

We crawled out of Tokyo. I watched the opposite line of cars, on the right, inching into the capital city as the rush hour neared its peak.

It was a sight at once symbolic of industrial supremacy and industrial plight. Japan was now the automobile king of the world, with annual production exceeding eleven million units a year, greater even than the United States in its heyday. Not capacity, but actual, physical production. And just as America had experienced clogged roadways and saturated streets, Japan was now emulating its once-benevolent brother.

True, the country exported nearly half its total production (and more than half of that went to America), yet the domestic Japanese market still absorbed the lion's share. And there they all were, sitting, idling, creeping slowly ahead, burning those precious gallons of Middle East politics.

I strained to catch a look at the once-historic landscape of the great Tokaido road, but in vain. For just as the traffic was bumper to bumper on the highway, the buildings were cheek by jowl in what was left of the countryside. The view was further blocked by enormous sheets of soundproofing material erected, wall-like, along both sides of the expressway, which gave the impression of driving through a roofless tunnel. It was one massive industrial belt, a Miracle Mile without the Miracle.

At about 9:30, after twisting and turning through the narrow streets of Zama city, we arrived at the plant. I glanced at the driver's odometer. We had travelled eighty kilometers. Fifty miles. In two hours. The car got approximately forty miles to the gallon. That was 1.25 gallons of gas, at $3 a gallon; put the tab at $3.75 for the way down and $7.50 round trip. Two fifty a head. Cheap. The equivalent trip on Japan National Railways would have set us back about twice as much. Somehow that didn't seem quite right. It ought to have been the other way around.

Whirr. Zap. Chunk.

After a brief lecture on the plant's layout by one of the Nissan staff, we were each given a pair of Captain Marvel safety glasses and walked through one of the assembly lines.

Rows of Sentras and Stanzas, suspended from their overhead hooks, crept along as quick-moving technicians, identically clad in clean maroon overalls with the bright Datsun insignia on back, outfitted them smartly with shock absorbers, brakes, gas tanks, dashboards, seats, and doors.

It was so quiet in the central assembly building that we could carry on a normal conversation without raising our voices. In Detroit, the first thing you notice when you enter an assembly plant is the incredible noise level. Hammers pounding, drills whining, metal sanders screeching, principally to remove defects from the steel, which is invariably damaged in shipment between the press plants and assembly. You don't talk, you shout, in Detroit.

"These letters," I asked, pointing to large, stencilled tags Scotch-taped to the doors. "Destinations?"

Tsukatani nodded. "USW, for example, is California. United States, West Coast. USS, South. GER, Germany. FRA, France."

As a few Stanzas destined for Great Britain crept into view, the workers in that station reached into a different pile of dashboard assemblies, installing ones that had the steering wheel access on the right-hand side. It all seemed so simple. Why couldn't we do that when we shipped cars to Japan?

If you've ever taken an unaltered VW or Peugeot across the English Channel from Europe and driven on British roads, you know the feeling. Especially when you try to pass. With the steering wheel on the wrong (left) side of the car, you practically have to pull out flush into the lane of oncoming traffic just to see whether you have room to overtake or not. Unless, of course, you have someone riding shotgun in the front seat. And even that will prove frenetic for both.

Yet Detroit calmly rolls its Cadillacs and Continentals off the assembly line with steering wheels irrevocably positioned on the left-hand side, just as they drive them in Bloomfield Hills. And when the monsters get to Japan, assuming they make it through the rat's nest of customs procedures, they no doubt contribute to Japan's growing perplexity with America. I'm surprised the Japanese authorities permit the damned things to be sold and driven without alteration. Just think how long it would take to clear our cars through customs if the Japanese government insisted on moving every steering wheel to the opposite side of the car. Not to mention the effect on price. Two nontariff barriers with one regulation. They're missing a bet.

We moved on down the assembly line, watching the serious shopworkers installing what the auto boys call soft trim—the interiors—pulling what they needed from neatly stacked trays and bins of seatbelt anchor pins, gearshift levers, window cranks, and hand brakes. Neatly stacked was understated. Everything was immaculate, as if some corporate mama-san came through periodically.

"Watch this," Tsukatani said, holding me gently by the elbow.

A maroon-clad technician grabbed a complete dashboard assembly from a stack of a dozen or so behind the yellow line paralleling the workflow and maneuvered it deftly into the moving frame. Holding it in place with his right hand, he reached up quickly with his left and pulled down an electric drill, which hung suspended from a springlike coil. It was outfitted with a togglebolt tightener that matched the size of the six bolts preinserted in the dash assembly to fasten it to the frame as it moved along.

Whirr. Zap. *Chunk.* Whirr. Zap. *Chunk.*

Six times he pulled the electric trigger; in seconds, the entire dash-board was mounted. He climbed out and released the electric drill. It sprang back to its waiting position just above head level. He glanced over at us and smiled, his face beaming with pride.

In Japan, dashboard assemblies come delivered to the plant com-pletely preassembled and ready to install. The speedometer, the idiot lights, odometers, fuel gauge, radio, heater switch, air vents, glove box, digital clock—all finished, tested, ready to go. Same with the seats: four bolts and they're in. And steering wheels, with all their compli-cated windshield-washer, turn-indicator, and headlight switches. All prepackaged and ready to install.

Whirr. Zap. *Chunk.*

In America, we still use what are called subassembly stations at most assembly plants. Over on one side, union workers sweat through the process of putting together seats. There are stacks of foam rubber, next to stacks of prefit leather or Naugahyde covers, next to steel seat frames. So the subassembler wraps the bulky foam around a seat frame and holds it in place with his chin while he tries to pull on the Nau-gahyde cover with both hands. It's a tight fit. It doesn't always work the first time. Fortunately for him, none of this stuff is moving while he works on it.

When the cover is on, he walks over to a wooden table and untangles a hand-held electric stitching gun from the maze of electric tools. Then he points it at predetermined spots on the Naugahyde and stitches the seatcover to the foam rubber on the steel frame. Just like Henry Ford showed the boys back in 1914. And for this he gets $19.65 an hour, fringes and vacation included.

On another side of this standard American assembly plant, a union worker may be putting together dashboard assemblies, which start with a frame, empty and full of holes, and resting on a small conveyor. (The conveyor is moving, so if you think he's headed for trouble, you're right.) The worker checks the sheet of computer-generated work orders for that day; looks at the dashboard frame; gets a number; matches the number against the computer sheet; determines what gadgets, sprockets, and gizmos that particular dashboard assembly is to receive; and starts pulling them out of nearby bins.

Radios. Speedometers. Clocks. Heater and air conditioner switches. Cassette decks. Wires begin to emerge in all directions, like worms wriggling out of the ground after a heavy rain. One by one the worker inserts the components, fastens them with a manual screwdriver, checking them off the computer sheet as they get done. Again, not much has changed since the days of Henry Ford. And for this, *he* gets $19.65 an hour, fringes and vacation included.

I thought about our once-famous Yankee ingenuity as I watched the Nissan man deftly installing his dashboard assemblies. All the grunt work had been done outside the plant by the subcontractor responsible for dashboards. One of those eight thousand "family" supplier firms Dr. Abernathy talked about. Nissan owned 20 percent, maybe 40 percent, of the little company that made dashboards to order, worked with them on quality control, set performance and design standards, and established delivery schedules so that every two hours another fifty dashboards would be brought in right to the assembly floor. Finished, tested, ready to go. No extra handling, no wasted time, no wasted space.

And they do that with *all* their component systems. Seats. Steering wheels. Engines. Transmissions. Interior trim. A different company in the Nissan group is responsible only for its own component specialty. The *kanban* system, as it is called, erroneously translated by us as the just-in-time system. *Kanban* literally means signboard or shingle and refers to the *kanji* character signs that hang outside shops and stores all over Japan, identifying the proprietor or owner. Ikeda. Tanaka. Nippon Denki.

So all these Ikedas and Tanakas and Nippon Denkis, some or most of whose capital may be owned by Nissan, go about their daily work of creating subassemblies for the great automaker under their own *kanban*. But they deliver only on precise, prearranged schedules, like hourly or twice a shift or four times a day. In Detroit, boxcars may unload outside the assembly plants once a month. Which makes for a lot of extra handling, a lot of wasted time, and a lot of needed storage space. All this finds its way into your American car in the form of either lower quality or higher prices or both.

Tsukatani and I walked forward as the nearly completed Sentra and Stanza frames moved on. Engines popped up from below and a team of four mechanics installed them promptly. They reminded me more of Swiss watchmakers than Japanese car assemblers. Then came the steering wheels. Then the windshields. Then the tires.

Whirr. Zap. *Chunk.*

Off they would roll, one after another, for a brief stay in the testing zone, where the engines, brakes, and electrical systems would be checked, and then out the back door to the multistory parking garage where thousands waited to be trucked to Yokohama to the car carriers that would soon float them to USW, GER, and FRA.

Datsun workers feel they are in direct competition with Toyota and Honda. The competitive spirit at Zama is impressive. On an earlier visit to a GM auto assembly plant in America, I had asked a line worker if he and his colleagues felt that same intensity of competition with Ford and Chrysler.

"You don't understand," he replied incredulously. "Those are our brothers and sisters working over there."

Noriko-chan

"We haven't seen the famous automatic welding machines yet," I said to Tsukatani as we climbed into the sedan.

He glanced at his watch, then looked up at me.

"*Robotto desu ka?*"

I nodded.

He spoke to the driver, and we headed for a back lot, where the pressed-and-formed steel sheets are secured to the body frame before the frames move on to painting and assembly.

Even the back lot was quiet. But there was a reason. Normally, with the Unimate industrial robots spitting and punching their spotwelds, the noise level would have been noticeably higher, but today there was a problem. The Unimates were down.

We strolled over to the far side, where some smaller automatic welders were busy doing their job. Sparks flew out in tiny explosions, like miniature Roman candles on the Fourth of July. Trunk hatches were being sealed to their frames. The pressed-steel shapes moved forward on a conveyor, stopped, and waited while a giant grasshopperlike nose danced back and forth spotwelding the pieces together. Always hitting the same spots, always applying the same pressure, always making the same weld. Every single time.

As I stood there watching those metal woodpeckers do their job, I thought for all the publicity they've gotten, they're really not that smart. In fact, they can only do what they're told, and although they do that very well, what magic they have rests in the little computer box off to one side. Electrical impulses command the welding head to twist left, twist right, up, down, to, or fro. Rather elementary. But it's important that the conveyor delivers the target metal to the right place and at the right time. Otherwise, you get a lot of small dots down the back of your trunk hatch that look like a zipper.

"What about the main robots, Tsukatani-san?" I asked.

His face turned red. "Well, you see..."

I could tell he was uneasy. Here we were at Zama, Japan's Potemkin Village, and the big Unimates were down. We walked back to the main welding area, where hulks of car body frames just sat, waiting. Rather impatiently, I thought.

"Second time this has happened in as many years, since I started bringing *gaijin* out here," Tsukatani said, frowning. *Gaijin* means foreigner. Literally, outside person. He ran a nervous hand through his long, black hair. "You know, we operate these robots straight through two shifts, sixteen hours a day, seven days a week, fifty-two weeks a year. It's amazing their frequency of repair is so low."

The Unimates were all frozen in position, some poised high, others low, where the line of cars had stopped. On the computer boxes, were the *kanji* for Kawasaki Heavy Industries, who had the license to manufacture Unimate industrial robots in Japan. Japanese companies operated over 80 percent of all the industrial robots in the world.

I stooped down to look at the Kawasaki logo, and as I glanced across the rows of silent robots, I noticed they all had pictures of young Japanese girls taped just under their ID numbers.

Keiko. Noriko. Miho. Seiko. Kumiko.

"These are popular singers, aren't they?" I asked, straightening up. Tsukatani nodded.

"Each shopworker chooses his favorite singer and puts her picture on one of the machines," he said. "Helps to personalize them somewhat, makes them less...less automated, somehow."

"How long before they go into action again?"

"I'll ask."

He disappeared momentarily to consult with a group of technicians huddled around a central control panel.

I stepped over to Noriko's picture and bowed.

"*Hajimemashite*," I said. "Pleased to meet you, Noriko-chan."

It was eerie. Suddenly I remembered the evacuation drills we took as youngsters in grade school during the fallout shelter scare. When we returned to our classrooms after tromping en masse to the cafeteria and sitting with our heads between our knees under the big tables, with the stench of sour milk and cottage cheese still hanging in the air, our desks always looked strangely silent and unused. Just like these inanimate robots.

"*Hajimemashite*."

The voice was but a whisper. It came from my right.

I looked up.

There was no one there.

"Who...?"

"It's me. Noriko," the soft voice persisted.

"But—"

"We probably don't have much time," she said. "Two short breaks in two years is hardly enough. What's your name?"

I told her.

"German?"

"American," I said, shaking my head. "*Sansei*."

"I see," she said. "But your Japanese. No accent. Most Americans who come through here have frightful accents, if they speak the language at all."

I glanced in Tsukatani's direction. He was still busy with the huddle of men in maroon.

"It's my teachers," I replied, turning back to her. "Excuse me." I reached up and gently removed a speck of grit from her forehead.

"Thank you," she said. "I'm not programmed to be able to do that."

"I understand. But why are all you women taking a holiday today? I came twelve thousand miles to see you in action."

"I know," she whispered. "But how would you feel if you worked sixteen hours a day, seven days a week, with no vacation or free time?" Her steel-blue eyes seemed to flash alive for an instant.

"Yes, but the corporation takes good care of you. All the electricity you need, free repairs, and attractive company," I said, gesturing toward her companions. "Plus you have a psychological edge over the American machines. You know you're wanted, that somebody cares."

"*Maa*," she sighed. "That's true. But it's really hard work. And repetitive. Nobody really knows how dull it can get, even for us Japanese."

"How long are you planning to break?" I asked. "I can only stay for the day."

Her dark eyes seemed to narrow. "You Americans are all so impatient."

"I know. But you should see the Germans."

She chuckled. Then her voice relaxed.

"We just took off an hour ago," she said. "I have the feeling we'll probably be out all day and won't start again until tomorrow. It takes us a while to reach consensus, you know."

"Oh dear," I said. "I don't want to miss your show."

"You'll just have to come back. You're in Japan frequently anyway, aren't you?"

She was right. So we made a tentative date to get together in the summer.

"I hope I'm still here," she said. "Lifetime employment is for the workers, not for us. We're lucky if we last two or three years, then they toss us out and replace us with somebody new."

"Hell, we do that with our *people*," I said. "Consider yourself lucky."

I could see Tsukatani out of the corner of one eye. He was on his way back.

"Look, we better say goodbye. My host is returning. What will you be doing if you're not here next year?"

"I'll probably get melted down and used in the steel plate for some

new oil tanker," she said. "But I think I can stay through summer.
Will you make it back by then?"

"I'll try," I promised.

Her eyes softened. "Thank you for stopping to talk. It made my
break much more enjoyable."

"The pleasure was mine," I said, bowing informally from the neck.

"*Sayonara*," she whispered. "Take care."

I turned to greet Tsukatani. His face was grim, his lips sealed in a
straight line.

"It doesn't look good," he said. "The robots will probably be out all
day. There really is no excuse."

"I know," I said, winking at Noriko.

I could have sworn she winked back.

Winning Is Everything

We stood at the exit, ready to leave, bowing to the Zama staff and
exchanging thanks.

Tsukatani announced that lunch would follow in a nearby restaurant.

I asked, in an aside, whether we could skip the restaurant and join
the workers in the plant cafeteria.

He shook his head. "We've never done that for a *gaijin* before," he
replied. Then he opened the door to the waiting sedan.

"I may never get back to see the robots," I said. "And I won't discuss
anything proprietary with the men."

He stood there a moment, thinking. It was a tough request. Not just
to eat in the company cafeteria, but to change the schedule. Japanese
are not fond of surprises.

I apologized for the change but persisted politely. Tsukatani disappeared inside for a few minutes. I jotted down the conversation with
Noriko in my notebook.

"It's OK," he said, returning with a relieved grin. "But we can't stay
long."

Tsukatani bought a fistful of meal tickets from the cafeteria matron
and we joined the boisterous line of hungry men in maroon. Loading
light green tupperware bowls and teacups and plastic chopsticks onto
our trays, we shuffled along. I picked the curry rice. Tsukatani chose
the *soba*.

Exiting the foodline, we sat down at a half-empty table. Tsukatani
poured us each a cup of green tea.

I turned to the man on my left and nodded.

He nodded back.

"How's it going?" I asked, stirring my rice with the chopsticks.

"Good," he said.

Then he paused.

"We'll win, you know."

Tsukatani and I finished our lunch in silence.

CHAPTER 4

WHEN STEEL REIGNED SUPREME

Certain Congressmen have given color to the view that importing is a privilege, not a right, and that bringing foreign-made goods into this country is not a suitable occupation for patriotic citizens.

—Percy W. Bidwell, *The Invisible Tariff*, 1939

The reaction of the automobile industry to the threat posed by cheap foreign imports was typical of responses other American industries have made over the years.

The first step, when the little VW appeared on the block, was to ignore it or treat it like a pesky fly. Go away, you bother me.

The second step, when imports increased their market share, was to place the blame on cheap foreign wages. If they had to pay the wages *we* do, they'd never be competitive.

The third step, when American firms became uncompetitive and domestic unemployment rose, was to mount a movement to keep them out. It's not our fault we can't compete, it's the imports that are killing us. So give us tariffs, give us quotas, give us some protection.

When protection is needed, management or organized labor, or management *and* organized labor, can petition the International Trade Commission for what is called a 201. Section 201 of our Trade Act of 1974 permits industries that suspect their poor competitive performance may be caused by substantial injury from imports to seek protection by persuading the ITC to give them some breathing space behind a protective wall of temporary tariffs. "Substantial" is defined as a cause that is important and not less than any other cause.

Section 201 is also known as the Escape Clause. It is ideally designed to enable domestic industries to "escape" temporarily from the competitive pressures caused by imports as well as to avoid penalties that would otherwise be imposed under international trading rules by enacting quotas or tariffs. Realistically, it enables protected industries to

41

"escape" from having to retool or regroup to become more competitive.

Well, in the case of America's two-ton gas guzzlers, the ITC decided that foreign imports were not a substantial cause of their plight. The economic downturn, shifts in consumer tastes, and an unwillingness to downsize were greater causes.

What to do? If you can't get a 201, try a 301.

Section 301 of the Trade Act permits an industry to file a complaint with the Office of the U.S. Trade Representative and request a presidential review. If the review concurs with the industry's position, then the president can recommend action to Congress. And then *Congress* can set up some protectionist walls for the industry to hide behind.

So guess who the most popular people are with industry associations, management, organized labor, and members of Congress? Lawyers.

Perhaps the American automobile industry was a little lethargic out there in Bloomfield Hills, you say. But they're the exception. Look at steel. Now there's where the tough guys are. They wouldn't let the foreign competition get ahead.

Steel. The quintessential smokestack industry. Hardworking immigrants in rolled-up sleeves. Building blocks for America, the backbone of our national defense. Bessemer furnaces. Belching chimneys. Pittsburgh.

One reason steel is called a basic industry is because the product is used in lots of other industries. Like autos, for example. And planes and tanks and rockets. Fundamentally, you can import as much steel as you'd like. It's just a matter of jobs and votes. But if you don't have a stable and competitive core business yourself, you may become too dependent on foreign supply.

"Nations do not have permanent enemies, nor do they have permanent friends," British prime minister William Gladstone once said. "They have only permanent interests." So one day your permanent friends are no longer permanent. And then where do you go to get the steel to make the weapons to keep your citizens safe from the enemy?

Automobiles are also a basic industry. Those assembly lines that produce Cavaliers and Escorts and LeBarons are the same assembly lines that produce T-1's and troop carriers and half-tracks. But if all our cars were imported from abroad because our auto industry is no longer competitive, how on earth would we ever put 15 percent of our labor force back to work? Silicon Valley couldn't possibly absorb them all.

In 1981, Professors Hugh Patrick and Hideo Sato of Yale completed a study that showed Pittsburgh wasn't so far removed from Bloomfield Hills, after all.

"Satisfied with the large, prosperous domestic market, the U.S. steel industry—like many other American industries—remained complacent about export markets for many years. As others became stronger and the competition grew, the industry was forced to struggle with smaller shares of its home market."

In the early 1960s, foreign steel had only about a 5 percent share of the U.S. market. Nothing to get excited about. Step One: Go away, you bother me.

By the mid-1960s, foreign steel had captured 17 percent of the American market, and Pittsburgh was beginning to get worried. Step Two: Complain. Cheap wages were blamed, and predatory pricing, and export subsidies. The foreigners were dumping.

By 1968, the situation had become intolerable, and Pittsburgh, which is unionized and vocal and politically powerful, put pressure on Washington. Step Three: Help! So in 1969, the State Department negotiated a three-year Voluntary Export Restraint Agreement with both Japan and Western Europe, which was extended in 1972 for another three years.

Again, the only loser was the consumer, who faced higher prices for steel as a result of limiting foreign imports to an artificially low market share. In 1972, the Consumers Union brought an antitrust suit against the State Department alleging violation of the Sherman Act by restraining foreign commerce in steel. They lost, but the case persuaded many people that VERs did pose certain antitrust risks if they were not initiated directly by the foreign governments involved. That's why Brock emphasized the auto VER had been "voluntarily" initiated by the Japanese and why the steel VER was subsequently allowed to lapse in 1975.

Now, when the VER expired that year, the United Steel Workers petitioned the ITC for, guess what? A 201. And the ITC upheld them, recommending import quotas for five years for certain specialty steels. The Office of the U.S. Trade Representative was requested to negotiate not a VER but an OMA: an Orderly Marketing Agreement, limiting foreign shipments to the United States. Japan agreed, but the European Economic Community did not, so the Ford administration slapped them with a three-year quota.

Backstage, in the autumn of 1976, Brussels persuaded Tokyo to slow down shipments of general steel to the EEC, which was having its own problems with Japan, and when the United Steel Workers found out about that, they filed a 301 with the USTR, complaining that Japanese steel would now be diverted from Europe to the United States. They lost, but in the process of turning them down, Washington decided that something had to be done to unmuddy the water. The nation's capital was awash in alphabet soup, and the USW were swarming around like a pack of angry bees.

Washington didn't have long to wait. Early in 1977, a small West Coast steel-plate producer brought an antidumping suit against a few Japanese firms that appeared to be pricing their exports too aggressively. And when U.S. Steel got wind of *that*, they began to prepare their own antidumping suit against the whole Japanese industry.

Responsibility for investigation of antidumping suits was lodged in the Treasury Department at the time, which began looking into the complaint. It takes four pages of fine print to define dumping in the 1974 Trade Act. Congress essentially redefined the standard Antidumping Act of 1921 by saying that if you sold your product in the U.S. market at less than your average cost of production, you dumped.

But how to define average cost of production? Treasury had to figure out a way, so they requested MITI to provide them with production cost data from the Japanese producers. The Japanese steel industry agreed, but declined to submit product-by-product information, reasoning that the Americans wanted to find out their production secrets. MITI advised them not to comply.

Here we have to step back and see what had happened to the Japanese steel industry since the war. With the fastest growing domestic economy in the world, Japanese steel producers had invested continually in new, large-scale, state-of-the-art technology. They had for years exported about a third of their production and, consequently, incorporated a global strategy into their planning and capital investment needs. The Japanese, thus, adopted advanced technology early, and by 1978, over three fourths of Japanese steel was produced in basic oxygen furnaces with continuous casting. Their mills were sited at deep-water ports and took advantage of long-term iron ore contracts, which greatly reduced their raw materials costs.

Nobody suspected the Japanese could be so smart. But then there was a lot we didn't know about Japan. For example, back in 1934, the Japanese could overhaul their steam locomotives in five days. It took us fourteen days, and the British four weeks. And by 1913, the Japanese cotton spinning mills were already superior to those in the West.

Our steel industry, by contrast, was characterized by oligopoly, obsolete production capacity and high union wages, escalating to 70 percent over the American industrial average by the late 1970s. Production facilities were still located in the Midwest, far away from major markets in the Southwest and the West. Not much attention was paid to exports: the industry averaged less than 3 percent a year and had been a net importer since 1959. The Americans kept most of their production in the old-fashioned, less efficient open hearth mills. Just over half of U.S. capacity consisted of basic oxygen furnaces by 1978, and only 15 percent of our mills had continuous casting. The steel companies also had an ideological fixation with paper profits that prevented them from pricing more aggressively in down markets and from spending more rationally to upgrade plant and equipment.

Meanwhile, back at Treasury, the Japanese were uncertain as to what they should do. To help clear the antidumping charges, they had to release their production cost data. If they didn't, they would be perceived as admitting their guilt. But if they did, then the lethargic Americans, who had been slower to invest in new process technology, would be in a position to see exactly how Japan had become so competitive.

So the Japanese held out, hoping for an OMA. Treasury proceeded to investigate the dumping suit on the basis of incomplete data, found the Japanese guilty, and slapped them with a hefty 12 percent countervailing duty on the shipments involved.

Guilty! Pittsburgh was ecstatic. Here was their chance. They closed several plants, which put more steelworkers out of work and brought additional pressure on Washington. U.S. Steel filed its own antidumping suit against the Japanese. And the steel lobby got busy in the corridors of Congress, threatening to hit the Europeans with an antidumping suit, as well.

Tokyo was understandably upset. If every time the Americans believed a foreign steelmaker was undercutting it in the U.S. market, they could bring an antidumping suit against the cheap foreign imports, clearly something had to be done. Step Three was getting out of hand.

The result: TPM. The Trigger Price Mechanism. Treasury came up with a formula that in effect determined the average cost of production for the most efficient foreign producer of steel. This became the trigger price. Any steel imported above that price, by anyone, would not be subject to antidumping investigations. But if you sold below that price, investigation would be automatic.

Well, you could hear the sighs of relief throughout the industry. The Japanese agreed to give average cost data for their six largest and most efficient producers, and in January 1978, the TPM went into effect. It lasted until 1982. And it basically fixed market shares for both Japanese and European steel in the United States because it effectively gave Europe a license to steal. While EEC production was nowhere near as efficient as Japan's, the TPM enabled them to protect their U.S. market share by pricing enough above the TPM but below average U.S. domestic prices to make their products more attractive. By March 1980, U.S. Steel had filed another massive antidumping suit against the Europeans.

The first Treasury *TPM Pricing Manual* was 268 pages long. Why did the American steel industry pick on Japan, you ask? After all, didn't the consumer benefit from the anti-inflationary aspects of cheaper steel? And didn't cheaper, higher quality steel make for cheaper and better cars? The TPM was estimated to have cost the American consumer $1 billion a year in more expensive steel.

We're back to fingerpointing again, only this time it's Pittsburgh rather than Bloomfield Hills. Convenient scapegoats die hard. The bilateral deficits with Japan had begun in the mid-1970s, and Japan was *perceived* by American politicians to be an unfair trader. The Japanese had protected many of their infant industries, restricted foreign investment in others, and kept certain agricultural products under strict quota, whereas the maze of nontariff barriers were just becoming public knowledge. The general lack of awareness about Japan at this time made these accusations sound perfectly plausible. Americans want to believe their politicians. If they can't, who can they believe? But this time it was not just a case of blaming the messenger for the bad news. The messenger *was* the bad news.

Still, after all the 201s, 301s, and TPMs, the American steel industry was no better off than before. Market shares of imported steel had stabilized at about 18 percent, of which the Japanese accounted for nearly half. The American companies continued to lose money, accelerate layoffs, and complain. They sought continued protection from Washington, and more Band-Aids in the form of regulatory and tax relief. The one thing they did not do was try to become more competitive by upgrading plant and equipment. A condition of TPM was that the steel industry would have to make "adequate progress toward modernization" within three years, or it would be terminated. Not much happened. When U.S. Steel had the cash to invest, it bought an oil company, not the latest basic oxygen furnace technology. Easy to see why. Even our own steel industry didn't see much future in steel.

Professors Patrick and Sato summed up the industry's gloomy prospects in 1981: "It faces fundamental structural problems: it has lost comparative advantage, and has the overhang of substantial obsolete capacity. Its wage rates are high (now 75 percent above those for all American manufacturing), and almost double Japanese steelworker wages. Union power has been strong, and it has reduced considerably the ability to compete against imports. Its application of process technology lags, [and] its rate of R & D is low and declining."

In 1982, Ira Magaziner and Robert Reich wrote a small book called *Minding America's Business*. Mr. Magaziner was a consultant with many years experience in Japan. Mr. Reich was director of policy planning at the Federal Trade Commission. Both had been former Rhodes scholars at Oxford. They also took a look at the steel industry and came up with the same conclusion.

"U.S. steel companies made small, incremental investments to obtain 'cheap' capacity rather than make the larger, more aggressive, and riskier investments that could have led to superior productivity. Overall, they sought to keep the return on investment—ROI—up by keeping the 'I' low, but this strategy has left whole plants uncompetitive. In the long run this scheme has been self-defeating."

They were even more critical of the American lethargy with regard to exports. "U.S. companies have never been aggressive in pursuing export opportunities. [They] export three times less tonnage to Latin America and four times less to Europe than do their Japanese counterparts. [This] lack of understanding of market development and of competitors was a serious problem in the U.S. steel industry. Business leaders spent too much time worrying about unfair trading and the need to diversify investments [out of steel] instead of planning investments to reassert technological and productivity leadership."

As the smoke cleared, it became obvious how the American steel strategy differed from the Japanese, and why the trade war grew hotter.

American steelmakers were in business to make money.

The Japanese were in business to make steel.

CHAPTER 5

A BIKE IS A BIKE IS A BIKE

Exports of Japanese bicycles in 1980 totaled $430 million, up 60% over the previous year.

> —Japanese Bicycle Industry Association

Surely, you wonder, there must be one industry in America that has resisted the temptation to run for protection when the going got tough. This business of petitioning Washington for import relief must be a recent phenomenon, characteristic of hemorrhaging balance of payments, surging Japanese exports, and declining industrial competitiveness.

What about bicycles? No, don't look at bicycles. Well, why not? Remember those old balloon-tire bikes?

In 1949, imported lightweights had only a 1 percent share of the American bicycle market. Output of U.S. factories was 50 percent greater than before the war, but by 1954 the domestic market had grown by over 200 percent.

In 1954, Americans bought over 1 million imported bicycles. The English firm of Raleigh alone made 1.3 million bicycles a year. By contrast, the *total* output of all American manufacturers from 1950 to 1954 was less than 2 million bicycles a year. By 1954, foreign imports had captured almost half the American market.

What was going on?

A Bike Is a Bike

Percy Bidwell was an economist who did lots of studies for the Council on Foreign Relations in his day. His most famous work was a 1939 publication called *The Invisible Tariff*, which we'll come back to later on. After the war, Bidwell looked into a number of domestic industries to analyze various cases for—and against—tariffs. From this came a spiffy little account called *What the Tariff Means to American Industries.*

The General Agreement on Tariffs and Trade had been negotiated and signed into practice in 1947. The United States had taken the lead in initiating tariff reductions and in trying to get other major trading countries of the world to do the same. Japan wasn't heard from much in those days as her exports were mostly dollar blouses, firecrackers, and toys. So what heel-dragging there was came from Western Europe. Remember, the EEC wasn't born until 1957.

Percy Bidwell looked at watches and he looked at electrical generating equipment and he looked at steel.

He also looked at bicycles.

Foreign imports in 1949 had only that 1 percent market share. Step One: Ignore them.

By 1950, imports of foreign lightweights had increased to 3.4 percent of the market. Step Two: Accusation and complaint. Cheap foreign wages, etcetera.

A year later, foreign imports had increased their share to 8.5 percent: a paltry 91,500 bicycles out of a total market of over 2 million. Step Three: Help!

So the American Bicycle Manufacturers Association appealed to the Tariff Commission in Washington (predecessor of the ITC in those vastly simpler days) to raise tariffs and impose an absolute quota on foreign imports.

The commission turned them down, having found no evidence of injury. Come on, boys, they said. Eight point five percent of the market? Who are you kidding? Roll up your sleeves, go back in there, and compete.

By 1955, foreign lightweight bicycles had captured 41 percent of the American market, however, selling 1.2 million bikes in a 2.9-million bicycle market. So the manufacturers tried Step Three again. This time they won. Four out of ten bikes sold coming in from abroad? You boys need some breathing space. (By the way, what have you been doing the past four years to let things get this bad?)

The commission recommended doubling the tariff on lightweights, and President Eisenhower agreed. But he wasn't happy about it, especially as it would mean higher bicycle prices for American consumers. In a letter to the Manufacturers Association, Ike said bluntly that the penetration of the American market by European lightweights was "attributable almost entirely to the ingenuity and resourceful efforts of foreign producers and [their] American importers."

The bicycle makers, not unhappy with the commission's decision to escalate tariffs, disagreed with the president nonetheless. "A bike is a bike," they said, "and they're all sold interchangeably in a single market." Never mind that domestic bikes weighed twice as much as their foreign competition. "There is only one major difference between bikes made in America and those coming in from any foreign source," they went on. *"That single difference is price."* (Their italics.)

You can hear old Percy chuckling even now. "Common observation throws considerable doubt on the accuracy of this statement," he opined with characteristic subtlety. "Practically every American boy or girl above the age of 10 knows the difference between an English bicycle—a light machine weighing 30 to 35 pounds, with clean lines not obscured by gadgets and accessories—and the balloon-tire models which make up the bulk of the product of American factories. Distinguishing features (of the English bikes) are the narrow tires that reduce road friction, caliper brakes attached to the handlebars and operating on the rims of both front and rear wheels, and a three-speed gear built into the rear hub."

Percy went on to describe the American bicycle in unforgettable terms. "The typical American machine, on the other hand, has balloon tires, 2⅛ inches in diameter, and weighs about 45 pounds. Its rear wheel has a single-speed, coaster-brake hub. Designers of the American balloon-tire bicycle have adorned it, in imitation of the motorcycle, with a variety of brightly colored or chromium-plated fittings and accessories, including false gasoline tanks, as well as horns, lights, and carriers."

Of course. Bigger is better, we all know that. And if the customer isn't buying our product, we'll dress it up. Nobody really wants those sissy foreign bikes with their skinny wheels. The only reason Americans are buying them is because they're cheap. Stick with the fat tires. They're USA all the way. Downsize? Forget it.

And Bloomfield Hills would one day be just as reluctant. Again, it was like downsizing the American dream.

"After waiting hopefully a few years for the craze to disappear, some American firms stepped up their production of lightweights in 1953," Percy wrote. "But when they could not meet foreign, particularly British, competition they discontinued those models."

Why?

The Public Didn't Want Them

Trying for two years to meet the competition hardly seems enough time to fight a pitched battle, let alone a major trade war. Where was that Yankee ingenuity, that Puritan work ethic, the determination to prevail that had just won World War II? Why were American manufacturers unwilling or unable to invest in the plant and equipment necessary to turn out lightweight bikes that would meet the competition head-on?

Mr. N. A. Clarke of the Westfield Bicycle Company had the answer. "My reason for not making more lightweights," he wrote, "is that my customers haven't ordered more lightweights. The reason they haven't ordered more lightweights is that they can buy much cheaper models that appear to be of an equal quality level with our own. These, of course, came from abroad."

Does this make any sense?

Webster defines vituperative as abusing or censuring severely or abusively. Old Percy was vituperative.

"Gaining a larger share of the expanded market," he concluded in 1956, "will pose a challenge to American ingenuity and initiative in both production and marketing. More investment in engineering research will be required and greater sensitivity to changes in consumers' preferences. The continuing pressure of foreign competition, if we assume that no further tariff increases are granted, may force a reorganization of the industry. It seems inevitable that marginal firms will be eliminated and that bicycle production, perhaps somewhat reduced in volume, will be concentrated in the best-equipped and best-managed plants."

Like autos and steel, American bicycle manufacturers were no longer competitive in their own market.

Have you visited a bike shop recently? In the first place, you have to hunt around just to find the three-speeds anymore, and the only balloon-tire bikes you may see are rust-laden models from the 1950s or those dirt bikes that have appeared in imitation of their motorcycle brethren. The market is now heavy into ten-speeds.

Peugeot and Motobecane: France. Sentinel and Raleigh (they're still in business): England. Rampar: Taiwan.

And who else but the Japanese.

Univega and Vista and Windsor and Fugi and Nishiki, all lightweight models, weighing thirty to thirty-five pounds, with clean lines not obscured by gadgets or accessories, and narrow tires to reduce road friction, and caliper brakes attached to the handlebars, operating on the rims of both front and rear wheels, and a ten-speed gear built into the rear hub.

All those sissy foreign types.

CHAPTER 6

FROM XENOPHOBIC TO *ZURUI*

Getsu-Getsu-Ka-Sui-Moku-Kin-Kin.
(Monday - Monday - Tuesday - Wednesday - Thursday - Friday -
Friday.)

—Japanese Imperial Navy Song

Let's play a game.

Pretend you're living in St. Louis, or anywhere west of the Mississippi for that matter, and one day the federal government tells you and everybody else living west of the Mississippi that you must move to California.

California?

California. All of you.

That's about 120 million people, give or take a few. (Remember, this is just a game.) So 120 million people pack their Samsonites, load up their big cars, and head west.

Two days later, you are sitting somewhere in California. (It's your choice whether you want northern or southern California, but once you've decided, you must stay there.)

Pretty crowded, isn't it? Perhaps you thought your two acres with a ranch-style house in St. Louis was your just dessert as an American. Manifest destiny, and all that. But the federal government has planned everything in advance, and a small house is waiting for you. Very small. So small, in fact, that you can reach out your window and actually touch someone.

Now that you've settled in and put your things away, perhaps it's time to go outside and walk around a bit. Wow, it's crowded!

But that's not the half of it. Suddenly, the ground beneath you starts vibrating and shaking and warping all out of shape. You rush back inside the house, taking care not to panic because you're not sure what's happening. Then you remember all those newspaper stories about an earthquake in California that's supposed to hit 8.0 on the Richter scale, and you figure, correctly, you're right in the middle of it.

But this proves to be no ordinary earthquake. It's a real humdinger that rips the entire state of California out right along those neat straight-edge borders with Nevada and Arizona, making Reno and Flagstaff our new West Coast ports.

So off you go, drifting aimlessly into the Pacific, waving goodbye to the rest of the continent. California is an island now, detached, insecure, defenseless.

You float for a week or so up into the North Pacific and eventually come to rest, slightly skewed, with Sacramento not far from Siberia and San Diego but a short hop from Taiwan.

You venture out again, with your neighbors, to have a look around, and this time you feel a little different. At first, among all these people, you felt hemmed in, pinned down, nervous. Now, you feel comforted, secure, safe. We're all in this together, you realize. Either we survive together or we die together. Individual preferences and idiosyncrasies suddenly become irrelevant.

You climb a low hill. Hey, look at that! What was once flat farmland and open space is now crunched up into craggy mountains the size of fists, punctuated by small valleys. Now you start to worry. What are you going to do for food? Goodbye beef, goodbye corn, so long amber waves of grain. Hello, fish.

Now the government's somewhat organized again and puts out an announcement explaining what has happened. California is now an island, and one that you can't leave. The farmland is gone, and less than 10 percent of that craggy landscape you just saw is flat enough to cultivate. The rich deposits of iron ore and oil and copper and coal are gone, the timber is gone, the wheat and the corn and the soybeans and the alfalfa and the maize are gone, the cattle are gone, the hogs are gone, the chickens are gone, the big rivers and dams are gone, all the wide open spaces are gone.

Practically nothing is left.

Shi-No-Ko-Sho

Okay, I told you it was just make-believe. You can go back to St. Louis now, to your two acres and your sprawling ranch-style house and your big car. It was just a game.

But that's Japan.

Shimaguni, the Japanese call it. Island Country. And under those conditions, what kind of people would you expect to find there? People who are competitive or people who are lazy? Cooperative or combative? Individualistic or harmonious and group oriented?

We might keep on pretending, but if you read the book or saw the movie, then you know the rest of the story. Along about 1600, after more than a hundred years of civil war, Tokugawa Ieyasu, having defeated everybody else, consolidated his power and said, "Hold on just a minute. We've been knocking ourselves silly during the past century, which is counterproductive, self-defeating, and stupid. We need to recapture our true spirit, recover our discipline, and make something out of this place."

Kind of like JFK's let's-get-this-country-moving-again speech.

So Ieyasu started by shutting the doors. No Japanese could leave the country, and no foreigners could enter Japan. It was forbidden to build boats larger than three tons, to keep people from getting the idea they could just sail away. The *daimyo*, feudal lords who had fought among themselves for control of the country, were required to leave hostages in Tokyo with the shogun when they were at home. The catchword was control.

Sakoku was another name for it. The Closed Country.

Historians, I hope, will forgive me for telescoping three centuries into a few paragraphs, but for all intents and purposes, the Tokugawas kept it this way for nearly three hundred years. Three hundred years.

The foreigners are barbarians, the Japanese said, only good for making pirates and missionaries, and we don't need either. *Keto*, the Japanese called them. Hairy barbarians. And so the Japanese concentrated on developing their own art and their own philosophy and their own schools and their own literature and their own form of central government and their own food and their own dress and their own strict behavioral codes and their own religion and their own military strategy and their own local economy. And they believed it was superior to just about anything anybody else had at the time.

How did they know? Well, when they threw the hairy barbarians out, they were smart enough to let the Dutch remain on a tiny island offshore from Nagasaki called Deshima to give them a window on the rest of the world. When the latest scientific and medical discoveries were made in Europe, the Dutch ferried word to Deshima. And it didn't take the Japanese long to catch up. Deshima was an important link for them. Especially for such practical barbarian inventions as firearms.

The Tokugawas were in complete control of things. The samurai sat at the top of the pecking order, wearing their swords, developing a code of martial arts, and living in cold rooms with grass mats and no heat. Then came the peasants who tilled the rice fields that fed the people. Then the artisans, who made the lacquerware and fashioned the swords and painted the glorious silk screens that are found in all those castles and temples today. And finally, the tradesmen—moneylenders, hoteliers, and restaurateurs.

Shi-no-ko-sho, in Japanese. Warrior, farmer, artisan, merchant. The four classes. A vertical society. The hierarchy. There was a place for everybody, and everybody knew his position. Oh, the peasants were fractious once in a while when some local *daimyo* demanded a little too much rice in payment for the rent, and they would riot and lose a few heads, but on the surface, at least, things were harmonious. The civil wars were gone.

The Tokugawas today express the wish that things could have stayed that way. Why change? They had the power, their society had made great strides in literacy and education, the *keto* were gone, and the country was at peace. Why break up a good act?

Well, the Americans were at fault. We saw what the Germans and the English and the French were doing in China, and we wanted to become involved. Manifest destiny, we called it. The West Coast had been reached and wasn't new anymore, so press on! If there's silk and opium in China, we figured, then there must be comparable riches in Japan.

Commodore Perry took off in his famous Black Ships and landed in Shimoda in 1853. The Tokugawas weren't anxious to have guests and told the Commodore to push off. But when Perry let go with a couple of blasts from his giant cannons, the Tokugawas agreed to meet with him. (They also sent runners down to Deshima to berate the Dutch for not warning them about those big guns.)

Perry and the Tokugawas talked, drank tea, and talked some more. They then sent Perry back home. But in 1854, he returned with a handful of trade treaties. The Tokugawas took one look and said, hey, these are all to *your* advantage. What's in it for us? Perry said, never mind, just sign them, please.

Tokugawa turned to his trusted advisors. "Do we want unequal treaties?"

"Of course not," they replied.

So the Commodore turned to his cannons. "Do you fellows want another blast?"

They signed. It took four years of negotiations, but by 1858, the trade wars had begun. And the Tokugawas would never forget that they had started off with one hand tied behind their backs.

The unequal treaties.

Build a better mousetrap and the world will beat a path to
your door.

—Ralph Waldo Emerson

"If you had to choose just one word to describe the Japanese, Ku-
nihiro-san, which would you pick?"

I was sitting in the book-filled office of Kunihiro Masao, cultural
anthropologist, author, television commentator, social theorist, member of former Prime Minister Miki's brain trust. It was early 1983,
Prime Minister Nakasone was about to leave for Washington, and skir-
mishes in the trade war between Japan and the United States were
heating up again.

The topic was cultural friction, those elements in the Japanese and
American cultures that fed the flames of mutual distrust. Our bilateral
merchandise trade deficit had reached nearly $17 billion in 1982, Jap-
anese politicians were accusing the *keto* of not working hard enough,
and American politicians were blaming the Japanese for economic problems in Bloomfield Hills.

"*Maa*," Kunihiro said, pausing to remove his hornrimmed glasses
and rubbing tired eyes. I could tell he was searching. When he removes
his glasses, he is thinking.

Then he looked me straight in the eye. "*Zurui*," he said. Then he
was silent again, reconsidering. "Yes, definitely *zurui*."

Of course, I thought to myself. *Zurui*. Cunning, crafty, clever. Or,
as we would say, inscrutable.

"Perfect," I said, making a quick note. "Americans are direct, forth-
right, and frank. We expect others to behave in our own image. And
when they don't—"

"You get angry and upset, impatient," Kunihiro interrupted, replacing his glasses. "We Japanese speak with vagueness, suggesting, hint-
ing. Americans like to kill mosquitoes with big hammers. You have
this excrutiating tendency to—"

"View the world in black and white terms?" I asked. We were in a
kind of rhythm, finishing each other's sentences like a pair of actors
in summer stock. "As in our relationship with the Soviet Union. It's
the old cowboy story of the good guys against the bad. With us, things
are either right or wrong, black or white. We're either saved or we're
damned, off to heaven or down to hell, pure and holy or sinful and
evil. There's no middle ground."

President Reagan's recent meeting with American evangelists suddenly came to mind. He had called Communism the focus of all evil
in the modern world and implored us to beware the temptation of pride

and to acknowledge the "aggressive impulses of that evil empire."

Kunihiro smiled. "Our problem is, we see only the middle ground. We have 465 shades of gray. The only black and white is in Fuji film." He shifted his broad frame on the small couch across from me and glanced out the window. "You want to win a holy war with the Communists," he continued. "And that's very hard for us to grasp."

I nodded. "Hard for *you* to grasp?" I asked. "It's not just the Communists. We want to win a holy war with *everybody*. With you, with the Europeans, with the Arabs. We've got this saintly attitude that pervades our character, and when things start to go wrong for us, we hunt for scapegoats. Confrontation is as basic to America as harmony is to Japan."

"You know what really struck me the first time I visited America twenty-five years ago?" Kunihiro said, turning back to face me. "Your roads. You had a system of national highways in place that was for us Japanese simply unbelievable. Remember, this was barely ten years after the war and we still had dirt roads out in the countryside. For me, that was somehow symbolic. Symbolic of the American work ethic, your desire to improve and upgrade, your emphasis on quality. And we learned all that from you. 'Build a better mousetrap—'"

"'—and the world will beat a path to your door.' Maybe it was easier for us to do back then," I sighed. "No international competition, only one adversary to worry about, and all our infrastructure still in place after the war."

Kunihiro nodded. "For us, the goals were clear. We had to catch up. Not to imitate, mind you, but to improve. And we had a long way to go. Just as in the early Meiji years, we borrowed, we absorbed, we assimilated. Because we had a philosophy that incorporated both/and, not just either/or. Plus we had the tradition of a strong central bureaucracy that controlled the introduction of essentials from overseas and protected our basic industries in their infancy."

I suddenly had a different feeling. Here I was, a hairy barbarian agreeing on substantive issues with Kunihiro.

"My contention," I countered, "is that our basic bilateral relationship is changing. Years ago, when we were so far ahead, it was easy for us to play the role of teacher: sell you the technology you needed, teach you the technical skills you had to learn, share the learning. Steel technology, automobile technology, Dr. Deming's quality controls. We were the master, the *sensei*. Japan was the student, the *deshi*. Our mistake was in thinking those roles would remain constant."

"*Zurui*," Kunihiro repeated. "That's where the cleverness comes in. We're *too* clever in some ways. We've surpassed you in many industries now. And you resent that. *Kiiroi kobito ni makeru hazu wa nai*."

We don't expect to be defeated by those little yellow people.

I nodded. "Especially when half our steel capacity is unused, a third of the United Auto Workers are unemployed, and 80 percent of the industrial robots in the world are in your country."

Kunihiro sighed now. "So what can we do? We've made speeches, we've written books, we've even sent teams of technical people to the States to try to right the balance. But it isn't easy. No one seems to care. Japan gets buried in the back pages of your newspapers, and the only time we make the news on TV is when your autoworkers take potshots at Datsuns."

"Toyotas," I corrected.

He shrugged his shoulders. "Anyway, you guys think you're always right and we're always wrong and that's the way it's going to be."

Zurui. I thought about it again. Kunihiro was absolutely right. Maybe what we needed was a little more *zurui* in our character, a little less contentiousness, more cleverness, less adversarial head-knocking.

But how do you get that message across to such a pluralistic nation as ours? I left Kunihiro's office feeling very doubtful. Freedom for the individual is our catchword, not harmony for the group. If someone wants to live in Bloomfield Hills on two acres with a sprawling ranch-style house and drive a huge car, who's going to tell him that he's facing the future with a philosophy from the past?

CHAPTER 7

RICH COUNTRY, STRONG ARMY

The keenest minds were concerned with such questions as the creation of trade and industry, not for their own sake, but rather to establish those industries one might call strategic. From the first, the military and strategic industries were favored, and were soon on a level with the most advanced Western countries.

—E. Herbert Norman, *Origins of the Modern Japanese State*

When the Tokugawas told Commodore Perry they'd just as soon not have any foreign salesmen visiting them, thank you very much, they didn't bother to reach the consensus their descendants are so famous for today. For if they had, they would have learned straightaway that not everyone was in favor of keeping the country closed.

Especially not the Satsuma and Choshu clans out in western Japan, about as far from Tokyo as one can get. They had been the shogun's most powerful opponents back in the seventeenth century, and he wanted to make it harder for them to return to power, so he put the Satsumas way down on the southern island of Kyushu and the Choshus off in Shimonoseki, on the western tip of the main island. A long way from Tokyo. It's as if the Republicans, winning the election, forced all the Democrats to leave Washington and go to Hawaii.

Well, the Satsumas on Kyushu had some natural advantages that the Tokugawas forgot about over the years as they consolidated power in the national capital. One was that they were so far away they could build up their own military power without fear of detection. Another was that Nagasaki was right next door, so they could keep closer tabs on the Dutch and such barbarian inventions as firearms. And third, they were close enough to China to carry on a lot of trade with the Central Kingdom.

So when they learned about the Commodore's visit to Shimoda,

59

they met with their neighbors, the Choshu, and said, hey, we've been out of power three hundred years, maybe it's our turn now. The two clans agreed it wasn't such a good idea to keep the *keto* out anymore because of what they saw happening in China: the Europeans were slicing up the Central Kingdom like Sara Lee coffee cake, and all the Chinese were getting was the tinfoil wrapper. We don't want to keep the barbarians out, they reasoned. We just want to *control* them.

Time for a little peasant unrest, the Satsuma decided. Stir up the farm folk, increase the local rice tax, spread some scary rumors, make them unhappy so they'll write a few angry letters to Tokyo. That'll keep things unsettled here. Then, with the Choshu boys, we can fight the Tokugawas, who should have their hands full with the Black Ships offshore and the disgruntled peasants in the countryside. Then we can deal with the foreigners on *our* terms.

Their strategy was pretty sharp. They knew already, from three hundred years of dealing with the Chinese, that foreign trade was the commercial equivalent of war. One of their key thinkers was a man named Honda Rimei (1744–1821). From his contacts with the Dutch on Deshima, Honda surmised that the wealth and power of Western nations depended fundamentally on foreign trade, shipping, and above all, manufacture.

As he saw it, "Since Japan is a sea-girt country, it should be the first care of the government to develop shipping and trade. Through sending her ships to all countries, Japan should import such goods as are useful at home, as well as gold, silver and copper to replenish her resources." He summed it all up in a neat little catchphrase for his Satsuma brothers. "Foreign trade is a war in which each party seeks to extract wealth from the other."

So if they continued to keep the Western barbarians out, the hairy devils would just come back with more gunboats and blast their way in, and the same thing would happen to Nippon as had happened to the Central Kingdom. This must be avoided at all costs. The only way they could ever hope to become as strong as the West, they reasoned, was to beat the West at its own game: build up Japan's military power to ward off the Sara Lee syndrome, and trade, trade, trade.

Fukoku Kyohei

When the clans won in 1868, they quickly brought the young emperor up from Kyoto and installed him in Tokyo to reinstitute the system of imperial rule that the shoguns had interrupted a thousand years before. They changed all their calendars back again and called the new era *Meiji Ishin*. The Meiji Restoration, or Enlightened Peace.

And the Satsumas and the Choshus, known as Satcho for short, packed up their things and moved to Tokyo, where they became known officially as the Meiji oligarchs. Itoh Hirobumi, their first prime minister. Field Marshall Yamagata Aritomo. Educator Fukuzawa Yukichi. Autocrat Okubo Toshimichi. Informally, they were the Meiji Boys. Their first priorities, after they had consolidated their military and political power, were to build up Japan's commercial and trading strengths and to develop the key industry sectors that would help them win their trade wars with the West.

Their rallying cry was *Fukoku Kyohei*: Rich Country, Strong Army.

E. Herbert Norman, born of Canadian missionary parents in Japan in 1909, was a prominent Japanese historian. Professor Norman was interested in the feudal remnants of Tokugawa—especially exploitation and autocracy—and how those feudal underpinnings would affect the new Japan's relations with the outside world. After completing his graduate work at Harvard, he produced a most telling book in 1940, called *Origins of the Modern Japanese State*, in which he described the principal concerns of the early Meiji oligarchs.

"In the first years of the Meiji era," he wrote, "the keenest minds were concerned with such questions as the creation of trade and industry, not for their own sake, but rather to establish those industries that one might conveniently call *strategic*, as the sine qua non of a modern army and navy, the creation of which was the central problem of the day. To put the sequence of emphasis in logical order, the Meiji leaders thought somewhat as follows:

"'What do we most need to save us from the fate of China? A modern army and navy. On what does the creation and maintenance of modern armed forces depend? Chiefly on heavy industries: engineering, mining, shipbuilding. In a word, *strategic* industries.'" (Norman's italics.)

As Norman interpreted Japan's formative years following three centuries of isolation, they were characterized by "a unique feature of Japanese industrialization: monopolistic and state control of strategic industries—*strategic* whether because of their connection with naval and military defense or because of their importance in export industries intended to compete against foreign products and hence requiring subsidy and protection."

Does this sound familiar? Current criticism of the Japanese government tends to focus on MITI—the Ministry of International Trade and Industry—as the hotbed of industrial policy, an evil concept that embraces everything from export subsidies to sectoral targeting. Most foreign critics tend to believe that MITI and industrial policy are post-war creations of the Japanese.

In fact, MITI grew out of the Ministry of Commerce and Industry when the old Agriculture and Commerce Ministry was split in two in 1925. The Ministry of Commerce and Agriculture had its origins back in 1888. So the concept of industrial policy in Japan is neither postwar nor prewar but *premodern*.

"The special attention paid from the first to the strategic importance of modernization," Professor Norman wrote, "in turn arose from the political necessity of throwing up a rampart of defense around Japan to ward off the danger of attack which had been hanging over the country ever since the beginning of the 19th century, while at the same time guarding against internal disturbance which might arise from the excessive burdens laid upon the population in paying for this modern-ization. This fostering of strategic industries does not imply that there was anything sinister in the industrial policy of the early Meiji Gov-ernment, nor is it intended to prove that modern Japan was planning from the start to embark on foreign conquest. But it is meant to show how political necessity, whether of foreign or internal origin, inevitably made the founders of new Japan sensitive to the *strategic* aspect of the industrialization of the country."

Zurui is the word. As here you have the Meiji oligarchs coming out of three hundred years of isolation and the first thing they do when they sit down at the conference table is to say, "Boys, we need an industrial policy."

Of course, a strong bureaucratic tradition helps get things done, and the Japanese, indeed, had a strong bureaucratic tradition. So they started borrowing from the West because that's where the power was perceived to be. But it is important to remember that Japan borrowed from the West not to imitate the West but to improve on it.

Japan's very best people were sent to Europe to learn law and engineering and commerce and manufacturing and government, to ac-quire transportation systems and educational systems and penal sys-tems, and to study philosophy and military strategy and science and the art of brewing beer. They wrote back to their peers in Tokyo that they had visited "courts, prisons, schools, trading firms, factories and shipyards, iron foundries, sugar refineries, paper plants, wool and cot-ton spinning and weaving mills, silver, cutlery, and glass plants, coal and salt mines, not to speak of old castles and temples—there is no-where we haven't gone."

And upon their return, they started putting it all in place, including the establishment of Tokyo Imperial University, which under the Tokugawas had been known as the Institute for the Study of Barbarian Books. It took a while, but then what would you expect after being separated from the world for three centuries? "It may have been easy enough to coin words for postage stamps and trousers and ice cream," wrote Miyoshi Masao at the time, "but it was no laughing matter to create expressions equivalent to liberty, right, or equality in a language long soaked in the hierarchic, authoritarian, and feudal ethos in which no such concepts existed."

So give the Meiji Boys credit. They set their priorities right from the beginning: create a strong army, develop a rich country. Their army defeated China in 1895 and their navy blew Russia out of the water in 1905. They put foreign trade at the top of the list to establish an industrial policy that enabled them to carve out strategic industry sectors for dominance and power. And they did it all with the same thoroughness and precision that had characterized their own domestic craftsmanship for centuries.

Space Heaters and Dollar Bills

"Well, who do you want me to bad mouth first, the barbarians or the little yellow people?" asked Kakimizu Koichi, newly appointed executive director of Japan's Overseas Economic Cooperation Fund. We were sitting in his office near Hitotsubashi in downtown Tokyo. It was early 1983, on the eve of Prime Minister Nakasone's departure for Washington.

I had first met Mr. Kakimizu in New York a few months before when, as director of the Customs Bureau of the Ministry of Finance, he had made a speech on the Japanese government's latest efforts to dismantle some of their famous import barriers. He retired from MOF shortly thereafter (the events were not related), received his *amakudari*, and joined the OECF.

Amakudari refers to the process of rewarding senior Japanese bureaucrats on retirement with ranking positions in business and industry or with directorships in institutions like the OECF. It literally means descent from heaven. Mr. Kakimizu had agreed to discuss with me the U.S.-Japan trade war.

I believe my response to his question was something like, "*Yoroshiku onegai itashimasu,*" which is a very polite expression that means, "I'll leave it up to you." Fortunately, Mr. Kakimizu had a sense of humor.

"The Americans still talk about market access," he said, warming

up. "As if Japan is still closed to the outside world, like it was over a
century ago under the Tokugawas. But they forget, or do not understand, the problems that are unique to Japan. May I give you one
example?"

"Please," I said.

He shifted his erect posture slightly and closed his eyes as he called
the details into memory. "As you know, our islands sit on a deep
geologic fault, and we are susceptible to severe earthquakes. Everyone
remembers how Tokyo was destroyed in 1923, but we get tremors in
Japan almost every day. What does that suggest to you?"

"Safety in building design?" I said.

"And safety in product design," he added. "The Japanese government
specifies very strict standards in product design because of that fact.
Like space heaters. Japanese homes and apartments do not have central
heating, so we use small kerosene heaters. If they topple over during
an earthquake, the fire hazard is great."

He gestured dramatically with his hands, throwing them up in the
air, simulating an explosion.

"So when foreigners want to sell space heaters in Japan, they must
conform to our standards," he said. "The Swedes make very good kerosene heaters, engineered even more stringently than we require. In
all simulated tremor tests, they never tip over. They are superbly
designed. The Americans, on the other hand, simply package their
domestic space heaters and ship them to Japan. Now, which do you
think we will approve for sale in our market?"

I shook my head. "No contest," I replied. That was easy.

"So attention to precision and detail are essential if a foreign manufacturer wants to be successful in this market. Let me show you
something."

He reached into a drawer and withdrew a plastic picture album.
Instead of vacation snapshots, it was filled with banknotes.

"I used to collect foreign money when I was at the Ministry," he
said. "Look at this yen note."

He handed me a standard 500-yen bill. There was Prince Itoh Hirobumi, a Meiji oligarch, with that familiar two-dollar look.

I tried to make the leap from earthquake-induced kerosene heater
fires to pocket money. That was not so easy.

"Look at the white borders," he said, "how even and exact they are,
on all four sides. Notice the *precision*."

I noticed. For the first time. Who ever pays attention to the borders
on greenbacks?

He pulled out a handful of various yen notes. They all had identical
borders and were, indeed, precise.

Then he lay down some American bills. George Washington and Ben Franklin were not surrounded by a force field of identical white borders. The borders were uneven, crude by comparison.

Mr. Kakimizu returned the bills to their transparent slots, looked at me and smiled.

The implication was obvious.

If our federal government was so sloppy when it made its own national currency, how could the Japanese expect American companies to be any better when they produced manufactured goods for export?

PART II

THE TACTICS OF TRADE WARS

CHAPTER 8

FOOD FIGHT!

I think it's another Pearl Harbor for the textile industry in my state. It's been torpedoed by Japanese competition and is in the process of sinking.

—Representative Mendel Rivers, in
the House Ways and Means Committee, June 11, 1970

Japan had chronic trade deficits throughout the entire postwar period to about 1969. That meant the Japanese were buying more than they were selling—importing more than they were exporting. The operant word here is *chronic*.

After the war, when the American liberators began their historic occupation of the Japanese islands—the first time Japan had ever lost a war, let alone suffered the indignation of having their country occupied by the *keto*—there were a number of problems that had to be solved straightaway. Inflation was out of control, the Communist Party had infiltrated the labor movement, and the yen was on a roller coaster ride.

Once those problems were tackled, and they were by no means easy, the postwar equivalent of the Meiji Boys at MITI sat down, and taking a good, hard look at their national pocketbook—which was pretty empty—arrived at a consensus. If we must import all the stuff we need just to survive—oil and food and vital raw materials, such as iron ore and coal—then we must find a way to pay for it. And about the only way we can get the necessary dollars is to export.

Now the real Meiji Boys had developed strategic industries that were crucial to two priority areas: national defense and exports. And each got 50 percent of the oligarchs' attention. But postwar Japan was stripped of its military capability and was prohibited constitutionally from building up its national defense again.

So this gave the postwar leaders only one alternative: to put all their time and effort into their export industries to build a base from which they could generate enough foreign exchange to pay the bills that were mounting up monthly from sourcing their raw materials and natural resources overseas.

MITI fought for—and got—practically ironclad control of all the policy measures they needed to implement the export program: foreign exchange allocation to importers, licensing of new plant construction, joint venture licenses and technology-sharing agreements with foreign firms, and probably most important of all, a dominant voice in the Fiscal Investment Loan Program, or FILP, that represented an off-budget allocation of citizens' deposits in the government's postal savings system. And, of course, FILP's major objectives were underwriting investments in the export industries.

So MITI concentrated on exports. The operant concept was value added. "We'll take all those natural resources we have to buy because we don't have any of our own, and we'll make products the foreigners need." In the 1950s, the key sectors were textiles and shipbuilding and steel. In the 1960s, these became man-made fibers and consumer electronics and automobiles. Products for the advanced industrial economies of the world. Products that were income elastic, as the economists say: their sales rise as incomes rise. Products that generated lots of dollars for Japan.

But even with this degree of concentration and emphasis, Japan had those chronic balance of payments deficits. There were strict capital controls on how much money Japanese residents could remit or take out of the country, quotas on imported goods remained in effect to keep import levels down, and tariffs were among the highest in the world, for the same reason. Cumulative merchandise trade deficits for Japan in the 1960s were around $7 billion. So one purpose of the U.S. Trade Expansion Act of 1962 was to help the Japanese sell even more of their goods in our market to generate needed foreign exchange. Things were tight.

Then in 1970, at long last, twenty-five years after the Pacific war, a plateau was reached. All that hard work and sacrifice and high savings and fixed investment and fast growth finally produced a trade surplus. Small, only about $400 million, but a turnaround at least. Nor was it just Japan with a surplus—because the dollar had become grossly overvalued, America had begun to generate huge trade deficits itself as a result of those competitively priced imports, dollars were flooding out to pay for the war in Vietnam, and domestic inflation was now exacting a toll.

So as Japan began generating trade surpluses, everyone cheered at first because this was the hoped-for result of those decades of struggle. But then the surpluses kept rising. By 1971, Nixon had to devalue the dollar because the yen, with other currencies, was seriously undervalued and the Japanese would not unilaterally revalue. (Why should they? At 360/1, it had taken them a generation to get out from under, and they were far from convinced that their new trade surpluses represented an established trend.)

But even with a revalued yen (308/1 after the Smithsonian Agreement of December 1971), Japan's good years continued. By 1975, the Japanese were running a bilateral trade surplus of $1.7 billion with the United States. By 1977, it was about $8 billion. In 1980, the difference had soared to over $10 billion. By 1982, the Japanese were selling us $17 billion more than we were selling them.

The Americans began to get restless.

Something had to be done.

If the Japanese were selling more to us than we were selling to them, that could mean only one thing: their market must be closed to our goods. Therefore, the Washington bureaucrats reasoned, we've got to figure a way to get them to buy more from us.

So the Washington bureaucrats huddled, and eyed each other, and all nodded in agreement: because the Japanese aren't buying enough from us, what can we persuade them to buy more of?

The answer: food.

The Food Fight

If you start a fire, you must also know how to put it out.

—General Kodama, Manchuria,
1933

Never mind that the Japanese were already the American farmer's largest single customer in the world. Never mind that by 1980, Japan already accounted for over $6 billion of our total agricultural exports of $40 billion. And never mind that one out of about every twelve acres in the United States was already producing food for Japan—more acreage than the entire cropland in Japan itself.

We were going to sell the Japanese more food.

Beginning in the late 1970s, bilateral meetings were held in Tokyo and in Washington to address what the Carter administration called "a serious situation." Because of growing Japanese trade surpluses, the Americans strongly suggested that Japan increase imports, restrain exports, and produce a specific list of long-term measures to cut its current account surplus, including liberalization of agricultural imports, specifically beef and citrus.

The Japanese responded by saying that they had more than doubled farm imports from the United States in the previous five years and the trend was continuing. But restraining exports for the Japanese was like getting Americans to think small. What else could they do?

For Washington, the answer was easy: buy more food.

You can almost hear the strategy session taking place at the White House.

"George, what do the Japs eat over there?"

"Fish, mostly."

"*Fish?*"

"Yeah. And a lot of it is raw."

"*Raw* fish?"

"Yeah."

"Hell, real men don't eat fish. Let's sell 'em some beef. What do they have for breakfast?"

George takes a look at his briefing book.

"Seaweed soup and soybeans."

"Say what?"

George repeats himself.

"Seaweed soup and soybeans? Nonsense! How can you start the day without a glass of Florida orange juice? We'll sell 'em more oranges, too."

And so it was that the United States began a program to pressure the Japanese into buying more beef and citrus. American citrus production had more than doubled between 1964 and 1971, from four million tons a year to ten million tons, and we had all these extra oranges sitting around. Florida accounted for nearly 75 percent of total U.S. citrus production, with California making up most of the rest. Oranges took 71 percent of total acreage, grapefruit 19 percent, with lemons and limes accounting for the balance.

The steer had become the greatest garbage disposal in captivity, and not terribly efficient at that. To get one pound of beef on our plates, the steer has to reduce sixteen pounds of grain and soy. The other fifteen pounds becomes manure. The Department of Agriculture estimates that the manure of American livestock has the potential protein equivalent of our entire soybean crop. That same livestock chews up 90 percent of our unexported grain, consumes the protein equivalent of six times the recommended protein allowance for us humans, and causes three times the water pollution contributed by industry. And we still import enough beef ourselves to put a hamburger on every American's plate, every day of the year. But we weren't going to sell the Japanese our steer, and export some of that pollution. We wanted to sell them steaks and chops.

Prime Minister Fukuda reshuffled his Liberal Democratic Party cabinet about this time, and the postwar oligarchs met to consider their response to our plan. Some weren't so keen to buy beef and oranges but thought they might be able to use more herring and cuttlefish, so they proposed liberalizing those quotas. Others thought the Americans wouldn't appreciate any suggestion to increase their fish exports because Nebraska and Kansas weren't exactly known for their seafood catch, so they proposed increasing the intake of off-season oranges and a little tomato ketchup. Off-season, because they were concerned about the plight of their own *mikan* growers.

Mikan are mandarin oranges that flood the fresh produce market in Japan between October and March each year. Smaller than our oranges, they more nearly resemble tangerines. They are also sweeter. The Japanese love them. Plus, they have lots of farmers producing lots of *mikan* and occupying jobs and supplying votes for Prime Minister Fukuda's party. And they are vocal.

"When we liberalized grapefruit and lemon imports years ago," one party politician said, "producers around the Inland Sea area suffered severely. Can we be sure the same thing won't happen again with beef and oranges?"

But the oligarchs at MITI, being rather hardheaded realists, knew that cuttlefish and ketchup wouldn't satisfy the Americans, so they knocked a few heads together and proposed doubling imports of beef for hotel use only and increasing the orange quota in the *mikan* off-season—when the *mikan* were all gone. That's called being very *zurui*.

You can imagine what Washington thought about that.

The bilateral meetings shuttled back and forth between the two capitals, with the hairy barbarians putting increased pressure on the little yellow people to come up with a better plan. On the thirty-sixth anniversary of Pearl Harbor, Ushiba Nobuhiko, Japan's Special Minister for External Economic Affairs, reportedly told Special Trade Representative Bob Strauss that "no country in the world can restructure its current account overnight."

The Japanese press responded to the American pressure with headlines like, "STR says Japan Should Set a Timetable for Turning Our Current Account into a Deficit." The Parliamentary League for the Promotion of Livestock passed a resolution saying there was no reason to make any more concessions to the Americans. And Japan's Fruit Promotion League took to the streets to protest the coming flood of imported oranges.

So Ushiba and Strauss sat down to play a little food poker. Strauss opened with a bid to increase hotel beef quotas to ten thousand tons. Ushiba countered with two thousand tons. Strauss plunked down a card that said Japan should increase its orange juice quota to fifty thousand tons plus an equivalent fifty-thousand-ton increase in oranges. Ushiba countered with another two thousand tons. Strauss banged a thick Texas fist on the table. "That's not enough!" he drawled. Ushiba merely folded his arms across his chest and said that to meet the Americans' demands, Japan would have to build 2.5 times more hotels and double the size of the average Japanese stomach.

They reshuffled and dealt again. After another pair of hands, with Strauss characteristically bluffing and Ushiba never cracking a smile, they finally reached a compromise agreement: Japan would import ten thousand tons of beef for hotel use, all right, but globally and not just from the United States. They also agreed to triple their orange imports to forty-five thousand tons but to increase the orange juice quota to just four thousand tons. So to sweeten the pot, the Japanese threw in tariff reductions on computers and color film. They knew the Multilateral Trade Negotiations then in progress needed to be concluded successfully, and they wanted a workable compromise as much as the Americans.

Bob Strauss got up from the card table and went to the microphone. "We have really redefined the economic relations between our two great nations," he said.

Ushiba was a bit more restrained in his comments: "I do believe that, whatever present dissatisfaction or confusion there may be, Japan can overcome it." He knew what the Livestock and Fruit Promotion leagues would have to say about the higher quotas.

When anyone starts playing with bilateral trade in food, several things need to be kept in mind. First, most countries view agriculture as a kind of extension of national defense, that is, when push comes to shove, they want to be sure they can feed their people. And Japan already depended on food imports for nearly half its total food requirements.

Second, *all* countries of the world are guilty of sinning against the free-trade Bible when it comes to agricultural imports, maintaining quotas that are not what the framers of the General Agreement on Tariffs and Trade had in mind in Geneva in 1947. The Japanese still had a long list of food quotas left over from the harsh days of the immediate postwar years when scarce foreign exchange had to be allocated for priority imports. But the United States had a long list of its own, including sugar quotas, which were well known, as well as quotas on imports of beef and mandarin oranges (certain western states feared the mandarin's citrus canker), which were not.

Third, no discussion of beef imports into Japan can take place without consideration of the *dowa* problem. *Dowa* is polite Japanese for the *burakumin*: social outcasts, or untouchables. Historically, these were the people in Japan who handled leather hides, did the tanning, and butchered what little meat the Japanese ate. They weren't at the bottom of the social hierarchy; they didn't even exist. Because beef never counted for much until the Black Ships brought in some herds for the American contingent at Shimoda. The outcasts handled that, too.

The *dowa* problem is so sensitive, it can't even be found in the most respected historical sources. Lafcadio Hearn never mentioned it, Basil Hall Chamberlain wouldn't touch it, Mock Joya probably never knew about it, and even old Sir George Sansom, in his famous three-volume history of Japan, doesn't give it so much as a footnote. The Japan Newspaper Publishers and Editors Association refuses to let their member publications even write about it. So to the Japanese, it is a very serious social problem because if they dramatically increase the amount of beef they import, then they need people to process it. And for obvious reasons, meat-handling jobs are not very popular at Japanese vocational schools. So this is one reason the oligarchs drag their heels.

About three months after the Strauss-Ushiba agreement, the American side noticed all the heel-dragging in Tokyo and decided that beef and citrus were simply *symbols* of Japan's closed market. The *real* reason American producers couldn't sell in Japan, they believed, was their perception that the Japanese market was closed to foreign goods. Remember, there had been all those quotas on cuttlefish and ketchup to save precious foreign exchange for iron ore and coal. So under severe pressure from Florida and California politicians to get rid of their excess oranges, U.S. officials now maintained that the Japanese concessions were insufficient.

In late summer 1978, a Japanese task force visited America to do a little fact-finding on their own. They didn't like what they heard. As long as the massive bilateral trade imbalance persisted, they were told, protectionist pressure against Japanese exports would continue in Congress. The bilateral deficit was perceived to be a result of Japan's unfair trading practices, and quotas on agricultural goods not only violated GATT but also symbolized unfair competition. They were told Japan should import enough American beef so that one quarter of their beef imports would ultimately be sourced in the United States. And Japan would have to increase again the off-season quotas for citrus.

Meanwhile, some of the independent Japanese trading companies, which were trying to get government licenses to import more American oranges, started hounding Fujii Trading Company, a small firm that for historical reasons had held about 16 percent of Japan's orange import quota. Fujii lobbied behind the scenes to keep its import quotas intact—there were only 91 licenses issued by the Japanese government for citrus—and rumors of scandal began surfacing in Washington about the feudalistic control exercised by Fujii over the import licenses.

So in the fall of 1978, Minister Nakagawa, head of the Agriculture, Forestry, and Fisheries Ministry, resumed negotiations with Strauss, after Ushiba had gone on record as saying that the Japanese had just concluded one agreement and saw no reason to change it.

This was another *zurui* move by the MITI oligarchs: when you're faced with a possible bad hand, change dealers. This forces the other side to explain all the rules of the game again and gives you a valuable asset—time. Also, the shift to Nakagawa gave the Japanese side a negotiator who was stronger with their cattlemen and *mikan* growers.

Nakagawa explained the plight of the Japanese farmers and likened them to America's autoworkers and steelmakers, urging sympathy. Strauss hammered home the bilateral deficit theme, and "in tones that reportedly shocked and upset Nakagawa, called Japan's [position] completely unacceptable." He had to appear tough to satisfy the demands of the California and Florida citrus growers. His fellow Texans and neighboring Oklahomans also got into the act, creating a Beef Cattlemen's Export Association. Knowledge of foreign markets had finally reached the Red River.

Meanwhile, American commercial interests continued to fan the Fujii rumor fires. Sunkist producers in California claimed that Japan had secretly agreed to allot 55 percent of any new orange import licenses among 400 Japanese banana importers with close ties to the Florida grapefruit industry. Sunkist didn't like this very much. So what started out as an international dispute between Japan and America had turned into a domestic squabble between the two dominant citrus states as well.

Japan hardened its position as their own Citrus Situation Study Group stressed that further expansion of imports would be disastrous for their own industry, that juice production in Japan also suffered from serious excess capacity, and that domestic producers resented American pressure to amend the agreement signed only months before. It resisted liberalization at all costs, and simultaneously criticized the United States for being "severe and rigid."

The Multilateral Trade Negotiations provided a necessary lift. Both countries were eager to resolve this latest food fight prior to the ministerial meetings scheduled for late 1978. More levelheaded opinion makers in Japan, notably the *Nihon Keizai Shimbun*, Tokyo's *Wall Street Journal*, and the *Asahi Shimbun*, Japan's largest daily newspaper, urged compliance with internationally acceptable levels for Japan's agricultural imports. As Prime Minister Fukuda had a party primary election coming up, he was anxious to get this issue resolved.

So a final agreement was signed two days before the thirty-seventh anniversary of Pearl Harbor. Japan agreed to increase both beef and citrus quotas substantially, although not as much as the Americans wanted, but they offered sizeable tariff reductions to make up the difference. The Japanese side stressed that citrus quotas were being expanded in the off-season only. The American side emphasized the importance of the new agreement in reducing trade and economic friction between the two countries at a time of serious bilateral imbalance.

The Americans were pleased to have improved their market access, but the Japanese were still selling a lot more to us than the other way around, swapping their Toyotas and Panasonics for our Tropicana and ground round. Market access, thus, became a kind of Holy Grail: it was one way to fend off protectionist pressures in Congress, which could be deflected by saying we were engaged in sensitive negotiations with the Japanese on various fronts and needed time to conclude them. Publicizing the market access issue was also one way to make those who weren't aware of the problem, aware of it. So it wasn't long before the Washington bureaucrats began looking around for another symbol of Japan's closed market.

Different Smokes for Different Folks

Back in 1857, when the first American consulate opened in Shimoda, Townsend Harris brought in a little beef, some knives and forks, and a few cigarettes. Because he knew the Japanese ate fish with chopsticks and drank rice wine, he wanted to be prepared. He also knew the Tokugawas had gotten rid of the Christians three hundred years earlier, so he wasn't expecting the Japanese to delight in things foreign.

They didn't then, and they don't now. It's not that the Japanese don't *like* foreign goods, it's just that they think they're, well, inferior. The Japanese borrow from other cultures to improve on them. Foreigners often had certain products and systems before Japan did, but that didn't mean the Japanese couldn't do them better.

Including cigarettes. The Japanese have been making their own brands for as long as anyone can remember. Hope. Peace. Hi-Lite. Cherry. Mild Seven. Yet American tobacco manufacturers have long been upset by the fact that their finest brands have been able to capture only 1.5 percent of Japan's $5 billion market. American tobacco manufacturers have nearly 30 percent of the Italian market, 25 percent of the Spanish market, and about 25 percent of the French market. So a 1.5 percent share of the Japanese market is simply not enough.

Japan is the fourth largest cigarette market in the world. China is number one, with a total consumption of 900 billion cigarettes in 1981. The United States is number two, with 637 billion. That's about 3000 cigarettes per man, woman, and child per year, or roughly 10 a day. Then Russia, with 490 billion, before Japan. The Japanese lit up 307 billion times in 1981. Their per capita rate is about the same as ours.

Why can't the American tobacco companies sell more cigarettes in Japan? Of course, they'd like to, but they're up against the Ministry of Finance, not MITI. Private companies don't make cigarettes in Japan. The Tobacco & Salt Public Corporation, a government-owned monopoly that belongs to the Ministry of Finance, does.

This is the heart of the problem. MOF is very conservative. It controls the budget and the tax collection, the Japanese banks and the Fiscal Investment Loan Program, an off-budget national investment account, as well as tariffs and quotas on imports, and *Nippon Sembai Kosha*, or the Japan Monopoly Corporation. *Amakudari*, the process known as "descent from heaven," whereby retired government officials land in attractive positions in private industry and the banks, works very well for MOF. They land their men at the monopoly, too, which means, in effect, MOF controls cigarettes in Japan. Not MITI.

Also, if a country has been phasing out quotas and tariffs for twenty years and practicing such barbarian techniques as deficit financing of the national budget, one's Ministry of Finance is going to squeeze revenues from wherever it can. And cigarettes is one place to start.

Foreign cigarettes in Japan used to have a 90 percent tariff, which made them very expensive. In 1981, the tariff was dropped to 35 percent, which just made them expensive. Then, in early 1983, it was dropped to 20 percent, which should have made them cheaper. But as we know, the Japanese are very *zurui*. To generate additional revenues for their deficit, they raised domestic taxes on *all* cigarettes when they lowered the tariff to 20 percent on foreign brands, so the price differential between foreign and domestic brands remained about the same.

The American tobacco companies are not happy. Because Japan is a $5 billion cigarette market, every 1 percent increase in market share is worth $50 million. They figure that with a European-style market share of about 30 percent, they could be selling $1.5 billion worth of cigarettes in Japan.

But MOF gives the *keto* only 20,000 out of 230,000 licensed tobacco outlets. Nor will they let us manufacture in Japan. So our hands are tied. We complain to MITI. But MITI doesn't control cigarettes. MOF does.

Not to be overlooked in all this is the fact that the Japanese are *already* America's number one customer for leaf tobacco. They buy over $300 million worth every year, which is about 10 percent of our total tobacco exports. America used to grow and sell 60 percent of the world's leaf tobacco. Now we're down to about 25 percent. The quality of our tobacco, like that of our manufactured goods, has been declining, whereas the quality of tobacco in other countries, like Zimbabwe and Brazil, has been improving.

Zimbabwe and Brazil?

Philip Morris is upset. They complain to Washington, who complains to MITI. MITI throws up its hands and says, "You have to talk to MOF." And Washington thinks the Japanese are just being devious again. But they don't realize they're up against one of Japan's strongest and most conservative government ministries, which protects its revenues in part by controlling cigarettes.

There's irony in the whole issue, of course. If Philip Morris and American Tobacco and all the other cigarette companies had even 10 percent of the Japanese cigarette market, their exports to Japan would still be worth only $500 million a year. Our annual bilateral trade deficit is approximately $20 billion. Plus the Japanese sell us such quality products as fuel-efficient cars and top-notch electronic equipment. And we want to sell them more cigarettes?

Perhaps former Finance Minister Watanabe Michio gave us the real answer. "The reason we don't smoke foreign cigarettes," he said in 1982, "isn't their high price. It's that they don't taste good."

The Japanese press chastised their finance minister for substantiating foreign claims that Japan was inherently biased against importing inferior foreign products. Within two days of his statement, Mr. Watanabe had switched to an American brand.

Think Tanks

Washington is full of think tanks. There are research institutes filled with otherwise unemployed academics, called ABC International, Inc., and little brainstorming collections of former government officials, called XYZ Associates, Inc., and private consultancies with the names or initials of their founders that crank out position papers on just about anything their clients are interested in paying for.

There are also the more staid, rock-solid, Establishment Think Tanks, where the ambitious carve out a power base while their party is out of favor and where serious, experienced scholars of the Washington scene crank out their books and reports. The Carnegie Endowment for International Peace is one. The Brookings Institution is another.

Brookings was incorporated in 1927 to combine three previously separate organizations: the Institute for Government Research, founded in 1916 as the first private organization devoted to public policy issues at the national level; the Institute of Economics, started in 1922 to study economic problems; and the Robert Brookings Graduate School of Economics and Government, established in 1924 to train qualified individuals for careers in public service. The new organization was named in honor of Robert Somers Brookings (1850–1932), a St. Louis businessman.

In 1982, the Brookings Institution published twenty-eight books (and issued twenty-two reprints of backlisted titles) in its three main areas— economic studies, government studies, and foreign policy studies. Brookings publications do not compete with diet books and exercise guides on local supermarket racks. Nor are such titles as *Transition to a Free Market: Deregulation of the Air Cargo Industry* or *The Administrative Behavior of Federal Bureau Chiefs* likely to appear on best-seller lists. But they are read avidly by government officials, legislative aides, and rivals at other think tanks.

Fred Sanderson was a guest scholar at Brookings when we met in early 1983 to talk about some of the problems in agricultural trade between the United States and Japan. He had done his Ph.D. in economics at Harvard, worked as an international food policy expert in the State Department from 1946 to 1973, and served as a Senior Fellow at Brookings for five years from 1977 to 1982. He published a book on Japanese agriculture in 1978 called *Japan's Food Prospects and Policies*. He was a recipient of the Rockefeller Public Service Award and the David A. Wells Prize from Harvard.

Dr. Sanderson had written urging us to preserve a "sense of perspective and proportion." Japan was now the American farmer's most important single-country market. In 1982, it accounted for almost $6 billion of our total agricultural exports of some $40 billion. One out of every twenty acres in the United States was producing food and feed for Japan, which represented more cropland than all of the cropland in Japan itself. Grains and soybeans alone accounted for about two thirds of this trade.

But in spite of Japan's position as our most important single-country commodity customer, our demands that the Japanese liberalize their beef and citrus imports—the market access issue—had become a cause célèbre, symbols of Japan's closed market. And the same confrontation and impatience and scapegoating had come to characterize the food fight as had characterized the hardware talks on autos and steel. If the Japanese bought more American beef, then their market was "open." If not, it was "closed."

So I asked Dr. Sanderson about the food fight.

"I think our strategy with regard to liberalization of Japanese agricultural imports is basically sound," he said. "And I don't think anyone really disagrees with the fundamental principle of expanding trade in food."

He stopped, smoothed a hand over his balding head, and continued.

"But I believe our tactics are sometimes ill advised and counterproductive. During my travels in Japan I heard endlessly from people, who are basically well-disposed toward our objectives, that they are uneasy about the stridency with which we put forward our demands; our tone of moral superiority, as if we didn't also have agricultural import quotas; and what is perceived as a lack of sensitivity for the problems faced by the Japanese farmer. Take the orange growers who have been asked to uproot 20 percent of their trees to deal with the overproduction of mandarin oranges for example. Would we expect American growers, in this situation, to be relaxed about increased imports, even in the off-season?"

The age-old complaint against quotas, of course, is that they artificially distort the patterns of free trade. Although still a form of protection, tariffs are preferred because they generate revenues for the government that can be used to offset discrepancies between supplier prices and world market levels.

"I think the Japanese are gradually moving toward liberalization," Dr. Sanderson continued. "We just can't expect them to remove all their quotas overnight. They need time. But they have also begun to focus on a system that I have myself calculated to be to their advantage. Once they eliminate beef quotas, for example, the Japanese can use deficiency payments financed by a temporary surcharge on imports. This would have the effect of reducing domestic retail prices by 30 percent, increasing demand by 45 percent, and more than doubling imports. All at no cost to the Japanese taxpayer. But it's hard to get them to review such a system in detail when we treat the subject so emotionally."

It was true. American emotionalism in the bilateral negotiations had offended the Japanese. Zenchu, the Central Union of Agricultural Cooperatives, had recently put out a poster showing a personalized Mt. Fuji in the form of Amaterasu Omikami, the Sun Goddess, warding off an attack on Japan by President Reagan, dressed as Superman, flying in with armsful of Florida oranges and Oklahoma beef.

I asked Dr. Sanderson if he had seen the poster. He had.

"My last visit to Japan occurred right after the abrupt adjournment of the agricultural trade talks in Honolulu, which seem to have shocked Japanese public opinion. The strong U.S. position had been characterized by the Japanese media as a demand for total and immediate liberalization of beef and oranges as a forerunner to an American assault on Japanese *rice*. Hence, the organized counteroffensive by Zenchu and the anti-U.S. poster."

What did Dr. Sanderson feel was needed now?

"Quiet persistence," he said, "coupled with patience and flexibility. This kind of approach stands a better chance of enlisting the support of those in Japan who have a stake in keeping the trade channels open and of moderating the presently rigid, stand-pat opposition of the farm organizations. Because once we are perceived as moving from beef and oranges to rice, the Japanese will harden their negotiating positions without question."

Quiet persistence, I mumbled to myself as I walked back out onto Massachusetts Avenue. Coupled with patience and flexibility. How can you talk quiet persistence to Washington bureaucrats who are under pressure from our politicians to fix the trade deficit *today*? And how can you advise patience to people whose idea of the long term is about six months?

I shook my head. Flexibility doesn't get you a lot of votes. But being tough on the Japanese does.

Zenchu

Zenkoku Nogyo Kyodo Kumiai Chuokai.

Zenchu, for short. The Central Union of Agricultural Cooperatives. Steadfastly opposed to liberalization of beef and orange quotas. Convinced the United States will flood their market with cheap rice once agricultural quotas are relaxed and put their rice farmers out of work. Concerned about protecting Japan's self-sufficiency in food, already dangerously low with a 50 percent reliance on foreign supplies (of which the United States furnishes half). Lead by a tough, gritty, rural trench-fighter named Iwamochi Shizuma.

Before leaving on my January trip to Japan last year, I wrote to Mr. Iwamochi requesting an appointment and saying I would call his office to confirm a convenient time once I arrived in Tokyo.

Zenchu's office is located in one of those gray, nondescript, seven-story buildings that were constructed in such haste right after the war. It's in the heart of the business district, a stone's throw from the *Nihon Keizai Shimbun* and the *Keidanren* (the Federation of Economic Organizations), two commercial powerhouses.

I had not yet spoken with Mr. Iwamochi's personal assistant on the phone, so when we met, he asked me what it was, exactly, I wanted to discuss with Mr. Iwamochi.

The issues I wanted to discuss had been set out in a couple of books recently published by Zenchu on Japanese farming and agricultural policy. One had been prepared by Zenchu's Central Bureau for Opposition to Quota Expansion and Liberalization of Agricultural Products and was called, predictably, *Why We Are Opposed to Agricultural Import Liberalization and Quota Expansion.*

So we sat for a few minutes, sipping tea and laying the groundwork for my discussion with President Iwamochi, a process the Japanese call *nemawashi.* Literally this means preparing the roots, as of a tree you are about to plant, but it is used now for any deliberate, preparatory massaging of people or problems. Caucusing on the Hill, for example, would be a form of *nemawashi.*

A light flashed on. We went through the outer door and down the hall. The famous Superman poster hung in the corridor, just outside Mr. Iwamochi's office.

President Iwamochi stood as we entered, and after the ritual of greeting, we settled into overstuffed chairs as yet another assistant brought in more tea.

I guessed Mr. Iwamochi to be in his mid-sixties. His hair was graying and he was slightly stooped. He looked tired. He turned to his seated assistant and asked about the nature of my visit. The assistant gestured toward me, so I explained it all again. By now I felt reasonably comfortable with the Japanese agricultural vocabulary, like "beef quotas" and "grain imports."

President Iwamochi looked at me and asked, "Where would you like to start?"

"Beef," I said.

"People don't seem to realize," he began, his eyes narrowing as he warmed up, "that any increase in our imports of American beef will ultimately mean a reduction in your feed grain exports to this country. So what you may gain in one area, you will lose in another. Also, you must remember that when our beef import quotas are liberalized, they will not be liberalized just for American beef but for all beef. So Australia will be ready to compete with you for increased sales. But what we find difficult to understand is why your government is putting so much pressure on an area that, even assuming complete liberalization, which is doubtful in any event, the maximum export gain is only about $500 million *before* any cutbacks in feed grain sales."

I said that I found it difficult to defend the seemingly irrational positions my government sometimes takes, but what else can you say when your bureaucrats focus on agriculture as a symbol of Japan's closed market? Agriculture is a political football in every country, I told him. Then I explained what a political football was.

"The U.S. government looks at two areas—beef and oranges—and decides we have a closed market, forgetting that imports of feed grains, soybeans, and wheat have been 100 percent liberalized for years and carry no tariffs whatsoever. In 1981, we imported nearly 90 percent of all our corn, 87 percent of our sorghum, 96 percent of our soybeans, and over 60 percent of our wheat from the United States. Americans also forget that Japan was your first billion-dollar market for agricultural exports—we now buy nearly $6 billion in food and fish products from you. That's over one third of our total food imports. If anything, we are *too* dependent on the United States and need to diversify our foreign food sources further. The soybean shock of 1975 is not easily forgotten."

Most Americans have probably not even heard of the soybean shock of 1975, but it is etched in the national consciousness of the Japanese. *Daizu shokku*. Hard to express in a meaningful way for people who don't eat soybeans. The Japanese use them for just about everything: in tofu, the bean curd; in food flavorings and seasonings; fried, as *yakidofu*; boiled, as *yudofu*; in soups and stews and noodle dishes of every variety. And in soy sauce, of course.

Soybeans are high in protein, have great food value, and are cheap. So when Washington cut off soybean exports back in 1975 because they feared shortages and didn't even consult their best customer before doing it, you can imagine the uproar in Tokyo. It's like Kansas City one day telling Bloomfield Hills there won't be any more beef for a while, but not giving them the courtesy of advance notice. Result: panic and paranoia.

We talked about the *dowa* problem and the plight of the *mikan* growers and the delicate issue of food self-sufficiency for a small island country isolated on the outer rim of the Pacific. Mr. Iwamochi's voice was calm and persistent. I learned later that he came from Akita Prefecture in the north, one of the great rural districts on the main island. He seemed to typify the old samurai expression: Walk quietly, but never forget your sword.

"Comparative advantage is also rather easy for Americans to talk about. You have unlimited natural resources, abundant agriculture, a great expanse of land, an educated population. But we Japanese have nothing except the manufacturing industries we built up after the war. We have to trade our advantage in manufacturing for your advantage in food. Otherwise, we cannot survive. But we cannot do that while asking our own farm population to sacrifice everything. We are already too dependent on foreign supplies. If anything, we must improve and develop our own farm sector further, to make it more competitive, but we can never compete with America. We don't have the land."

I asked Mr. Iwamochi about national dietary habits, whether the Japanese resented Americans pushing beef onto a fish and rice culture.

He shifted slightly in his chair, and for the first time I noticed that his feet weren't touching the floor. A foreign chair, no doubt.

"Japanese per capita consumption of food has not increased very much since the first oil shock in 1973. There are a number of reasons for this. One, of course, is the decline in real income of the average Japanese household. This has been true throughout the world, not just in Japan. But at the same time, while our per capita consumption of food has dropped, the increase in the intake of nutrition has not. This has nothing to do with expenditures on food. It is related to the fact that the Japanese diet has reached a high level both in nutritional quality and value. Our daily caloric intake has remained unchanged over the past several years at around twenty-five hundred calories, or about 20 percent less than the average caloric intake of the West. But it is enough for the body's needs. Some might say, perfect. And further evidence for the sufficiency of our diet can be found in our national life span: it is now among the highest in the world, with 78 years for women and 73 for men."

We were getting dangerously close to the comparative merits of cultural superiority,* and I felt it was time to wind down. As we stood in the corridor bowing our goodbyes, my eyes again caught the Superman poster on the wall. I asked Mr. Iwamochi if there might be an extra copy available, and he beamed with pride. Assistant number three procured one without delay. It now hangs on the wall behind my desk in Princeton, directly across from a wood-block print of a massive sumo wrestler whose daily caloric intake, I would hazard to guess, is somewhat more than the national average.

When I got off the subway near my hotel, not far from the American embassy in Akasaka, farmers were snake-dancing six abreast through the streets. Prime Minister Nakasone was leaving the next day for Washington, and beef quotas were on President Reagan's agenda. They wore traditional *mompei* work clothes and carried large banners painted with bright red *kanji*: "No More Foreign Beef!" "Protect the Japanese Diet!" "Food Independence!"

How misguided we were, it seemed to me, to try to force the Japanese to change their diet. Our missionaries never had much luck changing them from Buddhism to Christianity. What made us think we could convert them from fish to beef?

*The famous baseball bat case is described on p. 271.

CHAPTER 9

R2D2 AND THE POLITICS OF HIGH TECH

You have to deal with barbarians as barbarians.

—Senator William Mangum of North Carolina on the eve of Commodore Perry's departure

Government procurement codes were being negotiated in 1977 and 1978 as part of the ongoing Multilateral Trade Negotiations, but when our bureaucrats looked at the various offers proposed, they were stunned.

The United States had offered to open a total of $16 billion in its government procurement contracts to foreign bidding. The EEC agreed to open up $10 billion. Japan agreed to $3.5 billion. Not too *zurui*.

How could this be, the Washington bureaucrats said? There's got to be a reason. The reason was Japan's equivalent of R2D2: NTT. Nippon Telephone and Telegraph.

For most of the postwar era, the United States had a telecommunications system that was unique in the world. American Telephone and Telegraph was a private company subject to federal regulatory controls. In every other industrialized country in the world, including Japan, the *government* controlled telecommunications equipment, its procurement, and its use.

AT & T was, however, similar to a government monopoly, in that it had its own network of preferred equipment and hardware suppliers. But it depended on its own affiliate, Western Electric, for two thirds of its needs.

NTT, on the other hand, although a government monopoly, was one of three giant public corporations, or *kosha* (the other two being Japan National Railways and Japan Monopoly Corporation), owned by the Japanese government. These three accounted for nearly 90 percent of all staff hiring and equipment procurement of the total 112 *kosha* in

86

Japan. NTT was particularly visible because of all the high-tech equipment it bought.

But NTT was under the direct supervisory authority of the Ministry of Posts and Telecommunications. Now MPT is not MITI any more than MOF is. Not by a long shot. And NTT had, over time, exercised its own semiautomony and independence from MPT, so that, even though it was publicly owned, MPT had very little direct control over NTT's management or procurement practices. MOF and MITI were stronger, ranked higher in the bureaucratic pecking order, and fought intensely for turf. MPT wasn't in their league.

Being a kind of maverick, NTT had its own system of *amakudari*, the "descent from heaven" that enables senior government officials to parachute out of their formal posts on retiring at age fifty-five and land softly in private industry positions. MITI officials descend into steel, shipbuilding, and consumer electronics companies. MOF officials land in banks and insurance companies and the Japan Monopoly Corporation. But few MPT officials wind up at NTT.

So NTT not only developed a unique management style but also unique procurement practices, which helped them reinforce their independence. Hitachi, Fujitsu, Oki Electric, and NEC were recognized as NTT's family of suppliers. It was closed to the hairy barbarians, of course. But it was also closed to all Japanese companies except these four. One government official compared it to Tokyo University: almost impossible to enter, but once in, nobody flunked out.

Another reason NTT developed along independent lines was that it was profitable. Therefore, MPT had little control over its budget because NTT didn't need much money, and MOF was happy because it didn't use general account revenues. And NTT set up its own R & D labs as well, to put a little distance between themselves and MITI. Even MITI was frustrated. "NTT is beyond the reach of our industrial policy," said one of the postwar Meiji Boys.

But all this was relatively unknown in Washington, where "Japan, Inc." was used to describe anything to do with Japanese government and business. NTT was a public monopoly, therefore, ipso facto, the Japanese government (i.e., MITI) could tell it what to do. NTT was also fiercely domestic and very proud; after all, the Japanese couldn't make war materials anymore, so the high-tech spinoff from their consumer electronics sector was considerable.

In the fall of 1977, the Americans set up a Trade Facilitation Committee to investigate the growing complaints that selling to NTT was worse than taking coals to Newcastle, and in the spring of 1978, Congress established a Task Force on U.S.-Japan Trade under the auspices of the House Ways and Means Committee. The bilateral trade figures pointed up a growing sectoral deficit in high-tech goods as well. By 1979, the Japanese were selling about $100 million more in telecommunications equipment in our market than we were in theirs. Hence, the continued focus on market access. High-tech took the stage from beef and citrus, as NTT became another *symbol* of Japan's closed market.

Initial attempts to negotiate a higher level of open bidding for NTT didn't get very far. The Americans accused NTT of "stonewalling" and "engaging in double-talk." NTT's president, Akigusa, was unfortunately misquoted as saying that if NTT bought anything from the *keto*, it would be nothing more than "mops and buckets."

The Ministry of Foreign Affairs, which had no jurisdiction at all in the dispute, was nonetheless given responsibility for mediating the Japanese side of the negotiations. One MFA official summed up the initial round of talks very candidly. "NTT is being called a symbol of Japan's closed market," he said, "but, in fact, NTT is not symbolic of anything. Practically every other telephone system in the developed world uses a procurement system similar to NTT's."

Late in 1978, our Electronics Industry Association got into the act and sent a team to Tokyo to investigate some of these complaints. NTT argued that foreign equipment was incompatible, gave poorer service, and had a high failure rate. The American team returned home worn out and angry.

So once again Bob Strauss entered the picture to sit down at the card table with Mr. Ushiba. Strauss was concerned that U.S. high-tech firms were not getting a fair deal in their sales to Japan, and he wanted a bigger procurement concession out of the Japanese. Ushiba was bothered by NTT's intransigence as well, but there wasn't much he could do about it. The two started another poker game anyway.

Ushiba said that Japan's offer of $3.5 billion was not low when compared with the EEC because there were nine countries that made up their total $10 billion position. Strauss said that Japan's offer was simply unacceptable and would have to be doubled. He was spurred on by two things: one, you can't lose domestically being tough on Japan, and, two, big numbers look good on the Hill. About this time, Senator Lloyd Bentsen introduced legislation calling for nontariff barriers or import surcharges against Japanese goods if, in fact, the Japanese were keeping U.S. goods out of Japan. It was Texas against Tokyo all the way.

Time now for the postwar Meiji Boys to regroup. Prime Minister Ohira, who had defeated Fukuda in the previous primary following the bad news on citrus and beef, called a cabinet meeting to get to the bottom of criticism that U.S.-Japan relations had become a "problem" because of the NTT impasse. One of his ministers said that U.S.-Japan relations were okay, it was just "negotiations in which the United States *alone* takes the initiative that were a problem." He pointed to bilateral negotiations on nuclear energy, aviation, and defense that were not marked by acrimony or anger.

This was early in 1979; by May, Strauss and Ushiba had had a number of bilateral meetings. The Japanese side reluctantly made a counteroffer of $5 billion, which Washington rejected in public and Strauss ridiculed in private. Strauss felt the Japanese were being deliberately intransigent, and in a lengthy interview, he admitted he did not want the Japanese to be more flexible because he needed an opportunity to criticize them so he would be well received on the Hill.

"I'm doing the bastards a favor," he is reported to have said. "If I took their offer to Congress, they'd simply kick Tokyo in the ass and raise those sanctions against Japanese imports." Which is just another way of saying that domestic politics take precedence over international economic principles, but never mind. You can imagine how the postwar oligarchs reacted when they heard *that*.

Suddenly, as the poker pot grew, the Americans shifted their emphasis from how much the Japanese would source overseas to what specific items of equipment the foreigners should be allowed to supply. Then the specialists got involved, and lists were drawn up specifying certain sophisticated switching and transmission equipment as well as various odds and ends of cable and carrier material.

Ushiba, not happy with Washington's sudden change in tactics, nonetheless kicked the list back to Akigusa of NTT with a note saying that some of the demands had to be met to break the impasse. Akigusa finally agreed to let the foreigners supply some steel telephone poles as well as "mops and buckets," but he chafed at the specific high-tech demands. And in a gesture as traditional as it was unexpected, Akigusa then submitted his resignation to take responsibility for all the trouble with the Americans.

Now the negotiators were bumping up against another barrier, this time a scheduled summit meeting between President Carter and Prime Minister Ohira on May 1. After the cards were shuffled and dealt again, the most the two Pacific partners could resolve was an "agreement to agree." They signed a mutual reciprocity pact that granted access to each other's markets by January 1, 1981, and that enabled the president to close U.S. procurement to countries that did not reciprocate in the area of appropriate goods. Under the Trade Agreements Act of 1979, Congress, of course, defined "appropriate goods" as heavy electrical, telecommunications, and transportation equipment.

Negotiations proceeded after the summit. About a year later, however, in the spring of 1980, Prime Minister Ohira's cabinet fell to a no-confidence vote in the Diet. Ohira stood for reelection but died during the campaign. He was replaced by Suzuki Zenko following an intense factional struggle within the Liberal Democratic Party (LDP). Suzuki then appointed Okita Saburo, a former foreign minister and widely respected international economist, to be Japan's special representative for the continuing NTT negotiations. Okita was an electrical engineer whose English was superb. His father-in-law had been the first president of NTT in 1952, so he had the confidence and cooperation of NTT officials.

Okita patched together the ultimate agreement with Washington that was signed just prior to the mutual reciprocity trigger on January 1, 1981. The Japanese came up with a total of $8 billion in government procurement open to all foreigners, of which about a quarter related specifically to NTT through a complicated three-track system of open bidding for simple parts, negotiated bidding for more sophisticated equipment, and a process of designating specific suppliers for the most sophisticated items.

The postwar Meiji Boys said, in effect, you Americans can qualify to join the NTT family of suppliers. But by this time, they were getting just a little peeved about being singled out for so much criticism, especially as the Germans and the French and the British and the Italians all had similar systems.

Was it just a question of being too *zurui* or were there more substantive reasons why the Americans spent so much time and energy bashing the Japanese?

"No Country Is Very Pure"

Okita Saburo was born in the city of Dairen in Manchuria in 1915. Educated in the school of engineering at Tokyo Imperial University, he began his government career in the prewar Ministry of Communications, worked for a while with the Greater East Asia Co-Prosperity Sphere, and finally in the Ministry of Foreign Affairs.

After the war, he became head of the Economic Planning Agency's General Development Division. He retired from government service in 1963 to pursue private work in economics. From 1973 through 1977, he was governor of the Overseas Economic Cooperation Fund. And for nearly a year, from November 1979 to July 1980, he served as foreign minister in the second Ohira cabinet. He was later appointed Special

Trade Representative for the NTT negotiations. He wrote several books, including *Economic Strategy in an Era of Limited Choice* and *An Economist's 252 Days as Foreign Minister.*

I had met Mr. Okita once before in the mid-1970s while he was at the Overseas Economic Cooperation Fund, and now I visited with him once again in his new capacity as director of the *Naigai Seisaku Kenkyukai,* a government-sponsored research association on domestic and international policy issues. It was a wintry day early in 1983.

On the subject of trade, I asked his opinion of bilateral deficits in an age of multilateral relationships. Mr. Okita nodded slowly. At sixty-eight, he had just returned to Japan from a quick trip to Washington, and he was leaving again soon to address the Toyota Seminar at Columbia University in New York. He appeared weary.

"That is something I have stressed in all my meetings with foreign governments," he said. "When we talk about economic relations, we should compare the overall current account surpluses or deficits, not just the bilateral merchandise trade aspect, which is only a partial picture. World trade is multilateral in nature. Although the United States may have a deficit with Japan, it has a surplus with Europe and other parts of the world."

He buttoned the wool vest he wore instead of the more traditional *haramaki,* a wide woolen stomach band worn around the waist in winter to keep out the cold. His office was cool by Japanese standards, almost comfortable. Most offices in Tokyo are insufferably hot in winter, a throwback to the days when private homes lacked even kerosene space heaters, which prompted Japanese men to overcompensate during the day.

Mr. Okita reached into a file folder and withdrew a sheaf of papers, leafed through them until he found the one he wanted, and then passed it across his desk.

"This is what I mean," he said, gesturing toward the top sheet. "In 1980, for example, the United States had about a $12 billion merchandise trade deficit with Japan but a $17 billion surplus with Western Europe. Overall, America's merchandise trade deficit for the year was around $25 billion, but it had an overall surplus in services of $35 billion. That same year, Japan had a trade surplus of $12 billion with the United States but a $30 billion deficit with the Middle East and a combined $5 billion deficit with Australia and Canada. On top of which, Japan experienced a $10 billion current account deficit. So on an overall basis, the payments position of the United States in 1980 was better than Japan's."

I asked him why Washington chose not only to single out the bilateral issue, but also to blame Japan for many of America's domestic economic problems. In 1982, America itself had a current account deficit of $8 billion, so it wasn't so easy to use its revenues from invisibles and capital accounts to offset the merchandise trade deficit.

Okita shook his head and threw an empty palm upward. "I can't explain it. I do not fully understand why the United States is complaining so much or why the United States is criticizing us so much and bitterly saying that we are exporting and not importing. I think they have to look at the entire picture or, otherwise, this distorted impression will remain.

"In politics, merchandise trade imbalance has high visibility. It gets translated into jobs lost, into pressure on Congress to do something, into votes. But the broader picture has not been emphasized in your press or in public debate or in the halls of Congress. Therefore, these more misleading impressions give rise to somewhat one-sided criticisms about the Japanese position and policy."

There were those two simpler reasons, of course, which Bob Strauss, among others, knew well: that you can't lose politically being tough on the Japanese and that big numbers look good on the Hill.

I asked Mr. Okita about the yo-yo effect of exchange rates on the bilateral merchandise trade account.

He raised a finger in the air. "That is another factor which has received insufficient attention," he said. "In early 1981, the yen was stronger, around 200 to the dollar, but by August it had weakened to nearly 250, and a year later, in the fall of 1982, it was pushing 275."

As we talked, the yen hovered around the 235 level.

"Since the second oil crisis of 1979, Japanese productivity performance, success with inflation and exports have all been strong," he went on. "Consequently, you would expect to see a stronger yen. But the reverse has been true. Why? Interest rates in the United States have been twice as high as prevailing rates in Japan, which has encouraged capital flight to the dollar in search of higher yields. European currencies have done the same thing. All this demand for dollars creates an artificially strong dollar and a weaker yen. A weaker yen makes Japanese exports more competitive in dollar terms and the bilateral deficit becomes even wider."

As his secretary came in to announce another visitor, I asked the former foreign minister if he thought the United States was being just a little hypocritical in its behavior toward Japan.

He smiled. The smile was like that of an old bronze bodhisattva of seventh-century Japan.

"The world is full of sins," he said as he rose to say goodbye. "No country is very pure."

Shake hands is not so bad, but hug?

—Paul Hagusa, President,
Sharp Corp. of America

I was born and reared in Texas, and I think I know a little about the Texan mind-set. Now, if you're a native Texan and you bad-mouth Texas, you can't expect to have many friends left down there. But two things Texans tend to forget are, first, that other places exist outside Texas and, second, that once you leave the state for good, you have to surrender your visa at the border anyway.

Texas is definitely a state of mind. It is best exemplified by the bumper sticker that proliferated during the first energy crunch of the early 1970s when gas lines erupted everywhere but in the Lone Star State. There had been some discussion in Washington of diverting supplies of petroleum and natural gas from Texas, where it was in ample abundance, to New England, where it was not. And the bumper sticker that practically every Texan slapped on the rear of his car told the Feds what Texans thought about that.

It said, simply, "Let the bastards freeze."

Well, if Texans feel that way about other Americans, how are they going to regard the Japanese?

When Lyndon Baines Johnson was asked what he thought about Communists in Southeast Asia, LBJ said, "Let the bastards fry." He was going to nail that coonskin to the wall. No back talk, no sir, just gonna whomp those little yellow devils into shape. Well, they wound up chasing him out of office.

(Friends used to say, back in 1964, that if you voted for Barry Goldwater, we would get a land war in Asia. Well, lots of people voted for Barry Goldwater, and sure enough, we got a land war in Asia.)

And when John Connally was asked, after he turned Republican, what he thought about weak dollars and uncompetitive American products, Big John responded by going to London and knocking some European heads together. Let the bastards buy and hold dollars. Well, he found out the Europeans had several hundred years of more formidable experience than a political chameleon from Texas.

So when Bob Strauss, consummate politician and native Texan, was asked to be our Special Trade Representative under President Carter, we got someone who knew big numbers looked good on the Hill and who also knew you couldn't lose being tough on the Japanese. Let the bastards eat beef.

Strauss took over as STR after he had served as National Democratic Chairman and pieced the various party fragments back together. He was a successful lawyer and businessman and protégé of John Connally who had spent a lifetime involved with legislators and party politics, doling out favors, winning trust, threatening, cajoling, rewarding, conveying power. He was at home with governors and ex-governors, senators and ex-senators, state party chairmen and ex-party chairmen, congressional staff people, lobbyists, lawyers, and lieutenant governors—politicians all.

"Everything boils down to politics," he once said.

And he was our chief trade broker. When the STR was first created under the Kennedy administration, everybody wanted to avoid appointing another namby-pamby State Department diplomat to the post. Christian Herter told JFK that the STR "should be a politician, someone who understands the Congress, what the country's all about and makes it tick, and who particularly understands the process on the Hill." Herter was our first STR.

"Sugar is politics, not sugar," Bob Strauss was fond of saying. And in politics, as we know, appearances count a great deal. Perception is reality.

The problem in viewing our chief trade representative as a broker is that brokers generally have a vested interest in that which is being brokered. In this case, domestic politics. It is hard to see how either our international industrial competitiveness, in the form of manufactured goods exports, or spurs to domestic competition, in the form of foreign imports, can successfully command the attention of our politicians, whose concern for trade is secondary to national defense and day care.

Herter was probably right. The STR should understand Congress and what the country's all about. But should that official be a politician? As we have seen, when politicians get directly involved in the negotiating process, especially with regard to international trade and economic issues, the danger of Christmas tree legislation is not far behind. And if domestic politicians come to play such a direct and prominent role in trade, why not in national security negotiations or aviation treaties or long-term soybean-supply contracts? So all at once, we had a chief trade rep who was both a politician and a Texan.

Elizabeth Drew once wrote about Strauss in a lengthy *New Yorker* profile. She referred to his native intelligence, his shrewd understanding of people, his flexibility, his willingness to go by instinct, his sense of humor. Good qualities all. But she also mentioned that Strauss did not preoccupy himself with substance—an attribute of politicians—and made a big point of not doing so. His inability to relate to the Japanese was aptly caught in her vignette.

"Strauss," wrote Drew, "also disarms people with put-downs and sheer effrontery. In the recent trade negotiations, at a particularly sticky moment, he threw an arm around a presumably startled Nobuhiko Ushiba, his Japanese counterpart, and said, 'Brother Ushiba, you're crazy as hell.'"

Let the bastards freeze. One can only imagine how Ambassador Ushiba must have felt as the recipient of a Strauss bear hug. Here was a graduate of Japan's most elite university, career diplomat, former ambassador to the United States, cultural pride as deep as the ocean that surrounds his country, and a product of a noncontact culture that functions on hierarchy and personal distance. Ambassador Ushiba must still wake up nights with nervous memories of negotiating with the Texas politician. Domestic humor in cross-cultural situations is like nitroglycerin: one drop can be deadly.

But Texas is really nothing more than the national image writ large. Years ago, in another era, Stanley Hoffmann wrote a piece in *Foreign Affairs* called "The American Style: Our Past and Our Principles." He said that America suffers from a kind of happy simplicity resulting from a history that "is a success story, whose people tend to believe that the values that arise from their experience are of universal application, and they are reluctant to recognize that they are tied to the special conditions that made the American success possible."

We ran off the Indians and leveled the mountains and tamed the rivers and created huge industrial oligopolies and harvested the great agricultural wealth of the Midwest, all in a spirit of national independence and relative isolation from the rest of the world. Consequently, Hoffmann argued, we tend to equate world events with our own expectations for those events.

"Since it is inevitable that events will not fulfill expectations," he continued, "Americans tend to blame the world (i.e., others) rather than their expectations. In particular, a people that has never experienced defeat will be more likely to view the very possibility of even localized defeats as a catastrophe, than peoples that are used to alternations of success and failure and whose expectations are gloomily modest. This distance from history and our complacency about it converge in the frequently expressed conviction that we are on history's side, or vice versa, and our enemies are not."

This can be particularly true for Texans, whose principal *Weltanschauung* is that they hardly need the rest of America, let alone the rest of the world.

International trade spells interdependence, and interdependence, for most Americans, spells the end of an era—an era when America was number one, when Americans could do anything and just about everything, when foreign competition simply didn't exist.

We ran the world. For a while. But we're not running the world anymore, and we don't exactly find it to our liking. Why? Because we are forced to compete and to cooperate with others, like the Japanese who want to buy our wheat and soybeans and sell us their passenger cars and video tape recorders. We're uncomfortable.

As Stanley Hoffmann concluded: "It can be highly irritating to have to cooperate with others whose relative immunity from or vigorous resistance to pressure may give them a kind of compensatory equality, despite one's own size and predominance. But to others, especially Europeans, interdependence is the world's oldest story. They have always lived like sardines in a can—and are only too used to having someone behave at times like a shark. To Americans, interdependence is a kind of decline in sovereignty."

Like downsizing the American dream.

CHAPTER 10

VISIBLE AND INVISIBLE TARIFFS

We are importing lots of things we need: Parker pens, Cross pencils and French neckties.

> —Hasegawa Norishige, head of a U.S.-Japan Trade Committee, spring 1983

Agricultural quotas and government procurement are just two of many methods a country can use to keep imports down—or out. Quotas are, in principle, prohibited under the General Agreement on Tariffs and Trade, with only two exceptions allowed: national defense (broadly interpreted to include agricultural goods, which is why *everybody* has quotas for food) and balance of payments crises. When you're running chronic trade deficits, for example, you can slap on some import quotas to keep precious foreign exchange in the country. Banana republics are usually associated with this sort of behavior, although France and Italy, among other industrialized nations, have had recent bouts with deficits and used quotas to fix them.

But the tariff is the preferred method of keeping imports down or out of a market. Why? Because it is *visible*. The tariff rate is on the customs books of the importing country, and the importers know exactly how much tax they're going to have to pay when they sell. Most postwar efforts in favor of free trade have focused on reducing tariffs among the member countries of GATT.

Most. Until recently. During the Tokyo round of GATT negotiations, which occurred throughout most of the 1970s, the focus was on nontariff barriers to trade. Like government procurement. If you restrict your government purchases solely to domestic suppliers, then you can keep foreign goods out of that particular market sector. No tariffs, no quotas, just a little quiet government procurement. Remember Percy Bidwell? He called these nontariff barriers, or NTBs, the invisible tariff, and he wrote about them in 1939 when the world was still trying to figure out how to cope with Smoot-Hawley, the Tariff Act of 1930.

97

The *invisible* tariff. Invisible because you can't see it. Quotas are on the books, tariffs are on the books, but nontariff barriers are, well, they're sort of on the books, too, but you can't see them. And there are a potful of these invisible tariffs in use throughout the world. They're like a kind of commercial bacteria that attack imports and infect them with a disease called uncompetitiveness.

Domestic subsidies are one form of nontariff barrier. The government supplies funds to select industries or industry sectors by way of tax cuts, supplemental R & D payments, or special depreciation benefits. These all help chosen industries price their own products in the domestic markets below the foreign competition.

Restrictive customs procedures are another invisible tariff. You say you'd like to import pianos into our small, isolated island country? No problem. We believe in free trade, so we have no quotas or tariffs applicable to piano imports. (Watch my hands carefully now.) You are free to bring as many pianos into our market as you wish, and they will not be taxed at port of entry. There are just a couple of minor customs formalities we would ask you to observe. (Are you watching?)

One, the forms must be checked and personally approved by the Inspector of Customs himself. He is a very busy man, as you might expect, and you may have to wait a while for the forms to be approved. Perhaps six months. But we shall impose no limits on the number of pianos you wish to bring into our market.

Two, the pianos must be inspected. Surely that is not surprising, for you never know—worms might be in the woodwork and could attack domestic pianos or dangerous drugs might be hidden in the soundboard—so we just want to check them over, if you don't mind. The problem is, as we are a small country, we have only two qualified piano inspectors, both rather old, one of whom is perenially sick and the work load of the other.... Well, you understand. But you can bring as many pianos into our country as you wish.

A third and equally popular kind of NTB is the technical standard, or restrictive administrative regulation. Again, no limits on the number of pianos you can import. We all believe in free trade. However, because pianos are used in the presence of small children, we would insist that all sharp edges be covered with an approved rubber substance to lessen the likelihood of injury. What kind of rubber substance? We'll inform you when you get the pianos here, but the details will be available only in our national language.

You say you would like to include a few electric organs with your pianos? No problem. There are no limits on the number of electric organs you can import into our small island country. We believe in free trade. However, to minimize the chance of a dangerous electrical accident, we must insist that all your organs be calibrated to operate on 113.57 volts. Yes, we know the rest of the industrialized world accepts 110- to 120-volt standards, but we are a small country vulnerable to frequent earthquakes and we must avoid the risk of fire. Still, you may bring in as many organs as you like—there are no quotas or tariffs—provided they're all set at 113.57 volts.

These three nontariff barriers are perhaps the most common. But there are countless others, such as selective export subsidies (to help your export industries compete better overseas), antidumping regulations (set extra strict so every time you suspect importers of pricing too aggressively you can accuse them of dumping and sue them under the antidumping laws), controls over foreign investment (which limit the domestic industry sectors a foreigner can invest in, or the amount, or the term, or all three), and discriminatory foreign exchange rates (i.e., you can import as many pianos as you like, but when you sell them, we can only grant you one rate of exchange, and not a very favorable one, I'm afraid, when you remit the proceeds back home).

And they're all invisible. Word gets around, of course, so that if you're interested in selling pianos to Japan, for example, you know what you're up against and think twice before you start an export offensive in Tokyo. The Japanese, it just so happens, have used these kinds of procedures for so long and with such success that we have thrown up our hands in despair. The practices relate to the original export strategies formulated by the Meiji Boys back in 1872, and the Japanese have used them with discipline and great perseverance. It's all part of being very *zurui*. Too *zurui*, perhaps.

Just imagine the chaos that results when GATT member countries agree to reduce tariffs and then start cranking up the nontariff barriers. Perhaps the most famous recent case involved the sale of Japanese video tape recorders in France. Late in 1982, Paris was becoming incensed that Japan was flooding their market with VTRs. Never mind that there was no French competition for all those Sonys and Panasonics and Toshibas. France is France.

Now, no tariffs and no quotas. (Watch my hands.) You can sell as many Japanese VTRs in our country as you like. There's just one small administrative regulation we would ask you to observe. Instead of clearing the VTRs in lots, by shipment, at the port in Le Havre, you will have to truck them to our customs inspection center at Poitiers. It's only about three hours from Le Havre, and we'll give you directions. Once there, each VTR unit must be inspected individually, but we're sure you'll understand. *Merci.*

Chaos. And very *zurui* of the French. But not in the best interests of free trade as convoys of Japanese consumer goods choke the roads from Le Havre to Poitiers, and the importers wait interminably, drinking Pernod, watching each painstaking inspection, and then repackaging the goods for the long drive into Paris. *Merde!*

Imagine the reaction of Toyota officials, however, who could be confronted with a similar strategy from U.S. Customs in lieu of those thorny Voluntary Export Restraints. (We're not this clever, by the way, but we're learning.) With Japanese cars overflowing the piers at Oakland and Long Beach, all our Bureau of Customs has to say is, "Mr. Yamamoto, we're very sorry. But you'll have to ship these cars through the Panama Canal and up the Mississippi River by barge to St. Louis. We can't clear them for you here." How long do you think it would take for MITI to cave on something we want? And don't laugh. The Canadians pulled a similar tactic not long ago to assist their lumber exporters.

Well, it's not the businessmen and politicians who are responsible for all this chaos. It's the economists.

Remember the scene? Three intellectuals are sitting around debating the world's oldest profession.

One of them, a physician, states categorically that medicine is the world's oldest profession. "Way back, when there was only chaos and darkness," he says, "God created Man and Woman. That act of creation was a medical act; therefore, medicine is the world's oldest profession."

The second man, a mechanical engineer, shakes his head in disagreement. "Way back," he says, drawing on a smooth briar, "when there was only chaos and darkness, God created Heaven and Earth. That act of creation was an engineering feat. Therefore, engineering is the world's oldest profession."

The third man, an economist by character and training, disagrees strongly. "Economics is clearly the world's oldest profession," he says. "Where do you think all that chaos and darkness came from in the first place?"

Dr. Baldwin

Economists, I'm sure, try their very best to help us understand what goes on in the world of trade.

Professor Robert Baldwin of the University of Wisconsin is a good one. He has written an outstanding textbook on international economics, taught the subject, authored numerous books on trade, and served as chief economist in the Special Trade Representative's office during the Kennedy administration.

He is also known as a free trader. So when President Carter nominated him for appointment to the International Trade Commission, the labor unions forced his name to be withdrawn. "If he's not a protectionist, what good is he on the ITC?" they said.

Dr. Baldwin's writing has gone a long way toward clarifying all this chaos and darkness. He wrote *Nontariff Distortions of International Trade* in 1970, when he was at the Brookings Institution, and in 1979, he wrote *The Political Economy of Postwar U.S. Trade Policy.*

Baldwin isolated four factors that have influenced the attitude of Congress toward protectionism in the postwar era:

1. Pressures from major industry groups, such as the auto and steel industry, favoring free trade or protectionism.
2. Relàtive party positions of the Republicans and Democrats.
3. Relative party strengths in Congress.
4. The political affiliation of the president and the enthusiasm with which he pursues a pàrticular trade policy.

Baldwin also demonstrated, by means of the interaction of these various elements, how U.S. trade policy has seesawed back and forth since the war. The first phase strongly favored free trade and lasted until about 1950. Europe and Japan lay in ruins, and the United States acted vigorously to fight protectionism. The Democrats controlled the presidency and the Congress, and pushed through three renewals of the reciprocal trade agreements. In those days, the trade unions were on his side. There was no real foreign competition, so what did they have to lose?

From 1951 to about 1961, during the Eisenhower years, the Republicans gradually accepted the fact that liberalized trade was an important contributor to world peace. But the Democrats moved toward a more protectionist position that reflected the interests of their constituents, who feared adverse economic consequences from increased imports: Europe and Japan were no longer in ruins. Strong textile interests in the South and coal interests in the Northeast forced an easier Escape Clause in the 1955 trade bill that made it simpler to obtain favorable action if they were pummeled by imports. (This was about the time dollar blouses from Japan and coal from the Saar were being sold aggressively in the U.S. market.)

In 1961, Camelot came to town, and for the next five years, Washington was afloat in free-trade rhetoric. Trade was now seen as an effective means of containing communism as well, and President Kennedy reversed the protectionist trend of the 1950s by supporting free trade enthusiastically. When JFK sponsored his Trade Expansion Act of 1962, the halls of Congress exploded in unanimous support. "At rare moments in the life of this nation," JFK intoned, "an opportunity comes along to fashion out of the confusion of current events a clear, bold action to show the world what it is we stand for. Such an opportunity is before us now. This bill will 'strike a blow' for freedom." A far cry from the political Jap-bashing of the early 1980s. The postwar Meiji Boys should have been proud. And were.

By 1968, however, we were ready to enter the fourth and final postwar phase with a retreat toward protectionism. Protectionist pressures were increasing for a number of reasons: imports were giving U.S. goods a run for their money (Japanese steel, Korean footwear, German cars); American multinationals were investing heavily in overseas markets; Washington was reluctant to correct an increasingly overvalued dollar; and the labor unions had stiffened. To which Dr. Baldwin added another reason for the decline in competitiveness of American goods: a narrowing of the technological gap between the United States and other industrial nations. In other words, everybody was catching up.

When the Trade Act of 1974 was passed by Congress, it reflected this rising protectionist sentiment. The president's tariff-cutting powers were limited, criteria for import relief were further eased, various foreign products were excluded from preferential treatment, and the ability of the president to retaliate against unfair foreign trade practices was increased. Instead of striking a blow for freedom, we struck a blow for our own selfish interests. After all, we had helped Europe and Japan get back on their feet. Now it was time to help ourselves.

But we had still come a long way from Smoot-Hawley in 1930 when the average tariff level imposed on imports was 60 percent across the board. By the conclusion of the Kennedy Round in 1967, import duties in the major industrialized countries had been cut by an average of 35 percent on dutiable items and 20 percent on agricultural goods. By 1971, the United States had an average tariff rate of 10.6 percent, the EEC 10 percent, and Japan 9.8 percent.

The Tokyo Round in the late 1970s effected futher tariff cuts. The United States wanted to cut all tariffs by the same amount, but the Europeans wanted to apply what they called a harmonization formula and cut higher tariffs by higher amounts. It took a compromise from the Swiss to reach agreement. They proposed a formula that would divide each tariff rate by the sum of that tariff plus 0.14 percent. This achieved an average tariff reduction of about 40 percent, which most governments found acceptable. Why $T + 0.14$? As Dr. Baldwin quipped, "There was no economic rationale for this particular formula." But it worked.

Two things bothered me about these postwar developments. One was, the more Congress got involved in trade disputes, the more protectionist we seemed to become. The second was a distinct cultural bias to much of the legislation that was passed under the rubric of free trade. So I decided to call Dr. Baldwin to see if he could clarify some of this chaos and darkness.

I reached him at home one Saturday afternoon. He was very friendly, and his voice was calm and clear.

"Congress," I said.

"Yes, I know," he said. "Smoot-Hawley was the worst case of Congress becoming too involved in the details of trade negotiations, as opposed to the broader framework of trade policy. Once the special interests get their hooks on any piece of trade legislation, that's when the Christmas tree bills get passed."

I asked him about cultural bias.

He started with steel. "Pittsburgh had no postwar foreign competition, of course, and paid the steelworkers higher and higher wages until they averaged about 70 percent above the national norm. The older management was still in control and found they were in a no-win situation. They had an adversarial, almost a class-conscious, relationship with the USW and they couldn't cut wages because they needed desperately to avoid the strikes that would let foreign steel carve out even higher domestic market shares at their expense. So about the only route they had open to them was import protection."

I reminded the Professor about Percy Bidwell's bicycles. Then I asked him about textiles and autos.

"The jury's still out on those," he said. "The automobile industry is fortunately less entrenched than steel, and the textile industry has seen its own chances improve. It moved South, got rid of the unions, and injected some young blood into its management as it shifted into man-made fibers. They're still competitive. The real question for us, it seems to me, is whether we can remain competitive in the long run in these old industries or whether we will have to start shifting out of them."

Industrial policy, I thought. But I was getting ahead of myself.

CHAPTER 11

THE VIEW FROM MT. FUJI

I am therefore convinced that our policy should be to stake everything on the present opportunity, to conclude friendly alliances, to send ships to foreign countries everywhere and conduct trade, to copy the foreigners where they are at their best and so repair our own shortcomings, to foster our national strength and complete our armaments, and so gradually subject the foreigners to our influence until in the end all the countries of the world know the blessings of perfect tranquility and our hegemony is acknowledged throughout the globe.

—Hotta Masayoshi, from his "Memorandum on Foreign Policy," 1857

If you had been one of the postwar Meiji Boys sitting around the corridors of bureaucratic power in Tokyo in 1946, would you have done things differently? Remember, you have two thousand years of unparalleled imperial rule behind you, and you're part of an isolationist heritage that thinks the best game plan is an offense that exports and a defense that controls the inflow of foreign goods. Visibly or invisibly.

The country is in ruins, industry bombed out, food production destroyed, military power gone, the national currency worthless, and the populace quite understandably anxious about the future.

So you huddle around the *kotatsu* with your fellow strategists and admit that you must suffer occupation until your country has proved it can stand on its own two feet and won't make trouble anymore. But then. *Then.*

As a friend who worked in Tokyo during the Occupation put it, "No sooner had the wheels of General MacArthur's plane left the ground...." The postwar oligarchs at MITI practiced a little *menju fukuhai* with regard to their foreign liberators: they followed a superior's orders to his face, but reversed them in the belly. Meaning they said, "Yes, sir," when the Occupation authorities initiated economic reforms, but they kept their fingers crossed when they said it.

104

The Ministry of International Trade and Industry ultimately became synonymous with power and control in postwar Japan. Initially part of the Ministry of Agriculture and Commerce founded by the original Meiji oligarchs, it was spun off on its own in 1925 as the Ministry of Commerce and Industry. As we shall see a bit later, it went through several key reorganizations on its way to becoming the Ministry of Munitions during the war until, in 1949, it achieved its present name and structure.

MITI dominated the development of postwar industrial policy in Japan. It controlled foreign exchange allocation, approved or disapproved plans for expansion of industrial production capacity, and developed plans for strategic industries to push the value-added concept of importing raw materials and then processing them for reexport. But Japanese industrial policy was predicated on the premise that to export, their industries had to be fiercely competitive, and for their industries to become fiercely competitive, they needed a period of protection in their infancy from foreign competition. The postwar Meiji Boys figured that once the process of domestic Darwinism had sorted out the strongest and the best from among the principal competitors in industry, those survivors could be expected to succeed overseas.

Chalmers Johnson teaches government and politics at the University of California at Berkeley. He has studied Japanese government institutions and public corporations for a long time and authored a valuable book titled *MITI and the Japanese Miracle*. He wrote, "No technology entered the country without MITI's approval; no joint venture was ever agreed to without MITI's scrutiny and frequent alteration of terms; no patent rights were ever bought without MITI's pressuring the seller to lower the royalties or to make other changes advantageous to Japanese industry as a whole; and no program for the importation of foreign technology was ever approved until MITI and its various advisory committees had agreed that the time was right and that the industry involved was scheduled for nurturing."

MITI—the mere mention of whose name was enough to stop a child's tears.

So you go to work on your strategic domestic industries, protecting them while they're young and vulnerable, at the same time selling what you can in overseas markets to generate some foreign exchange. In the early 1950s, this was mostly cheap toys, dollar blouses, and Christmas tree ornaments. In the late 1950s, it was ships, industrial machinery, and power-generating equipment. In the 1960s, it was consumer electronics, steel, and man-made fibers. In the 1970s, it was semiconductor chips, automobiles, and computer technology. Each successive stage fueled by the same strategy: value-added processing, infant-industry protectionism, and exports of the most competitive products to overseas markets.

As the postwar Meiji Boys watched their strategy unfold, they knew they were on the right track. For the twenty-year period between 1952 and 1972, Japan had the highest rate of industrial growth in the world, consistently in double digits. Much of this could be explained by their catch-up psychology, to be sure, but much of it was also due to the sectoral targeting and strategic industry positioning of MITI.

Plus they saw the way American capital was gobbling up companies right and left in Europe, and they didn't want that happening to them. Preservation of cultural pride was another way of saying, let's keep the barbarians out.

By 1963, when Japan joined GATT, its overall quota restrictions on imports had been cut from 432 categories to 27. And in 1968, when it became a member of the Organization for Economic Cooperation and Development, it reduced its capital restrictions to conform with policy. Well, almost. Because we know that to cut a tariff is not the same as to encourage sales of foreign products in your market. Although the Japanese had put through a number of capital liberalization programs between 1968 and 1972 to show that they had joined the community of advanced industrial nations, not until 1980, well after the European economies had fully liberalized, were they able to eliminate all restrictions on inward and outward capital flows.

Even so, there were foreign success stories in Japan by companies that chose to invest and manufacture directly in Japan rather than export to Tokyo from home base. But their sales never showed up in the merchandise trade accounts, and as bilateral trade deficits widened in the late 1960s and early 1970s, the increased sales of these American companies simply had no impact on the merchandise trade balance because of the peculiarities of balance of payments accounting.

In time, Coca-Cola, IBM, Caterpillar Tractor (through its joint venture with Mitsubishi Heavy Industries), 3M (in a joint venture with Sumitomo), Chesebrough-Pond's, Procter & Gamble (initially through the acquisition of a Japanese detergent company), Texas Instruments (although MITI exacted a high price for their market entry), and the major oil companies (these established refining and distribution joint ventures with Japanese partners and supplied their ventures with crude oil from their worldwide network of upstream production)—all became success stories. By 1982, the combined sales of American companies in Japan had reached an annual level of about $25 billion.

Lots of sales *in* Japan, but not so much *to* Japan, which is how the merchandise trade figures are tallied. If just half the sales of American companies in Japan had consisted of exports rather than in-country revenues, the bilateral trade deficit that year could have been cut by 75 percent. But dividend remittances and repatriation of capital do not appear in the merchandise trade accounts. They show up in the capital accounts, which are not as politically visible.

So when Washington bureaucrats criticize the Japanese market for being closed, the postwar Meiji Boys say, well, that might have been more accurate thirty years ago, but not today. Besides, it's not our fault you choose to set up manufacturing subsidiaries overseas rather than export to foreign markets.

Most American firms that produce and sell in Japan have a better track record with their products than their counterparts who try to export. IBM Japan, for example, has until recently been the leading *Japanese* computer manufacturer with a mainframe market share of just under 25 percent. Fujitsu, Hitachi, NEC, Mitsubishi Electric, Omron Tateishi, and Oki are all competing like hell, but IBM has been the traditional market leader. Its products are designed specifically for the Japanese market. You want a computer that will print in *kanji?* IBM's got one. You want a word processor that has *kana* capabilities—one that can cope with the Japanese phonetic alphabet—just call your IBM sales representative in Tokyo.

Not so with the metal benders. Westinghouse and General Electric tried for years to sell refrigerators in Japan, with remarkably little success. True, in the early years consumer goods imports attracted high tariffs to discourage the Japanese from spending their scarce foreign exchange that way, but over time the tariffs were cut (T divided by T + 0.14) and prices dropped. Yet sales never took off.

Japanese houses are small. Tiny, in fact. By our standards. (When the Japanese look at our houses, they are often appalled at how big they are. Huge, by comparison.) The Japanese don't have spiffy Armstrong kitchens with those Magic Chef radar ranges and Jenn-Air convection ovens and Whirlpool electric dishwashers and Hot Point garbage disposals and all the energy-wasting conveniences of Bloomfield Hills. Until well after the war, many of their kitchens still had traditional dirt floors. There wasn't much demand for Johnson's floor wax.

Nor was there space for a big icebox, so the Japanese designed and produced a small, compact refrigerator that would fit under the kitchen counter. When mama-san went out to do her grocery shopping, she bought enough fish for dinner at the local fish shop, picked up some vegetables and fruit from the *yaoyasan,* got a little seaweed, purchased a few bottles of Kirin beer, and stuck it all in the minifridge when she got home. Before, during, and immediately after the war, the Japanese were too poor to afford refrigerators anyway, so they had to do their food shopping daily. It was part of the lifestyle. Not only did the wives procure fresh food, but they also caught up on the local news as they visited at each specialty shop and chatted with the merchant.

And they would do the same thing day after day after grocery-shopping day. If the Americans from Westinghouse had left their hotel or the American Club during their initial visit to Japan, they would have seen that there were no A & Ps or Safeways. They might even have seen how small the houses were. The Bloomfield Hills concept of loading up on a week's worth of groceries at a time just wasn't in the cards. Had the Americans strolled through a Japanese department store, they could have seen the kind of refrigerators Hitachi and Mitsubishi and Panasonic were putting out.

So after we began sending our mammoth refrigerators to Japan, mama-san could take papa-san to the foreign products corner at Mitsukoshi or Takashimaya to view the proud exports from the Great Rice Country. And overwhelmed by their size if not by their price, papa-san would simply shake his head.

The Europeans also had their problems trying to export to Japan. One Danish furniture maker went to great lengths to get his chairs approved for clearance through Japanese customs and to hire the appropriate middlemen to market them through department stores.

Months would go by without a sale. "I don't understand," he said. "Our nifty teak furniture ought to be just the ticket for modern Japanese homes."

On flying to Japan, he learned from his distributors that there had been quite a high level of trial sales. Customers were buying his chairs and taking them home on approval, but then returning them after a day or two. He simply couldn't understand it.

So they got the names and addresses of a few dissatisfied customers and did a little cross-cultural exploration. He and his wholesaler called on a number of families and saw the reason for their dissatisfaction almost immediately.

The chairs had been designed for European bodies. When the Japanese customers tried them out in the department store, things were fine. But once the chairs were in the home, where the Japanese remove their shoes, the new owners felt uncomfortable when their feet didn't touch the floor. Who wants to sit like a child in an adult chair?

There are other such stories, of course. Detroit, trying to sell those big gas guzzlers in Japan with wrong-side drive, has to be a candidate for the reverse Horatio Alger Award.

Also, as the postwar Meiji Boys say, most Americans don't or can't or won't learn the Japanese language. Japan sends its commercial missionaries all over the world to spread the good word about the superiority of Japanese cars and consumer goods and steel, and they do it in the local language. We all make fun of how the Japanese butcher English when they do business over here, but you ought to hear their laughter when the hairy barbarian tries a word or two of Japanese. They can be as derisive as the French.

Plus, Americans simply aren't patient when it comes to selling in the Japanese market. Rule number one when exporting to Japan is, take the amount of time you think you'll need and double it. Then sell the hell out of your product. Our short-term orientation doesn't help us much when the Japanese are geared to look at market development efforts in terms of decades. For better or for worse, impatience is one of our prime cultural characteristics.

Americans also complain that they can't crack the convoluted Japanese distribution system, which is politely known as the spiderless cobweb. One middleman or jobber or wholesaler, and we're in business in Bloomfield Hills. Not so in Tokyo. Whereas consumer goods are handled an average of 1.5 times between manufacturer and retailer in the United States, the average in Japan is 4.3 times.

An anomaly, the Japanese distribution system serves a purpose beyond just getting products on the retailer's shelf. In periods of recession, it serves as a shock absorber for unemployment. Lose your job, start wholesaling Nikka whiskey or Kewpie mayonnaise. Things look up, go back to work. Either way, those official unemployment statistics remain low. Manufacturer to regional distributor to district wholesaler to local jobber to retailer's rep to retailer—4.3 times. Around the horn. Everybody takes a cut, and the system helps replace unemployment benefits, which are scanty.

Americans should not forget that their products stand a better chance of success in the Japanese market if they are somehow identified in the consumer's mind as being Japanese rather than foreign. Ragu spaghetti sauce, very popular in America, sells well in Japan not because the Japanese consumer knows or even cares that it is a Chesebrough-Pond's product. It sells well because the name of Chesebrough's Japanese partner, Kikkoman, is prominent on the front label. So mama-san thinks those wonderful soy sauce people have brought out another new product; she tries it, she likes it, and she tells all her friends about that wonderful spaghetti sauce from Kikkoman. The Chesebrough name appears, in *kana*, on the back label. In small print.

So you take one part nontariff barrier, two parts poor product design, one part Japanese language, one part American impatience, two parts Japanese distribution system, and three parts cultural pride—mix well and bake.

What do you get?

A closed market.

CHAPTER 12

OF POTS AND KETTLES: AMERICAN HYPOCRISY

O wad some Power the giftie gie us
To see oursels as ithers see us!

—Bobbie Burns, 1785

Oh to others the giftie be,
to see myself as I see me.

—Contemporary American version

"Putting it bluntly, the United States is a 'knight in shining armor' compared to other nations of the Free World," Lewis Lloyd wrote in *Tariffs: The Case for Protection* in 1955. "Foreign trade barriers are as bad or worse than ever. Stringent exchange controls are the norm. Strict licensing or quota systems are in effect. Citizens are not free to travel abroad. Cartels everywhere are rampant."

Lloyd was writing at a time when protectionist pressures were on the increase in this country. He put forth a number of proposals for a new U.S. trade policy, among which were the following:

1. America should not lower its tariffs any further.
2. When negotiating, we should get a clause placing limitations on other nations' use of trade restrictions.
3. Administration of tariffs should be returned to the Congress.
4. Our participation in GATT should be only on the basis of consultation. "We should not bargain away the rights and interests of our citizens at an international bargaining table," he wrote.
5. Our foreign trade policy must always give due weight to problems of defense and national security.

110

Well, the postwar Meiji Boys stifled a few grins when they read that, and they probably weren't alone in suspecting that Lloyd's research was a bit on the meager side. It was he, for example, who proclaimed proudly that "in the 20 years since 1934, the United States has progressed to the point where it now has lower trade barriers than any other major trading nation in the world, except Japan."

This was 1955, remember. Not exactly Tokugawa, but if you were a Japanese citizen and wanted to travel abroad, you had to get all kinds of permission from the government just to get a passport and some foreign exchange. Strategic-industry targeting had resumed, cushioned behind a wall of infant-industry protection, high tariffs, and MITI's iron-fisted control.

Lloyd was not dismayed. He was one of the earliest defenders of Bloomfield Hills. "Critics can argue lower auto tariffs with impunity," he said, "because the average American cannot afford to buy a foreign make of car. Not because American cars are necessarily and fundamentally cheaper, but because there is, in the United States, no system of service stations with parts and experienced mechanics to repair foreign cars." The MITI oligarchs just smiled. They would start changing all that soon enough.

But what about Lloyd's claim that America was a proverbial knight in shining armor? Does this contention hold up? Let's take a look at various trade barriers of our own, beginning with ASP.

The American Selling Price was one of the most ingenious nontariff barriers ever created. Unique to the United States, it was hated by foreigners with a fierceness not known since Smoot-Hawley.

ASP helped protect the American chemical industry. It worked like this. If you were a foreign exporter selling chemicals, for example, most importing countries would levy their tariffs on your product price, ex-factory, before adding insurance, freight, and profit. But in America, the tariff was applied to the domestic price of comparable *American* chemicals selling in the U.S. market. Hence the designation ASP.

So if your chemicals were priced at $50 a pound, say, FOB/Hamburg, and the tariff rate was 50 percent, then you would normally expect to pay a tax of $25 and sell the products at $75 plus insurance, freight, and profit.

But not in America. Here, if the selling price of comparable products was $100, then you paid the tariff on that price, not on your price. So the tax would be $50 instead of $25, and your base price here would be $100, which even before adding freight and profit makes it harder for you to compete with the American giants. Pretty neat.

Professor Baldwin had this to say about ASP. "The U.S. practice most annoying to foreigners," he wrote in *Non-Tariff Distortions*, "is the use of the American Selling Price, whereby certain imports are valued at the price of similar products produced in the U.S. rather than, as is usual, at their wholesale price, the export value of the foreign-produced products. No other major trading nation uses a valuation system based on domestic prices for its non-agricultural products; introduction of such a system would be in violation of the standards set down in GATT. The U.S. practice predates its membership in GATT and is grandfathered."

Grandfather clauses and waivers are the best way to avoid compliance with new rules. In a related practice, the United States used to tax whiskey imports on the basis of 100-proof contents. Most whiskey exported to and sold in this country is 80 proof, so the exporter in fact paid an extra tariff on plain water. Very *zurui*.

Washington finally agreed to relinquish ASP in 1979 as part of the Tokyo Round of GATT negotiations.

What about quotas?

Quotas are prohibited by GATT, except for balance of payments or national defense purposes. Agriculture qualifies as an extension of national defense—the other half of the guns-and-butter equation—so food quotas are on *everybody*'s books. And America is no exception.

Absolute quotas are in effect in the United States on a large number of agricultural imports: raw cotton and cotton wastes, for example, wheat and rye, mandarin oranges, cheese, butter substitutes, dried milk and cream, and peanuts. We also have the flexibility to apply quotas on fresh, chilled, or frozen beef, veal, mutton, and goat meat when imports exceed a certain level.

And don't forget sugar. In 1966, one estimate showed that if sugar quotas were eliminated entirely and duty and excise taxes abolished, the annual cost of sugar consumed in America would decline by $785 million. The cost attributed to quotas alone was $560 million. Today, Americans pay three times the world price for their sugar.

Next, subsidies.

And lots of them. We'll leave aside the question of agricultural subsidies for the moment because Washington does not subsidize food exports per se; but there is a fine line between subsidizing the domestic production of wheat, for example, which you also export, and subsidizing the direct sale of wheat to foreigners. Like the fine line between ASP and normal import tariffs.

Export credits (such as those implemented through our Export-Import Bank), insurance, guarantees, even foreign aid to banana republics tied to the purchase of domestic U.S. products are all forms of subsidy.

The American shipping industry receives federal subsidies to compensate for its high operating costs. There is also a standing requirement that 50 percent of all U.S.-government-financed cargoes be shipped abroad in U.S. flagships, which has been estimated to cost the taxpayer hundreds of millions of dollars annually in taxes. Another regulation requires that all U.S. coastal trade be carried out in U.S.-built, -owned, and -operated vessels.

What else? Government procurement.

Until the Buy American Act of 1933 was superseded by the GATT government-procurement codes under the Multilateral Trade Negotiations concluded in 1979, American suppliers were given a 6 percent price preference over foreign suppliers, with a 12 percent price preference to American firms in so-called depressed areas (such as Appalachia or The Bronx). In fact, the Department of Defense was giving a 50 percent price preference to American firms for all nonmilitary procurement. You can imagine the domestic political uproar in the 1930s when it was discovered the Department of Defense had bought a diesel engine from Switzerland and was using Russian matches in its dining rooms.

What else? The American system of measurement.

The United States is the only major industrial country in the world that has not adopted the metric system, excluding, of course, Her Majesty's imperial gallons and the Ayatollah's linear cubits. This means that foreign automakers have to stamp out separate speedometers for their export dashboards, imported machine tools have to be calibrated in feet and inches rather than meters and centimeters, and foreign steel has to be weighed in pounds and ounces rather than in kilograms. A very nice invisible tariff because it increases costs for the producer, but we don't necessarily call it that.

And finally, escape clauses.

The famous administrative Swords of Damocles. If all else fails, American producers can invoke Section 201 (which triggers an ITC investigation) or Section 301 (which triggers a USTR investigation) of the Trade Act of 1974, approved and implemented by the Trade Agreements Act of 1979. Domestic American manufacturers can also claim injury from imports for national security reasons, and petition for relief. Or should they suspect foreigners of dumping in the domestic market, they can run to Sections 321 and 331, and request the Department of Commerce to invoke countervailing duties.

Harassment: a typical American countermove. When in doubt, sue. This also is very much in keeping with the American character, which not only has a tendency to be confrontational but also has a bent toward hypocrisy as well.

Visitors to America have been quick to point out our fatal flaws. De Tocqueville was among the most famous, but other educated foreign guests have penetrated our surface strengths to find the contradictions lurking not far below.

When the first Japanese embassy was established in Washington in 1860, Muragaki Norimasa went up to the Hill to watch Congress in session.

"We had a good view of the hall below where a heated debate was taking place," Muragaki wrote. "Even when discussing the most important problems facing the country, they wore their usual narrow-sleeved black coat and trousers, and cursed and swore in the loudest voices. The way they behaved, with the Vice President presiding on the elevated platform, the whole scene reminded us, we whispered among ourselves, of our fishmarket at Nihonbashi."

This predisposition to see ourselves as knights in shining armor was also rejected by Mrs. Trollope when she made the first of several visits to this country in 1832.

"We were in Washington at the time that the measure for chasing the last of several tribes of Indians from their forest homes was canvassed in Congress," she wrote in *Domestic Manners of the Americans*, "and finally decided upon by the fiat of the President. If the American character may be judged by their conduct in this matter, they are most lamentably deficient in every feeling of honour and integrity. It is among themselves, and from themselves, that I have heard the statements which represent them as treacherous and false almost beyond belief in their intercourse with the unhappy Indians.

"Had I, during my residence in the United States, observed any single feature in their national character that could justify their eternal boast of liberality and the love of freedom," Mrs. Trollope went on, "I might have respected them, however much my taste might have been offended by what was peculiar in their manners and customs. But it is impossible for any mind of common honesty not to be revolted by the contradictions in their principles and practice."

You can almost feel her quill pen snap against the writing paper.

She concluded: "They inveigh against the governments of Europe because, as they say, they favour the powerful and oppress the weak. You may hear this declaimed upon in Congress, roared out in taverns, discussed in every drawing-room, satirized upon the stage, nay even anathematized from the pulpit: listen to it, and then look at them at home. You will see them with one hand hoisting the cap of liberty, and with the other flogging their slaves. You will see them one hour lecturing their mob on the indefeasible rights of man, and the next driving from their homes the children of the soil, whom they have bound themselves to protect by the most solemn treaties."

Pretty strong stuff, 150 years ago.

Knights in shining armor, indeed.

CHAPTER 13

MANUAL TYPEWRITERS IN THE COMPUTER AGE

The average judgment formed by those who have lived some time among the Japanese seems to resolve itself into three principal items on the credit side, which are cleanliness, kindliness, and a refined artistic taste, and three items on the debit side, namely, vanity, unbusinesslike habits, and an incapacity for appreciating abstract ideas.

—Basil Hall Chamberlain, 1895

Simply put, a bilateral merchandise trade deficit results from an excess of imports over exports. The Japanese, say, sell more to us than we sell them.

Washington's cure: sell more to the Japanese.

But there are problems with this prognosis. First of all, Washington is convinced that Japan's market is closed to us and that we have to mount a new Christian crusade to open it. Second, Tokyo is convinced Americans don't try hard enough, haven't studied the market, aren't patient, and won't learn their language.

Plus, Washington puts all its efforts into selling food and telephone equipment, admitting that even if Japan were the fifty-first state and had no quotas or nontariff barriers, the maximum dent in the $17 billion bilateral deficit would be about $2 billion. Add tobacco, and you get maybe $2.5 billion.

That still leaves $14.5 billion, which is a lot of pork bellies and orange juice. Also, once the agricultural quotas are off, it's a free-for-all, with Australia and Brazil just sitting in the wings waiting for the opportunity to sell more to Japan.

What to do?

Deficits are a two-way street. Sure, we can try to sell more to Japan, but that's probably a dead-end street. Like trying to get the Japanese to stop eating with chopsticks. A better strategy is to try to persuade the Japanese to export less.

116

Now, I suspect you're going to say the postwar Meiji Boys would never go in for something like that, addicted as they are to exporting.

But I think they see the *kanji* on the wall now. Because there have been enough Voluntary Export Restraints imposed on Japanese goods in the past fifteen years to convey the message. One estimate last year put some 60 percent of all Japanese exports subject to some form of restraint. And even though Japan has made end runs around the VERs by exporting cars in assembly kits, for example, or transshipped steel into the United States via Mexico and Canada, they know the days of their export drives are over.

Also, the more we try to get them to buy from us, the more they will try to sell to us. Otherwise, where are they going to get all that foreign exchange to pay us with?

But there's another way the Japanese can export less, and that's by investing directly in the U.S. market—transplanting a proportionate share of their productive manufacturing capacity here rather than exporting from home base. Then, no matter how many cars they sell here, most of the dollars stay in this country rather than flowing out to Tokyo. They're called retained earnings. Dividend remittances and repatriation of capital will of course occur, but with impact on the capital accounts and not on the merchandise trade accounts. And the impact on jobs would be staggering.

I prepared a short paper a few years ago for the Japan Society in New York on Japan's expected direct foreign investment in the 1980s. I proposed that it was meaningless to talk about the bilateral trade deficit in aggregate terms and suggested that a sectoral approach was necessary.

For example, Americans spent a total of $255 billion on imports in 1982. Of that amount, we spent $68 billion on oil and $17 billion on food. That left $170 billion for what economists call "non-ag, non-fuel."

Of that amount, we spent $35 billion on manufactured goods, about 20 percent of the "non-ag, non-fuel" sector, of which about $7.5 billion went to Japan for such popular items as iron and steel and Bridgestone tires.

We spent another $35 billion on transportation equipment, about 20 percent of the sectoral total, of which nearly $15 billion went to Japan for Toyotas and Datsuns and Hondas.

And we spent $41 billion on machinery, about 25 percent of the sectoral total, over $13 billion of which went to Japan for Canon copiers and Hitachi computers and Mitsubishi Electric generators.

Or, looked at another way, Japan supplied us almost half of all our imported transportation equipment: 55 percent of all imported autos, buses, and trucks; 49 percent of imported autos alone; and 96 percent of all imported motorcycles.

Japan sold us 37 percent of all the iron and steel we imported that year as well as 39 percent of all metal and machine tool imports; 49 percent of imported office equipment and computers; over half our telecommunications, video, and sound equipment; 22 percent of all electrical equipment; 26 percent of heavy industrial machinery and equipment; 25 percent of professional and scientific instruments; and 31 percent of all clocks and watches.

Five key industry sectors alone accounted for over two thirds of our manufactured goods imports from Japan in 1982.

Transportation equipment, $14.4 billion, 36 percent of the total

Telecommunications equipment, $4.8 billion, 12 percent of the total

Iron and steel, $3.9 billion, 10 percent of the total

Electrical machinery, $2.3 billion, 6 percent of the total

Office equipment and computers, $2.2 billion, 5 percent of the total

These five industry sectors represented $27.6 billion out of a total of $39.8 billion worth of imports from Japan into the United States in 1982—69 percent of all manufactured goods imports from that country.

We had to be out of our minds, fussing about their taking more beef and oranges and tobacco. We're supposed to be pragmatic. We invented Teflon and put a man on the moon, didn't we? So why didn't we encourage the Japanese to bring some of their automobile plants and machine factories and computer operations over here instead of exporting the damn stuff from Yokohama? (And not through coercion, which local content legislation would require—or, as the *Wall Street Journal* correctly phrased it, "loco content." One would think, through our experience with prohibition in the 1920s, that we had learned our lesson.)

The answer was simple. One, the direct investment process takes a lot longer to show results than stepped-up orange quotas or government-procurement contracts. And two, you aren't *perceived* as being tough on the Japanese when you're inviting them to invest in America. And this, as we know, can be politically disadvantageous.

In fact, numerous Japanese manufacturers had already begun to shift part of their productive plant and equipment capacity to the U.S. market. Though reluctantly, to be sure. When you're addicted to exports, withdrawal takes time. But Honda was making motorcycles in Ohio as early as 1973, and Kawasaki followed suit in Nebraska in 1974;

Kikkoman was producing soy sauce in Wisconsin in 1975; YKK was making zippers in Georgia that same year; and by 1976, practically all the major Japanese television makers had assembly plants over here: Sony, Hitachi, Matsushita, Mitsubishi, Toshiba.

The Japanese automakers were on the way. By 1978, Honda had started expansion of its motorcycle plant in Marysville, Ohio, to produce four-wheel Accords there by 1982. In 1980, Nissan announced the establishment of a new truck factory, wholly owned, in Smyrna, Tennessee. And by early 1983, GM and Toyota had come up with plans for a joint venture to make a replacement for the Chevette, based on the Corolla, at GM's Fremont, California, plant. Assuming the Justice Department would give its blessing and pronounce this arrangement free of antitrust restraints, which it ultimately did.

But the trend was set. Hate to have to do it, set up shop with all these hairy barbarians. Their product quality is inferior to ours, and they have all those labor unions who behave like wild men, and you can't take one damn step without calling your lawyer. Still, it's better than that endless abuse our brothers are taking, so let's hold our breath and swallow the nasty brew. The main things is, *we can protect our market share.*

So the stage was set. Here were all these representatives of the Greater East Asia Co-Prosperity Sphere setting up shop and we blew it. A little lip service was given to encouraging Japan's automakers to consider some factory transplants in the late 1970s; but even when it came to the auto industry, our primary efforts were directed at getting the Japanese to source more of their domestic spare-parts requirements in this country and taking them back to Japan.

What moxie it must have taken some Department of Commerce official to try to persuade his counterparts at MITI to use those life-threatening Firestone radials instead of their own Bridgestones on Japanese cars! Whether he is still in Washington, no one knows, but he was not successful.

Five key sectors, $28 billion. Even allowing for a three-to-five-year gap in execution, we might be farther ahead today if we had taken all that highly charged energy out of beef and oranges and, instead, worked at persuading the Japanese to make direct investments in our market. Because this spells value-added and is pronounced market share, which is the staff of life to a commercial nation like Japan. A strategy based on simply getting the Japanese to buy more from us is a little like using manual typewriters in an age of 128K micro word processors.

Even if we exclude steel, which obviously doesn't lend itself to transoceanic transplants, and convince the Japanese to shift just a portion of their production capacity for these key sectors into the U.S.

market, the bilateral trade deficit would be much lower, American employment would be much higher, and all this Jap-zapping would be politically defused.

Imagine the reaction of the Japanese business community in Tokyo if a senior official from the White House or the Commerce Department were to visit Honda's plant in the United States to say how pleased we are that the Japanese have invested in America in this way—creating new jobs and products for our country. Cooperation rather than confrontation; a positive rather than a negative approach; a friendly instead of an adversarial relationship.

But that's not how votes are obtained in Detroit and Pittsburgh. And, as we know, it doesn't look as good on the Hill.

The U.S.-Japan Trade Study Group

The U.S.-Japan Trade Study Group, a bilateral, semiofficial committee established in Tokyo in the late 1970s to look into the questions of market access, invisible tariffs, and bilateral deficits, came up with some interesting observations of its own. The findings were released in spring 1983 under the heading *Japan: Obstacles and Opportunities.*

Some of the conclusions were a little offbeat, such as the suggestion that to penetrate the Japanese market more thoroughly, U.S. firms ought to concentrate on five Japanese industry sectors: financial services, computer software, medical management services, videotape rentals, and truck leasing. They called these The Opportunities. With the exception of software, there's not much in the way of export potential in these sectors.

But they also looked at The Obstacles, and here their analysis was a little better.

For example, the United States accounts for 50 percent of all technological agreements with Japanese companies. Assuming royalties or licensing fees of around 3 percent of sales, total annual remittances from Japan to the United States are equivalent to some $35 billion in sales to the Japanese market. But American firms choose to sell their technology rather than to export the equipment directly. And these royalty remittances are not factored into the bilateral merchandise trade balance. They show up in the invisibles accounts together with insurance, freight, and tourist expenditures.

Second, the United States sells Japan about $20 billion worth of crude oil each year from third countries, principally from the Middle

East through the major oil companies. The profits on these crude oil sales are not reflected in the bilateral merchandise trade account, and neither are the shipments, which show up in the bilateral accounts between Japan and Saudi Arabia or Iran.

Third, U.S. direct investment in Japan is about equal to its investment in Belgium, which has a GNP of only $116 billion, or about one-tenth the size of Japan's $1,127 billion. In 1980, Japan accounted for only 2.9 percent of total U.S. foreign direct investment of $213 billion. American investment was 4.5 times greater in the UK, whose GNP is only half the size of Japan's. Germany had 7.2 percent of total U.S. overseas investment, France 4.4 percent, and even Holland and Switzerland had higher levels of direct investment from the United States than Japan.

Fourth, although it was true in the 1960s that Japan had a higher number of quotas than other industrialized countries, that is no longer true. Today, they have only 27, of which 22 are agricultural. These 27 quotas represent 2.5 percent of all marketable goods in Japan. Germany has 14 product categories under quota, France 46. Other than agricultural goods, Japan has 5 excludable quota categories, the United States 6, Germany 11, and France 27.

Fifth, in response to complaints that foreigners are not permitted to participate in the writing of technical or product standards, the Japanese now allow them to do so. This is of limited value, however, unless you can speak or read Japanese.

Finally, the study group concluded with the observation that the Japanese have in the space of one generation become the most demanding consumers in the world, from among the poorest to the second richest after the United States. And still, the Americans sell big cars with wrong-side drive, equipment not measured to the metric system, appliances not adapted to lower voltage and frequency requirements, office equipment without *kanji* capabilities, clothes not cut to fit the smaller Japanese body, hamburger meat that isn't fatty, and ketchup that doesn't run.

As one of the study group participants, an American, summed up his frustrations, "Unless we can contain the Japanese by taking a larger share of their market, we can't expect to beat them at home or anywhere else."

Another participant, Ohmae Kenichi, who is the managing director of McKinsey's Tokyo office and author of *The Mind of the Strategist*, was somewhat more blunt.

"Bilateral trade figures are just not a very reliable indicator of performance," he once told me. "Global, yes, but bilateral? Do we measure merchandise trade transactions bilaterally between Texas and California?"

But it's easier to search for scapegoats than it is to devise a competitive counterstrategy. Such as persuading the Japanese in a positive way to shift part of their production capacity overseas by investing directly in our own market.

CHAPTER 14

EUROPE'S NOBLE ELITE

How do our characteristics strike the Japanese? From hints dropped by several of the educated, and from the still more interesting, because frankly naive, remarks made by Japanese servants, the Japanese consider our three most prominent characteristics to be dirt, laziness and superstition. What is a stranger who hails from a land of fifteen working hours daily and of well-nigh three hundred and sixty five working days yearly, to conclude from the habits of European artisans and from post offices closed on Sundays either totally or during portions of the day? For all these and yet other reasons, Europe and America make a far less favourable impression on the Japanese visitor than seems to be generally expected. Be he statesman or be he valet, he is apt to return to his native land more patriotic than he left it.

—Basil Hall Chamberlain, 1895

Back in the late nineteenth century, when the Meiji Boys fanned out all over Europe to study the art of building railroads, designing blast furnaces, and brewing beer, the Noble Elite of the Continent thought it was all rather quaint. Here were these little foreigners running around in groups, bowing and smiling and acting just as innocent as children.

The Europeans felt it was fitting and proper for the Japanese to borrow from their own superior industrial systems, political institutions, and military structures because Europe represented the Advanced Industrial Powers of the world. And the Japanese knew they had to borrow to catch up, but they also knew they wouldn't be satisfied in just pulling even.

They had to *surpass* the Western powers. Anything less wouldn't be, well, Japanese.

So the relationship was one-sided from the beginning. The West was the teacher, Japan the student. *Sensei-deshi.* Master-apprentice. This

suited the Japanese just fine because of the unique, hierarchical way
in which they viewed the world. Europe and America were at the top
of the heap, respected and admired, because they had political and
military power. Russia, China, and Korea were at the bottom and got
no respect. In fact, China got knocked off by Japan in 1895, Russia in
1905, and for its part, Korea got occupied for a generation from 1911
to 1945.

The Noble Elite of Europe travelled to Japan during the Meiji era,
of course, but not so much to trade as to vacation. Japanese silks were
greatly prized, the lacquerware brightened their dreary drawing rooms,
and those samurai swords were handsome indeed. "The land of gentle
manners and fantastic arts," was how one European resident described
the land of the rising sun. But when the Europeans tried to do business
with the Japanese, they came away simply shaking their heads.

"European bankers and merchants in Japan complained not so much
of actual, wilful dishonesty," wrote Basil Hall Chamberlain in 1895,
"as of pettiness, constant shilly-shallying and unbusinesslikeness almost passing belief. Japan, the globe-trotter's paradise, is also the grave
of the merchant's hopes."

Chamberlain recorded the comments of another prominent English-
man, Sir Edwin Arnold, who visited Japan shortly after the turn of the
century:

> When Sir Edwin came to Tokyo, he was entertained at a banquet by a
> distinguished company including officials, journalists, and professors; in
> fact, representative modern Japanese of the best class. In returning thanks
> for his hospitality, Sir Edwin made a speech in which he lauded Japan
> to the skies—and lauded it justly—as the nearest earthly approach to
> Paradise or to Lotus-land—so fairy-like, said he, is its scenery, so ex-
> quisite its art, so much more lovely that almost divine sweetness of
> disposition, that charm of demeanour, that politeness humble without
> servility and elaborate without affectation, which place Japan high above
> all other countries in nearly all those things that make life worth living.
> (We do not give his exact words, but we give the general drift.)
>
> Now do you think that the Japanese were satisfied with this meed of
> praise? Not a bit. Out comes an article next morning in the chief paper
> which had been represented at the banquet—an article acknowledging,
> indeed, the truth of Sir Edwin's description, but pointing out that it
> conveyed, not praise, but pitiless condemnation. "Art forsooth, scenery,
> sweetness of disposition!" cried the editor. "Why did not Sir Edwin praise
> us for huge industrial enterprises, for commercial talent, for wealth,
> political sagacity, powerful armaments? Of course, it is because he could
> not honestly do so. He has gauged us at our true value, and tells us in
> effect that we are only pretty weaklings."

Japan is a long way from Western Europe. About twelve thousand miles, to be exact. "Distance from markets" is one explanation economists traditionally use to explain the preponderance or absence of trade between countries. But if Japan is twelve thousand miles from Europe, then Europe is twelve thousand miles from Japan. So what distance alone does not explain is why the Europeans sell as little as they do to the Japanese and the Japanese sell so much to them.

By 1979, Japan's trade with Asia was 50 percent greater than Europe's. Not surprising, because Asia is in Japan's backyard and years ago there was that local fraternity called the Greater East Asia Co-Prosperity Sphere.

Japan has six times more direct investment in Korea than Britain, France, Germany, and Holland combined, and five times more than these four countries in Indonesia. Japan has more invested in Hong Kong and Singapore than the UK today, and her trade with China is greater than all the European countries put together.

What in the world have the Noble Elite been doing all these years?

Pulling out of Asia, for one thing. European companies had a total of sixty-seven representative offices in Japan in 1961. By 1975, this had dropped to forty-five.

Not investing overseas, for another. In 1979, total EEC investment in the Japanese market was less than $300 million, whereas Japan had $2.5 billion invested in Western Europe—a sixteen-to-one per capita difference.

The EEC was running sizeable bilateral trade deficits with Japan. From a small deficit of $1.3 billion in 1973 to a slightly larger deficit of $4.1 billion in 1976 to $7.1 billion in 1979 to $10.9 billion in 1980.

Brussels is no different from Washington: when you see red ink, hunt for scapegoats.

So the Europeans said the Japanese were economic animals, lived in rabbit hutches, exported unemployment, engaged in social dumping, used unfair trading practices, kept a closed market (all this sound familiar?), saved too much, discriminated against foreign goods, and were simply workaholics without enough common sense to take a little time off once in a while. If the Japanese would just relax and not work so hard, they said, our trade relations would get back into balance.

This time the Japanese fired back with a little uncharacteristic honesty and forthrightness of their own. They accused the Europeans of being lazy, of not trying hard enough to sell in Japan, of being undisciplined and extravagant, of allowing the Puritan work ethic and other hallowed traditions to evaporate, of being hopelessly fragmented within their own economic community. "They're mongrels," the Japanese muttered under their breath, "and slothful." If the Europeans would just work harder, they said, their trade relationships would get back into balance.

And the Japanese had a point. If the number of European businessmen travelling to Japan is any indication of their seriousness of intent to export to that country, the figures for 1975 were revealing. That year, Europeans sent more Christian missionaries to Japan than businessmen and bankers: the Japanese Foreign Ministry issued 1103 religious visas to Europeans and only 1033 of the commercial type.

Statistics are peculiar animals. More recent data isn't available and categories in the Foreign Ministry documents have changed. Besides, Christians have had as little luck in the Japanese market as their commercial brethren: converts to the faith represent less than 1 percent of the population, a statistically insignificant market share.

Nevertheless, if we run the numbers and do the same kind of sectoral analysis of Japanese exports to Europe as we did for those to the United States, we come up with amazingly similar results. In 1980, Japan's total exports to the EEC were $16.4 billion. Of that amount, machinery and equipment accounted for $12.1 billion, or 74 percent of the total. And the five key sectors that we segregated earlier in the U.S./Japan case accounted for $8.5 billion in the Europe/Japan case, or 70 percent of Japanese manufactured goods exports.

The actual breakdown for 1980 looked something like this:

> Transportation equipment: $3.4 billion, or 28 percent of manufactured goods
>
> Telecommunications and sound equipment: $2.3 billion, or 19 percent
>
> Office equipment and computers: $1.7 billion, or 14 percent
>
> Iron and steel: $653 million, or 5 percent
>
> Electrical machinery: $440 million, or 4 percent

In these five strategic sectors, Japan's comparative advantage was not only apparent but paramount. These were the five sectors the Noble Elite should have isolated and pressed the Japanese to make further direct investment in the European market through joint manufacturing ventures, wholly owned production subsidiaries, acquisitions, and minority capital participations in existing European firms.

But it's easier to search for scapegoats than to see one's own shortcomings. Because in Europe's case as in America's, bilateral trade deficits are largely a measure of international industrial competitiveness.

Japanese banks have been very aggressive in establishing a European

presence. Duesseldorf is one of their major centers on the Continent.
There are so many Japanese businessmen in Duesseldorf that the city
is now known as *Nippon Mura*. The Japanese Village.

Takeuchi Toshio was an old friend and deputy general manager of
the Bank of Tokyo's Duesseldorf branch in the late 1970s. He was
singularly responsible for helping me to become the first barbarian
member of the Japanese Club there.

Mr. Takeuchi and I used to practice our German together at the
Nippon Club, while we drank sake, ate raw fish, and played mahjong.
His German was practically flawless; he had been a student in Ger-
many, and this was his second assignment there for the Bank of Tokyo.

We talked a lot about trade. The Japanese trading companies had
been falling all over themselves exporting sheet steel from Kobe to
Wolfsburg cheaper than Thyssen could supply VW from its nearby plant
in Duisburg.

One night, after Mr. Takeuchi had won all my mahjong tiles again,
I asked him why the Japanese played such hardball with the Germans.

"Because if we don't," he said, putting the mahjong tiles away, "we
know the competition will."

So Europe, as with the United States, has been plagued by problems
with its declining industries: shipbuilding and steel in Germany, steel
and video tape recorders in France, automobiles in Britain, consumer
electronics all over the Continent. New investment in more productive
plant and equipment in any of these sectors has simply not kept pace
with the Japanese.

Europe's failure to compete with Japan in ships, cars, and steel par-
allels their failure to hold market share in the United States as well.
The EEC has been caught between the labor-intensive Newly Indus-
trializing Countries and knowledge-intensive Japan.

After analyzing these trade problems, their own blue-ribbon panels
have come to realize that they cannot be competitive in their own
markets, in Japan, or in any overseas markets until they attack the
problems of industrial competitiveness.

Otherwise, like the Washington bureaucrats, the Noble Elite will
continue to blame Japan for problems that are in large part their own
making.

Chamberlain, in reminiscing about the superior negotiating skills
of the Japanese during their attempts to eliminate those unequal treaties the Meiji Boys had been forced to accept, credited certain unusual
qualities the Japanese used to achieve their diplomatic victory in 1894.

"Diplomacy," he wrote, "is not a game of chance. It is a game of
skill, like chess, at which the better player always wins. The Japanese
negotiators, who, to be sure, had more at stake than their opponents,

entirely overmatched them in brains. By playing a waiting game, by letting loose Japanese public opinion when convenient, and then representing it as a much more potent factor than it actually is, by skillful management of the press—in short, by talent, perseverance, patience, and tact, exercised year by year, they gained a complete victory over their adversaries, and at last avenged on the West the violence which it had committed in breaking open Japan a generation before."

Sensei-deshi. Master-apprentice.

But who was master now?

CHAPTER 15

THE CHICKEN WAR

Italians don't like wings or legs—send only breasts and thighs.

—Telex from Rome during the Chicken War, 1962

We got ourselves into another little food fight early last year when we exported some wheat to Egypt at $25 a ton under the world price. Washington made up the difference by means of a small payment to our wheat farmers. That's known as an export subsidy, and GATT frowns on export subsidies.

But Washington said it was only doing to Europe what Europe has been doing to us through their Common Agricultural Policy since the 1960s. And, as we don't usually subsidize food exports, GATT likes us. We're the knights in shining armor. We only subsidize food while it's in the ground, which is why the Europeans don't like us.

"We're on the verge of war," a French official visiting Washington said early in 1983.

Well, we've been in trade wars before. We're fighting one now with the Japanese. But perhaps the most famous was the Chicken War of the 1960s that brought out a little of our traditional hypocrisy, the kind Mrs. Trollope wrote about in 1832.

We have to go back to 1955 when, except for a little thermonuclear saber-rattling between Washington and Moscow, all was right with the world. Chevrolet had brought out the first swept-back windshield, President Eisenhower was playing golf on the banks of the Potomac, and all America had discovered the finger-lickin' goodness of Southern Fried Chicken.

Way back in 1929, when the avowed goal of our national industrial policy had been to put two cars in every garage and a chicken in every pot, annual per capita consumption of chicken was 5 pounds. Poultry farmers produced only 34 million broilers weighing an average 3½ pounds each, and it took 12 pounds of feed and sixteen weeks of feeding to get them there.

But by 1955, Chicken Little had been subjected to the most revolutionary breeding techniques known to man. He had become the fast-food chicken, no longer clucking around the barnyard but force-fed on the assembly line. That year, it took only eight weeks and 8 pounds of hybrid feed to produce the 3½-pound broiler, and the chicken factories flooded the market with 2.2 billion of them.

Producer prices had dropped from 35¢ a pound to 14¢ as the broiler-makers raced down the experience and learning curves. Annual per capita consumption jumped to twenty-eight pounds. Junior no longer had to ask, "What's for dinner tonight, Mom?"

While the United States was experimenting with chickens, Western Europe was struggling with a new form of political democracy. On March 5, 1957, after years of formative debate, self-doubt, and considerable skepticism, six perennial enemies of the past formally agreed to become tentative friends in the future. They formed the European Economic Community.

Would it last? Could this unique experiment in political self-expression survive the nasty national rivalries that had characterized the Continent for centuries? Many were doubtful, not the least of whom was Charles de Gaulle, who distrusted the Americans, hated the Germans, and kept the British at a safe distance. As the phoenix rose from the ashes, Europeans looked to the United States for moral support, money, and food.

Would we be up to the task? Could we commit the people and the funds and the resources necessary to ensure the future political stability of a United States of Europe? Of course we could. We had funded the Marshall Plan to rebuild national economies, we had established the Truman Doctrine to keep the Communists away, and we had sent food—$1 billion worth of agricultural exports in 1955 alone. Of which $2.5 million was poultry.

By 1959, the American poultry growers realized they had to do something with all these chickens that were coming off the assembly lines or the country would soon be faced with an acute oversupply. So the poultry farmers huddled and decided to do what every other mercantile country in the world does when it faces a situation of serious domestic excess.

Export. Sell the chickens to somebody else, anybody, get them out of the country, we're stacked floor to ceiling with the best and cheapest broilers in the world.

In 1959, America sold Europe $19 million worth of chicken. In 1960, poultry exports to the EEC jumped to nearly $30 million, and the

American broilermakers were ecstatic. In 1961, they sold almost $50 million worth of poultry to Europe. The poultry flotilla from Baltimore to Le Havre made the lend-lease program look positively stingy by comparison.

Too good to be true, of course. The Europeans had not gone through years of belt-tightening, self-doubt, and recrimination to watch their own poultry farmers succumb to the flood of cheap American imports. So they renewed their own subscriptions to *Agricultural Digest* and soon were adopting the new feeding and breeding techniques themselves.

On January 14, 1962, the EEC ministers concluded over two hundred hours of marathon meetings and agreed to a new set of regulations that would become the Common Agricultural Policy of The Six. They also adopted Regulation 22, which established a policy on poultry that effectively kept imports down until the technologically inhibited European farms could catch up with their American competitors: a creative blend of agricultural quotas and infant-industry protection.

CAP was signed into law after forty-five separate meetings, 137 hours of plenary discussion, 214 hours of drafting in subcommittees, three heart attacks, and 582,000 pages of documents. In short, CAP was authorized to take over responsibility from the member states for guaranteeing a reasonable level of income to farmers, national protection would be replaced by a Community system and there would be free trade in food among The Six.

By now, of course, Camelot had come to town, and Eisenhower's soporific nature had been replaced by a more aggressive, activist style. When The Six put CAP into effect, Washington roared its disapproval of Europe's protectionist aims, and under pressure from the National Poultry Growers' Association, went on the attack.

The Chicken War was on!

In 1962, before they effectively shut the barnyard door, the American poultry growers sold nearly $55 million worth of poultry products to the EEC, over 150 million pounds of chicken to Germany alone.

The following year, because of CAP, our exports to the EEC dropped back to $30 million. So we did what any self-respecting American would do under the circumstances, we sued.

Washington took the EEC to court in Geneva under the complaint rules of GATT and requested the dispute be put to arbitration. America wanted to sell chickens and, arguing that Europe had thrown up restraints to free trade, claimed over $50 million in damages. The Europeans countered by saying that their own farmers would be put out of business without some temporary protection, but they offered compensation of $19 million.

The Europeans contended that American domestic farm policy was intertwined with direct and indirect subsidies and that Washington was being hypocritical when it spoke of taking the lead in furthering free-trade interests. The EEC Commissioner for Agriculture, Pierre Lardinois, took a page out of his boss's book of distrust when he criticized the American sermonizing about the virtues of free trade.

"We have the impression," he said in Brussels, "that America is purposely treating agricultural trade as a one-way flow. You preach free trade when it comes to other people's internal markets, but you practice rigid protection at home." He then went on to cite the laundry-list of quotas on agricultural goods that Washington maintained.

But the United States opted for confrontation, its first and most powerful weapon in settling trade disputes, arguing that trade in both hard goods and food had to be negotiated as parts of the same package— the "linkage" argument we always find so appealing. The EEC insisted the issues were separate. As one U.S. observer put it, "By using the tactics of confrontation, we made a good solution to the problem more difficult to achieve."

The GATT Council deliberated for months, weighed the evidence, listened to the witnesses, and read the testimony. They awarded the United States $26 million.

On December 4, 1963, President Johnson issued a proclamation raising tariffs on certain Dutch chemical starch imports, French brandy, and Volkswagen truck chassis to generate the revenues we had been granted by GATT.

The villain was neither the chicken nor CAP, but rather the tactics of confrontation used by Washington to fight the war that left a bitter taste in everyone's mouth. The United States maintained a self-righteous posture and continued to preach its sermons of free trade. The EEC dug in its heels, resisted the Americans' adversarial approach, and hardened its already-stubborn attitude toward the Common Agricultural Policy. The real loser was the technological chicken, who had to stay at home.

After our NATO allies declared a truce in the Chicken War, American poultry farmers regrouped to review their strategy. The door might be closed to chickens now, they thought, but not to turkeys. By 1972, when they had put our Thanksgiving bird on the assembly line and got their unit costs down, they fired the first shots of the next battle. The turkey war.

Ross Talbot, a political scientist at the University of Iowa, reminisced about the Chicken War and wrote an account of it all after the feathers had settled. "A trade conflict brings an issue into the open, and causes the attentive citizen to reflect on and perhaps be concerned

about the activities and decisions of powerful and antagonistic bu-
reaucracies," he wrote in 1978. "Unfortunately, it seems that the political education involved generally takes on the malady of a one-eyed
myopia, each major part visualizing 'clearly' its own particular interest,
but the vision in the other eye is 20–200 when it comes to seeing the
interests of the other party.

"The chicken war did bring to light some of the rather excessive
aspects of the EEC's overindulgent bureaucracy. But the American side
often had a naive-like provincialism about the whole matter, a sort of
blissful unconcern with economic and political realities intermingled
with an uneasy conviction that southern fried chicken was one of the
unwritten natural laws of the universe."

Like Kansas beef and Florida orange juice.

PART III

GREED VS. POWER: CONFLICTING STRATEGIES

CHAPTER 16

THERE JUST HAS TO BE A REASON

Real money comes from Supercurrency. The most pure forms of Supercurrency are the great companies with broad markets selling at high multiples of earnings. Grandad and Uncle Harry had a partnership. They took the money home. Uncle Harry turned it into a company, and it was then worth whatever a private buyer might pay for it. But Uncle Harry sold it to Eli Lilly or IBM or Xerox or Coca Cola, and now Uncle Harry's side of the family is rich and peels off the Supercurrency—shares of IBM or Coca Cola—whenever it wants a new boat.

—Adam Smith, *Supermoney*

But there has to be a *reason*, you say. The greatest superpower in the world can't be losing world markets to the Japanese without some explanation. If our national wealth continues to decline, how will our sons and daughters be able to afford country club memberships in the future? Or those wonderful long vacations we used to take in the not-so-distant past?

We're back to the economist and his ubiquitous assumptions. Let's say you don't buy the fact that the Japanese are fair traders doing a more competitive job at selling in world markets. But let's *assume* this to be so, that they're hung up on being number one and winning the commercial equivalent of the Super Bowl every year, that their market is not closed, and that exporting aggressively is a matter of national survival.

I repeat, let's just *assume* this to be true.

How does success translate into a difference in strategy and tactics? And in italics, so that you won't forget it:

Because Japanese companies are in business to make products, whereas American companies are in business to make money.

That's it. It's like a theorem. It helps you focus on the principal cultural and philosophical differences between the Japanese and ourselves as we compete for global markets.

137

The Japanese are in business to make products.

Good products, better products, best products. If our product doesn't sell, then analyze the hell out of its quality, we must be doing something wrong. If foreign countries put up import barriers, then we'll transship through a neighboring country or export the products in knockdown assembly kits or set up a joint venture to make the products overseas. If a competitor comes out with a better product that outsells ours, we'll buy it, reverse-engineer it, build a prototype, adapt it, improve it, cut the price aggressively to hold market position, and sell it even harder. Because we're really not doing anything different today with integrated circuits and video tape recorders and automobiles than our ancestors did with kimonos and silk screens and lacquerware: a burning cultural addiction to making high-quality products and holding a significant market share.

The Americans are in business to make money.

Money, more money, most money. If our product doesn't sell, then analyze the hell out of our advertising campaign, Madison Avenue must be doing something wrong. If foreign countries put up import barriers, then we'll critize the local government, accuse them of not playing fair, and simply sell somewhere else—like at home, where the returns are greater. If a competitor comes out with a better product, we'll hype up our ad campaign and attack the competition, huddle with our accountants and lawyers to figure out new tax dodges and restraint of trade suits, petition Washington for regulatory relief, and lay off employees. If our product makes a loss, we'll sell the product-line off. If the division makes a loss, we'll sell the division off. And if the company's in trouble, we'll sell the company off. Because we're really not doing anything different today with products and divisions and companies than we did a hundred years ago with oil and railroads and banks: a burning cultural addiction to protecting the bottom line.

Land First, Sea Second

Although Japan is an insular nation surrounded on all sides by the sea, it is basically an agricultural nation. Since the olden days of rivalry between Minamoto and Taira clans, the main role on the battlefield was always played by the mounted warriors who charged about over the ground. It is true that there were some marine forces centered around the Inland Sea, but they always played a secondary, not a primary, role. This "land first, sea second" thinking assumed an even more clearcut form when Japan moved into the Tokugawa Era. The culture of Japan was thus formu-

*lated on the pattern of land management—rice—first, sea
management—fish—second. And the Imperial Japanese
Navy way of thinking was exclusively defense-oriented,
while the Imperial Japanese Army way of thinking was bel-
licose and offense-oriented.*

—Mino Hokaji, Editor in Chief,
Business Japan

Quiet, please. We have been invited to attend a meeting of the
Forward Planning Group of American Widgets and Sprockets, Inc.,
headquartered in Fairview, Connecticut. No, their headquarters building just *looks* like the Fairview Country Club. The clubhouse is down
the road about two miles. Ted and Jim and George and Mary and Faith
are gathered around an expensive mahogany table in the conference
room, seated in thick plush swivel chairs. A battery of audiovisual
equipment whirrs impatiently at the back of the room. On a long
credenza to one side of the table sits a cornucopia of food and drink.

At the far end of the room hangs a picture of the company's founder,
Ralph W. Johnson, Jr., next to a picture of their current chairman, Ralph
W. Johnson IV. On the opposite wall, framed, is one of Benjamin Frank-
lin's innumerable pithy sayings: "Time is money."

Ted is group vice president responsible for sprockets. Jim is from
Finance, George from Legal. Mary represents Cash Management and
Faith the chairman's office. The subject under discussion: overseas
sales to Tierra del Fuego.

"Jim, you run those numbers on our hurdle rates?" Ted asks.

"Got 'em right here, Ted. We're looking for an 18 percent return on
our investment in the division, as you know. Our immediate goal is
10 percent after-tax, and there are several factors working in our favor.
We can get a full investment tax credit under the double-taxation treaty
between Washington and Tierra del Fuego, which will help, and Price
Waterhouse says there is nothing in the local regs to prevent us from
taking accelerated depreciation the first three years."

Ted flips open his yellow pad and scribbles down a few numbers.

"In addition," Jim says, "if we do a little switch-invoicing and book
local sales through a third market, we can benefit from the flow-through
of some heavy tax-loss carryforwards. And there's always the possibility of leasing the production equipment down there instead of buying
it outright. Then we can sell the safe-harbor cross-border tax benefits
from the leases to the highest bidder. GM and Exxon might be strong
buyers."

"How do the discounted cash flows look?"

"Not bad. I figure with the tax bennies, some switch-invoicing, and leasing just half the production equipment, we come up with a melded DCF rate of about 8 percent pretax, but a sparkling 15.5 percent after-tax over three years." Jim looks up, beaming.

"The chairman will never buy a project that takes that long to pay out, Jim. You know that."

It was Faith.

"If we're going overseas, we've got to get into a market and out of it in a year, max eighteen months. The risks are simply too great otherwise."

"Faith, when Ralph sees these numbers, he'll be ecstatic. None of our domestic investments pays over 15 percent after-tax. Think what our bonuses will look like if the numbers are anywhere near what I think they'll be."

"But three years, Jim? You're asking me to go to the mats for *three* years?"

Ted turns to George. "You got some feedback on our 'what-if' exercise?"

"Spent the day in Washington yesterday pulling all the loose ends together," George says, opening a crisp Naugahyde folder. "One. If the local government slaps any import restrictions on sprocket parts before our investment is fully paid out, we can shift to a joint venture and manufacture the components there. I've got my staff working on a draft J/V agreement that we can put on the shelf, just in case—spells everything out. Nominally fifty-fifty, but we retain control by dominating the voting shares."

George reaches behind him, takes a Coke and pops the tab.

"Two," he says, taking a long swig. "If the Central Bank locks up capital flows by restricting dollar remittances, we simply shift our borrowings to pesos and bury the foreign exchange losses in a reserve account. The paper F/X gains can come right through to our income statement. We're putting a boilerplate loan agreement on the shelf, too."

Ted frowns. "What about technology-licensing problems?"

George smiles. "That's three. If the government tries to block sales of our sprocket technology, we'll sue the shit out of them. They'll be hamstrung, tied up in the local courts. Just like our Nicaragua case two years ago. These banana republics are all alike."

"Good," Ted says. He turns to Mary. "Interest rate outlook?"

"The dollar is stable in the exchange markets right now," she says, scanning a sheet of numbers. "Assuming the chairman buys a three-year payout on this deal, which we all agree is doubtful, we've got the funds up front and ready, locked into thirty-day commercial paper at

8 percent, an at-notice account at the Chase fluctuating at a rate of about 7.75, and some Tuesday-Friday Euro repos yielding us 7.90. We can mix and match pretty much at ease."

"The numbers look pretty good. Faith, I'm worried about Ralph. How can we convince him?"

Faith shook her head. "It won't be easy. You know he has a meeting next week with the Financial Analysts Society in New York to review our results for last quarter. We're down in a down market—the Japanese came in with their computer-controlled sprockets and took us completely by surprise—so the FAS won't want to hear about a three-year project offshore."

"But the numbers!" Jim interrupts.

"Tomorrow's results won't do us any good today," Faith says, glancing across at Jim. "Once the market learns we're going overseas with a long-term payout on the heels of a lousy quarter, just imagine what will happen to our share price. It's dangerously low already."

George nods. "So much for my stock options this year," he says.

"We've got to resist anything that may deflate earnings," Faith continues. She flicks a switch, and the room lights dim. Another button, a slide appears on the screen. "Look at our recent profit performance. Disastrous." The sloping line resembles a child's playground slide.

Groans and moans fill the room.

Faith clicks the swtich again. "Here, earnings per share. Buoyed temporarily just because we went into the market to buy treasury stock, which reduced the number of shares outstanding." Another click. The group cheers as a rising trend line appears. "Relax, guys. This happened only because we sold the manual widget division last quarter and laid off a third of the sprocket work force." She throws the room lights back on.

"I'm telling you, now is not the time to approach the chairman on this deal. Because even if he reluctantly agrees, he's still got to convince the board."

Jim snaps his fingers. "I've got it," he says. "We can set up a shell in Tierra del Fuego—George here can prepare the legal documents. We use a paper company to report paper profits, but ship the product from our Florida factory, stamped in Spanish. They'll never know the difference, and our share price will get a boost."

George nods. "We've got a Curaçao holding company registration on the shelf," he says. "It could work."

Ted nods slowly in agreement. "And if we play our cards right, we can hold onto the shell for a year or so, sell it in the M & A market, take an accounting gain on the divestiture, and flow the profits straight through to the income statement. We cut the directors in on their golden parachutes, to protect them against any adverse reaction, but Wall Street should rejoice and our share price will rebound. I like it. Mary, what about the proceeds?"

"No problem. We can stuff the funds into our short-term Eurodollar account pending repatriation. Assuming stable rates, we should be able to get something between 8 and 9 percent."

Ted turns to Faith. "Ralph's got to go along. What do you think?"

Faith chews on an eraser. "I don't know. If we can structure the deal as a long-term leveraged buy-out and take some convertible preferred from the buyer as scrip, but get in and out within a year, he might agree. Remember, he needs board approval. And even if he gets it, he still has to persuade the division heads to go along."

"If he swings the board, we'll help him ram it down their throats," Ted says.

"I'll get right to work on the new numbers," says Jim. "Boy, those earnings are going to look terrific."

"And I'll redraft the documentation," says George. "We can have something ready by tomorrow morning."

"Go to it," says Ted. "We're not getting any richer just sitting here."

We pause momentarily while the stagehands shift some scenery and replace the set. The polished mahogany table goes out, and a gray Formica-top steel table takes its place. The plush swivel chairs roll off stage, and straight-backed wooden chairs are placed around the table. An electrician disassembles the sophisticated A/V equipment and hangs a plain blackboard on one wall, placing an eraser and chalk on the rail. A small, ceramic vase of flowers now sits in the center of the table surrounded by five tiny teacups nestled in a cluster of bamboo coasters.

At the far end of the room, toward the top of the wall, hangs the company name, in vertical *kanji*: Matsushima Heavy Industries, Ltd., Tokyo, Japan. On the opposite wall is a scroll that depicts, in cursive script, the company's motto, paraphrasing the famous Zen monk Kembo and signed by the Matsushima chairman: "Through perseverance and persistence, we can overcome all adversity."

There is a knock on the door. Hearing no response, Matsushima Heavy Industries' director of planning, Mr. Katoh, enters, followed by his overseas division specialists: Kawamura, section chief responsible for Latin America; Suzuki, deputy director of planning; Nakagawa, assistant director, Export Division; and Yamada, section chief, Industrial Sprockets Division.

The five Matsushima men turn and bow silently to the Zen scroll, then take their seats at the table. Suzuki and Nakagawa set programmable Casio calculators next to their file folders. Yamada pulls out an abacus.

"*Yoshi*," Katoh says. "Let's start. We will discuss the Tierra del Fuego sprocket project today." He turns to Nakagawa, his face grim. "What is our market share position, and who are our closest competitors?"

Kawamura opens his folder, then ducks his head slightly in deference to the Bucho—the planning director. "Our company currently holds just over 15 percent of the market," he says. "We have captured this position over the last three years, starting from zero, with the close cooperation of our Export and Sprockets divisions, after investing heavily in new production equipment here to accelerate manufacturing output."

He runs a finger down a column of names and figures.

"Ishibashi Heavy Industries is still the market leader there, with about a 20 percent market share, followed closely by Okita Manufacturing at 17 percent. We understand the hairy barbarians are considering a delayed market entry, but our contacts in the government say they have no concrete plans yet."

"Who, for example?" Katoh asks.

"American Widgets and Sprockets."

Katoh laughs. "They'll get embroiled in red tape trying to set up some kind of stupid licensing agreement. Their market entry will be considerably delayed. We should not view them as a threat."

"What if they begin to export, Bucho-san?"

It was Nakagawa.

"Nonsense! Did you drink too much sake last night? The Americans have no experience in exporting small industrial products, Nakagawa-san. Winter wheat and soybeans, those are their strengths."

Katoh turns back to Kawamura. "We have been discussing market strategy at the working level long enough. It is agreed that we must increase our market share—for our chairman, for our company, for our country. Our new slogan will be *Ni Nen, Ni Bai*."

Yamada of the Industrial Sprockets Division sucks in a large quantity of air with a loud hiss. "Double in two years?"

"Exactly. In the next two fiscal years, we will overtake the market leaders with a share in excess of 30 percent. Is that understood?"

"*Hai*." The group answers as one.

Suzuki rises, bows, and reads a brief report.

"We will establish a beachhead with our new computer-controlled sprocket units, to get a jump on our competitors and take the most advantageous position. Then we will attack local manufacturers with an aggressive price-cutting campaign designed to lock in a minimum market share. When that has been accomplished, we will defend that floor level with our compatible products. As Saigo Takamori once said, 'We will never retreat, even under the toughest conditions.' Victory is our only option; surrender is unthinkable."

"*Domo*, Suzuki-kun. In the words of Musashi, 'We must persevere, even if it takes us a lifetime of lifetimes to succeed.'"

"However," Suzuki continues, "the Ministry of Industry and Commerce in Tierra del Fuego has given us preliminary indication of a change in import regulations. Beginning next year, we may have to export finished sprockets from Japan under a voluntary restraint agreement. I have revised figures here from both our Export Division and our Industrial Sprockets Division indicating two ways we can circumvent the new regulations: one, shift production to partially completed assembly kits and, two, divert some shipments of our new computer-controlled sprockets from the EEC. Either way, we escape the quotas on finished sprockets. We will need everyone's cooperation for success, especially to double our market share."

With a short bow, he sits down again.

"Re-exports?" Katoh asks.

Nakagawa nods. "*Mondai nai*," he says. "No problem. We have obtained permission to set up a task force in the country's capital to study the possibility of importing standard sprocket components from Japan under existing quotas. Then we process them in Tierra del Fuego and export them as finished sprockets through Matsushima Trading to third-country markets. This will push us farther down the experience curve. We shall also receive an export-tax rebate, which we can credit against our Market Development Reserve here in Japan."

Katoh nods in agreement. "Very good. Has our Exim Bank agreed to finance those shipments?"

"We have a preliminary agreement from them," Kawamura says. "As long as Tierra del Fuego remains a 'developing country,' sprocket component exports will qualify for preferential rate financing."

Everyone laughs politely, including Kawamura. "Developing countries always move slowly, like an old woman in summer," says Katoh. Everyone laughs again.

The door opens, and a staff assistant enters, a pot of steaming hot tea in one hand. She makes her rounds quickly, bowing silently, filling the five teacups. She bows again as she leaves.

Katoh blows on his tea to cool it. "How has MITI responded to our production estimates, Suzuki-kun?"

"The third New Industrial Structure Plan was released just last week. We have been approved for general additions to domestic capacity through next fiscal year. However, we may be forced to acquire one of the failing sprocket companies to add to our division to maintain order in the market."

"Anything else?"

"MITI has approved our application for joint research and development efforts with Okita Manufacturing. Also, we now qualify for an allocation of funds from the national mahjong tournaments that will help us finance our research."

Katoh bangs the table with a clenched fist. "Excellent, Suzuki-san. Excellent! As Confucius said, 'We must avoid the three poisons of greed, sloth, and anger.' The Americans are so stupid as to allow their underworld to monopolize legal gambling. If they put one tenth of their gambling revenues into exports or education, they would be much more formidable competitors."

"We should be thankful they don't, Bucho-san."

It was Yamada.

"My production people informed me last week that the customs inspectors are taking longer and longer to clear our sprockets into their country. This cannot be allowed to continue."

Katoh glances at Nakagawa. "We have taken steps to improve this, Yamada-kun," he says. "First, we have informed their embassy here in Tokyo that beginning next week, every bottle of Tierra del Fuego wine imported into Japan will be subject to inspection on a unit basis, must be maintained at a constant temperature of forty-five degrees, and must have a full contents declaration, in Japanese, on each label. Second, we have asked MITI to invite their chief of customs to Tokyo as our guest to discuss ways of streamlining customs clearance." He looks up at Katoh and winks.

"Very *zurui*, Nakagawa-san. What have we done to counter their criticism that a wooden component in our sprockets violates certain of their religious customs?"

Yamada is quick with a response. "We sent a special team to Tierra del Fuego to study the problem, Bucho-san. I have their report right here."

"What does it recommend?"

"The Alternative Component Report is very thorough. It recommends using the tusk of the mountain aardvark instead of wood. This provides the same consistency as wood, does not conduct electricity and, most important, will not offend their religious beliefs."

"You are sure, Yamada-kun?"

"Have you ever heard of aardvark-tusk religious artifacts in Tierra del Fuego?"

"I am unfamiliar with religious artifacts anywhere. My job is to be sure that all barriers to increased sales of our industrial sprockets are removed so that we can make our production and market share targets. If we cannot, then Chairman Matsushima will be severely displeased. The export planning group will lose face, and our entire company will suffer. That must not happen."

"It will not happen, Bucho-san. We are working closely with the Export Division to ensure a smooth transition from wood to tusk. Do not worry. We are putting our best technicians and engineers on it. We will persevere."

"*Yoshi,*" Katoh says. "There can be no excuse for failure. Is that clear?"

"Of course," Yamada responds.

"Everyone?"

"*Hai.*"

And so it goes. Historical precedent, Zen strategy, Confucian ethics, strong company loyalty, cultural flexibility, export priority, and an undying faith in product superiority. What may have started as rival divisional attitudes at the working level ends up in consensus: everyone is on board to support the plan aggressively.

It's the age-old story of power against greed.

CHAPTER 17

CONTRASTING IDEOLOGIES

Inventors, scientists, engineers, and academics, in the normal pursuit of scientific knowledge, gave the world in recent times the laser, xerography, instant photography, and the transistor. In contrast, worshippers of the marketing concept have bestowed upon mankind such products as newfangled potato chips, feminine hygiene deodorant, and the pet rock.

—Bennett and Cooper,
Business Horizons, June 1979

Professors Robert Hayes and William Abernathy of Harvard were among the first to put their fingers on the diminishing heartbeat of American business in an attempt to find out what was wrong. They had observed the patient's loss of market share over the years, the lower rate of productivity growth, the drop in product quality, and the general decline in international industrial competitiveness compared to businesses in Europe and Japan.

So the two doctors sat down to write up their hypothesis, which they published in the fall of 1980 in the *Harvard Business Review*, industry's equivalent of the *New England Journal of Medicine*. In an article titled "Managing Our Way to Economic Decline," they detailed the various symptoms of our industrial sickness and tried to formulate a few fundamental recommendations for recovery.

They found that the poor patient, addicted to a kind of corporate junk food called profitability, was suffering from two rather serious complications. One was "analytic detachment," whereby the patient listened to the advice of lawyers and accountants rather than engineers and production managers. The other was "short-term cost reduction," which meant the patient was putting more and more emphasis on using existing assets as efficiently as possible without developing those new products, technologies, and production processes that would open new markets or restructure old ones.

147

They also found the patient just a tad irritable. "Why risk money on new businesses," he snapped, "when good, profitable, low-risk opportunities are on every side?" He swung his legs over the side of the bed.

Nodding paternally, the two doctors set their clipboards down and gently forced American business back into bed. "You're not going anywhere," they said, "until you realize the seriousness of your condition." They strapped his arms and legs to the bed frame.

Dr. Abernathy looked at the hospital charts and read off the results as Dr. Hayes picked up his clipboard.

"Growth in labor productivity still way down," he said. "The lowest of all my patients, in fact, at 2.8 percent over the past fifteen years." He glanced at a neighboring chart to compare statistical norms. "Japanese productivity in manufacturing still the marker rate at 8.2 percent," he mused. "Germans in at 5.4 percent."

"That's ridiculous," the patient sputtered. "I feel as good as I ever did."

"That's not what these charts tell us," said the good Dr. Abernathy. "Your outlays for research and development peaked years ago, my friend. You used to spend upwards of 3 percent of GNP on R & D. Now you're down a third, close to 2 percent. Even the Japanese are on your level now."

"Trend line?" asked Dr. Hayes, scribbling on his clipboard.

"Still down," whispered Dr. Abernathy. He flipped over another chart.

"And your capital investment as a percentage of GNP? Atrocious! How can you say you've never felt better when France and Germany have been investing in capital equipment at a rate 20 percent greater than yours? And the Japanese *double* yours." He looked down at the sickly patient, shaking his head. "It's disgusting, that's what it is. Your return on equity is no higher today than it was twenty years ago. You may be rich, but you're not spending your money very wisely."

"Nonsense!" the patient roared, propping himself up on his elbows. Dr. Hayes moved to tighten the straps. American business fell back against the mattress. "I'm just responding to free-market forces, the invisible hand, letting the chips fall where they may. If I'm as bad off as you say I am, it can't be my fault. Talk to the government doctors. They're the ones who let those cheap foreign products into the country."

"There, there," said Dr. Abernathy. He placed a comforting hand on the patient's forehead.

"Fever?" asked Dr. Hayes in hushed tones.

Dr. Abernathy nodded. "Probably evidence of his drive for short-term success. Monthly board meetings, quarterly results for the financial community, constant attention to earnings per share," he whispered. "He's getting delirious, I'm afraid."

Dr. Hayes picked up a pad of blank prescription forms and uncapped his fountain pen. "I'll prescribe some medication that should help his long-term competitive position," he said.

"What are you going to give me?" the patient asked, trembling now.

Dr. Abernathy cranked the bed. "Something to help you focus on longer term capital investment. It won't taste good, but you can swallow it. It will also improve your product quality. Next year when we run these tests, we want you to be much better."

"We're also going to give you some export stimulants," Dr. Hayes said.

"No, not exports! Anything but that!" American business shivered.

"This won't hurt a bit," Dr. Abernathy said as he adjusted the syringe. He rubbed the patient's arm with a little alcohol and quickly inserted the hypodermic, releasing the powerful drug. Within minutes, the patient was sleeping quietly.

Dr. Abernathy sighed. "What do you think?"

Dr. Hayes shook his head. "It's touch and go," he said. "I mean, good health is 90 percent prevention, 10 percent cure. If he wants to compete, he's got to feel that desire *burning* again."

"You're right," said Dr. Abernathy. "Technological competitiveness is a horse of a different color today. This guy's got to learn it's no longer a one-man race." He tucked a sheet under the patient's chin and snapped out the reading light.

"Survival is a long-term goal," said Dr. Hayes, standing by the door. "Once he realizes that good health is more than just financial performance, he may do all right. But he's got to think in terms of new products, new processes, new markets. Or he'll die just like his ancestors."

"Young and rich?"

"You said it."

Where the Jobs Are

"It's even more basic than that," the B-school student said to his friend as they sat in the lounge drinking coffee one afternoon. "It's like, where am I going to make the most money?"

I saw one of the charts the good doctors were using, the one that showed changes in professional origins of corporate presidents for 100 top American companies. The trend lines were crystal clear: since the mid-1950s there had been a steady increase in the percentage of company presidents whose primary interests and expertise lay in finance and the law, not in production. By the late 1970s, fully one third of the corporate presidents had been trained in those fields, with another third in marketing and other backgrounds, and only the remaining third with technical and engineering skills.

Copying the chart, I took it to my friend George, who is a former corporate president himself. He's retired now, so he can sit back and enjoy his golden parachute with the silver strings, which gives him an enviable perspective on affairs of business today. But he was once the chief executive officer of a major manufacturing company and still sits on the boards of a half-dozen corporations as well as a number of management associations and advisory committees.

I asked him what he thought about the chart.

He looked at the three divergent lines and shook his head.

"I dispute it," he said. "Did you see the Arthur Young study?"

I said no. "An accounting firm doing a study on CEOs?"

"Yeah. The Arthur Young report showed that two thirds of the top corporate presidents came up from the operating side, and fully 82 percent of them expected their replacements to be from the operating side as well."

"Who did they survey?"

"Oh, you know, the usual front-runners. IBM, GE, 3M, that crowd."

"George, you know those names *always* surface when people want to show what American business is doing right. They're the only companies left that are."

It was true. *In Search of Excellence* had isolated the same names, indicating that the value-infused, best-performing companies were led by people who grew up with the core of the business. The market leaders were seldom headed by accountants or lawyers.

"Hewlett-Packard, Rockwell International, Westinghouse, Texas Instruments, Eastman Kodak, Procter & Gamble—"

"George, will you cut it out? They're the exceptions that prove the rule. What about Roger Smith at General Motors?"

George stopped and thought. "Finance."

"Right. And David Roderick of U.S. Steel?"

"Lawyer," he said.

"And Jimmy Ling and Hal Geneen and Roy Ash?"

"Okay, okay, you made your point. But I still think the trend is toward throwing the bankers and the lawyers off corporate boards."

"So who's taking their place?"

He paused. "Senior management from other companies. They're in real demand. And consultants. You ought to see the fees they get. Make my golden parachute look like a dishrag."

"And where are the top B-school students heading?" I was getting pumped up now.

"Well," he said, frowning. Sometimes George's parachute gets stuck in the treetops and keeps his feet off the ground.

"The demographics are different today," he went on. "You have to realize that 40 percent of the B-school students now are women."

"So what does that have to do with anything?"

"Lots. Like, they're not interested in large corporations. Many of them are married, and their husbands have separate careers, so they don't want to sacrifice their lives to the company, go overseas, live apart."

"Great," I said. "So they sacrifice their lives to tennis and their country clubs because they have double salaries and can afford all that stuff. Whereas the Japanese and Germans push our products out of world markets because when *their* companies tell them they have to go live overseas to compete, they say 'When do I leave?' Come on, George, you can do better than that."

"We've got great students here," he said. "Capable students, bright students, some of the best in the country."

George also teaches a course at one of the East Coast B-schools.

"So how are they any different from the kids in Texas?" My old stomping grounds.

"Well, I would guess their top 10 percent might rank with our bottom 10 percent."

"Careful, George, your silk stockings are showing. But what do they want when they get out of school? Where are these leaders of tomorrow heading?"

George paused again. "Okay," he said, "they're going into consulting and accounting and investment banking and finance. Because that's where the jobs are."

That's where the jobs are.

I suddenly had a vision of the future. I saw Americans becoming the world's bankers and lawyers and accountants based on skills and expertise they had acquired over a generation ago when people looked to us for guidance and advice. Now the only people looking to us for guidance and advice were underdeveloped countries. Because the Japanese and the Germans and the Swedes were out there producing the hard goods and our production jobs were evaporating because we were no longer interested in competing.

For every ten thousand people in Japan, only one is trained as a lawyer and three are trained as accountants. True, Japanese society is very harmonious as all that bowing and hissing substitutes for lawsuits and litigation. And I suppose when a national population becomes so skilled in using the abacus that it can beat the latest electronic calculators, you don't need as many accountants. But in the United States, for the same ten thousand people, we train twenty to be lawyers and forty to be accountants.

And why not? That's where the jobs are.

Why do we need engineers and scientists and technicians when our most important priorities are reshuffling assets? Wonderful service industries spring up like dandelions in April to cater to the demands of American business: spinning off unprofitable divisions, diversifying through acquisition, coating the balance sheet with new accounting interpretations, creating paper companies offshore for tax-avoidance purposes, taking competitors to court as a delaying tactic, and devising new financing schemes that provide funds with a zero coupon but sell at half of par value to convince the shareholders that borrowing costs are really lower and to persuade the IRS that repayment at maturity is really untaxable distribution of principal, not taxable interest.

In the meantime, as all this creative talent is playing paper games and enriching itself in the process, the best minds in Europe and Japan are tinkering with improved industrial sprockets because they know without better products they won't survive, and living with lower current returns on equity because they know they have to upgrade their plant and equipment today to be able to compete effectively tomorrow, and plowing more retained earnings into research and development because they don't have any accidental spinoff from the Pentagon like we do, and sending their brightest managers to America *not* to study in the B-schools and the law schools but to take advanced degrees in science and engineering because that's where the future is.

Jackson Grayson, president of the American Productivity Center in Houston, said back in 1978 that American business "has coasted off the great R & D gains made during World War II and constantly rewarded executives from the marketing, financial, and legal sides of the business while it ignored the production men. Today, courses [in business schools] in the production area are almost nonexistent."

Derek Bok, president of Harvard University, said in his 1983 annual report that law schools attracted too high a percentage of the most able college graduates, a situation he called "a massive diversion of exceptional talent." Law schools waste money, he wrote, "and absorb more young people in America than in any other industrialized nation. The law attracts an unusually large proportion of the exceptionally gifted. Far too many are becoming lawyers at a time when the country cries out for more talented business executives, more enlightened public servants, more inventive engineers, more able teachers."

He drew on the Japanese parallel, too. "In Japan, a country only half our size, 30 percent more engineers graduate each year than in all the United States. But Japan boasts a total of less than 15,000 lawyers while American universities graduate 35,000 lawyers *every year*. As the Japanese put it so succinctly: 'Engineers make the pie grow larger. Lawyers only decide how to carve it up.'"

But that's where the jobs are.

I left George's office more depressed than when I went in. I gave him the doctors' chart and asked him to keep it with his Arthur Young study so that the next time he took a B-school student to lunch he'd at least have both sides. After all, even umpires sometimes disagree.

Zen and the Art of Asset Shuffling

> *No target's erected,*
> *No bow's drawn,*
> *And the arrow leaves the string:*
> *It may not hit,*
> *But it does not miss.*

—Ninth-century Zen archer

Grimm used to be a name that was associated with fairy tales. Today, it's a name that's associated with mergers and acquisitions.

Excuse me, did you say...?

W. T. Grimm & Co. Every year Grimm & Co. puts out a little-noticed summary of all M & A transactions over the previous twelve months called *Mergerstat Review*. And in a nutshell, it tells you what all those lawyers and accountants and investment bankers have been doing since graduation.

Buying and selling companies. Or divisions. Or paper shells. Or product lines. Taking public companies private. Or private companies public. Upstream mergers, downstream mergers, whales eating fishes, fishes eating whales. Horizontal acquisitions, vertical acquisitions, market extension acquisitions, product extension acquisitions, pygmies and cripples.

Pygmies and cripples? Of course. Acquisitions of companies so small you can practically pay for them with pocket money, and acquisitions of companies so sick you can buy them at bargain basement prices.

The *Mergerstat Review* lists them all. In 1981, a total of 2395 mergers and acquisitions was completed. Twelve months. Two thousand, three hundred and ninety-five deals. Assuming 220 business days in a

year, that's over 10 a day. No new products, no new production processes, no cutting-edge technological innovations, just a little asset-
shuffling.

For the sum of $82.6 billion.

"Setting a new record for the third consecutive year," *Mergerstat*
announced in a tone reminiscent of prewar manufacturing statistics,
"the total dollar value paid in 1981 surged to an overwhelming $82.6
billion, almost double the 1980 dollar total of $44.3 billion. The last
twelve months can accurately be designated as the year of the 'mega-
deal.' There were 12 transactions valued at over one billion dollars
during 1981, while 1980 witnessed only four such transactions. Completed transactions having a purchase price of $100 million or more
numbered 113 in 1981, compared with 94 last year. An uninterrupted
increase in large-scale consolidations has been taking place since 1975."

Not only are we reshuffling assets, we're doing it with vigor. With
all this creative talent out there looking for new ways to deploy old
assets, what would you expect? The lawyers skim $200 an hour off
the top, the accountants also get paid while the meter runs, and the
investment bankers take their cut off the selling price. Not only is that
where the jobs are, that's where the Jaguars and the horseback-riding
lessons and the swimming pools are.

For example, steel is going to hell in 1981. The Japanese long ago
replaced us as the world's most efficient low-cost producers. American
wage rates out of line, industry management out of touch, losses out
of sight.

Oil is selling for $35 a barrel in 1981. But the oil companies have
all those undervalued reserves in the ground and they're continually
finding more. Earnings up, pump prices stable, supply plentiful.

Question: what to do?

Answer: if you're a steel company, buy an oil company.

So U.S. Steel paid $6.6 billion to acquire Marathon Oil in 1981. They
had all that cash sitting around, and they weren't going to invest in
steel anymore because the shareholders were interested in making
money. And if you can't make money in steel, you get out of steel and
into something you can make money at. Like oil.

"The decline of Homestead—U.S. Steel's cornerstone mill—offers
a tangible symbol of the company's disillusionment with its namesake
business," wrote the *New York Times*, "and its strategic decision to
pursue less troublesome ways of making money."

"In five years, it won't be here," said one twenty-five-year, laid-off
employee at the mill. "It's obsolete. We can't even get money for
repairs."

In 1978, steel represented 74 percent of U.S. Steel's total revenues;

15 percent came from related manufacturing, 7 percent from chemicals, 4 percent from other sectors.

By 1982, after the acquisition of Marathon, the company was on its way to Nirvana. Only *28 percent* of its total revenues now came from steel, with 51 percent from oil and gas, 5 percent from manufacturing, 2 percent from chemicals, and the rest from other sectors, including transportation, utilities, resources, and fabricating.

U.S. Steel is no longer a steel company, it's a conglomerate producing diversified commodities and services. It will probably change its name before long to something like USS Inc. or United Services, Inc. or Unisco, take out double-page ads in the *New York Times* and the *Wall Street Journal* showing a muscular forearm with the sleeve rolled up to the elbow, fist clenched in the traditional symbol of machismo and power, to announce the creation of a new company that stands for profitability and growth, concepts that would attract any paper-profit entrepreneur.

But there are problems with such a strategy. All the divisions of the company can experience down cycles at about the same time. That strategy has put more than one jerry-built conglomerate out of business over the years.

"Their problems are formidable," said one analyst. "They understand commodities, but they would have trouble running a computer company."

Robert W. Johnson, former chairman of Johnson & Johnson, put it more succinctly: "Never acquire a business you don't know how to run," he once said. As *In Search of Excellence* so dramatically documented, America's best companies "stick to the knitting"—they run businesses they know how to run. What our conglomerates were learning as they diversified through acquisition was that the businesses they had acquired (and didn't know how to run) in the sixties were causing them problems in the seventies, so maybe they ought to be divesting them again in the eighties.

Not so with U.S. Steel.

"What we're doing is for the long term," U.S. Steel's lawyer-chairman David Roderick said in an interview, sensitive now to the more competitive strategies of the Japanese. "We're not just concerned about 1983 and 1984. We're looking at where we want to be in the year 2000, and we're running our company that way."

It's a safe bet that U.S. Steel, or whatever its new conglomerate name may be, won't be selling much steel in the twenty-first century.

The twelve megabuck deals of 1981 contributed $38.4 billion, or 46 percent of the dollar merger and acquisition total. The Marathon transaction was only the second biggest. Du Pont/Conoco was number one, at $8 billion. Elf Aquitaine of France acquired Texasgulf for $4.3 billion. Connecticut General bought INA for $4.2 billion. Fluor bought St. Joe for $2.7 billion. Nabisco bought Standard Brands for $1.8 billion. Baldwin-United, the old piano maker, bought MGIC Investment Corp. for $1.2 billion.

After a while, you can't see all those 000s after the numbers anymore, they just stop making sense. Like wheelbarrows of deutsche marks during the Weimar years, the whole process becomes meaningless. In Berlin, in 1927, you didn't leave your bicycle unlocked outside a *bier stube* because somebody might steal it to pay for a loaf of bread. In Cincinnati, in 1981, you didn't leave your company unlocked outside business hours because somebody might buy it to pay the shareholders' dividends.

By 1982, thanks in part to a worldwide recession and government deficits not seen since the Pharisees, the American merger and acquisition market had slowed for the first time in years. Still, transactions totalled $53.8 billion, and Grimm said there were 2346 of them during the year. That's still more than 10 a day. It was the megabuck deals that finally began to turn people off.

In March 1983, what the *Wall Street Journal* had called one of the sweetest success stories of the 1970s began to sour. It was one of our megabuck heroes. Baldwin-United.

"Baldwin-United Corp. has grown over the past 15 years from a tiny piano and organ maker into one of the nation's largest financial services companies," the *Journal* wrote.

Did you say *financial services?*

Baldwin-United bought insurance companies, banks, savings and loan associations, and mortgage-banking companies. It became known as the "multi-bank music company." Its CEO, who came up through the operating side, however, was called a financial wizard by his peers.

Until last March.

The story was a familiar one. Old Man Baldwin (D.H.) started out in Cincinnati in 1862 importing Steinways, and when he lost his distributorship in 1887, he started making his own. We took a different view of foreign competition in those days. We were still taming rivers back then.

D. H. did pretty well for himself because the Baldwin piano became a household name over the years. No doubt Mr. Baldwin began to think about exporting his pianos and organs after a while, once the U.S. market was saturated, and no doubt even then the Japanese customs inspectors drove him nuts.

By the late 1960s, deterred by those nontariff barriers and never-present Japanese piano inspectors, the Baldwin management team decided that pianos and organs were becoming less and less profitable. And because they weren't really in business to make musical instruments but to make money, they did what any respectable American company would do.

They diversified.

In 1968, Baldwin bought a bank in Denver. Banks looked pretty good in those days. So they bought a few more, and along with them some insurance companies and other financial intermediaries. In 1977, Baldwin merged with United Corp., an investment firm, and changed its name to Baldwin-United.

By 1981, Baldwin-United's net income was $85.5 million, almost forty times its prediversification earnings in 1967. You think the shareholders weren't happy that Baldwin was out of pianos and into money?

The company had hit on its big winner in 1979, with an enthusiasm reminiscent of Jimmy Ling and National Student Marketing, when its life insurance subsidiaries started selling a popular nonmusical product called a single-premium deferred annuity. This behaved like a tax-deferred savings account: payments in, avoided tax; payments out, years later, got taxed but supposedly at a lower rate.

Baldwin-United sold about $8 million worth of these annuities in 1979, more than $200 million worth in 1980, and $1.5 *billion* in 1981. Best product they ever devised. Better than uprights, better than church organs, a sweeter sound than electric guitars.

So with all that cash now sitting around, they made history with a couple of megabuck deals in 1981, buying S & H Green Stamps and then MGIC Investment Corp. for a combined $1.6 billion. But they had to borrow about $600 million to do it.

Meanwhile, insurance regulators began snooping around and learning that the Baldwin companies were loading their portfolios with the stocks and bonds of other Baldwin companies. Things like this make regulators nervous. One Baldwin insurance company had a quarter of its portfolio invested in Baldwin-affiliated securities that were yielding *2.09 percent* when mortgage rates were in the upper teens.

And that's a sure-fire formula for failure.

In March 1983, Standard & Poor's lowered its ratings on Baldwin-United's debt, and MGIC stopped selling its commercial paper because there were no takers. No one wondered why. By late April, Baldwin-United had stopped selling its single-premium deferred annuities at the request of regulators, negotiated a necessary extension of its bank debt, and sold its 58 percent interest in a computer software company in Texas.

Then the CEO resigned, taking a leave of absence to find a way to prop up his ailing company. In May, he found Victor Palmieri, who had turned the Penn Central around after its debacle in the early 1970s, and persuaded him to try his hand at rejuvenating the once-famous piano maker. But by late September, even an experienced corporate rebuilder as Palmieri recognized the futility of this exercise, as Baldwin-United, besieged by its major creditors, filed for bankruptcy.

That same month, almost by coincidence, the International Trade Commission released a sixty-five-page report documenting the challenge posed by foreign imports to American piano makers. It found that the Japanese had again been outproducing its U.S. competitors by making better use of advanced technology, such as computer-controlled machinery. In 1900, the report said, there had been dozens of American companies producing quality pianos. One was D. H. Baldwin. Today, there are only fifteen.

So financial performance for the sake of financial performance is not the way to go. *In Search of Excellence* made this point rather tellingly, too. The value set of America's excellent companies integrates the major notions of autonomy and entrepreneurship, a bias for action, serving customers, productivity through people, and sticking to the knitting, among others. "Profit is like health," one manager said. "You need it, and the more the better. But it's not why you exist." Companies whose only articulated goals are financial have not even done as well *financially* as those having broader sets of values.

But they're the megabuck heroes.

Zen and the Art of Japanese Investment

"What do I tell foreigners who ask me about Zen?" Ya-*mamoto Shichihei mused in his recent book* The Spirit of Japanese Capitalism.

"For the Japanese, working is not just a matter of economic achievement. By Zen standards it amounts to something like religious training. We still believe the teaching of Suzuki Shozan that by doing our daily work we are doing the Buddha's work, as well. Thus when a manufacturer makes good products he is showing one face of the Buddha to bring profit to the world. When a salesman makes his rounds, he is on pilgrimage. Each in his own task can gain salvation through doing work well, as long as he keeps away from the three poisons of greed, anger, and idle complaint.

"That's what I tell people who ask me about Zen. If they want to study how Zen works, let them look at the Japanese trading companies."

How is it that our attention seems to have shifted away from trade and trade wars to profits and money and greed? What's the connection?

The connection is this. If America is focusing on paper profits and not investing in a big way in new products or new product and process technologies in its own *domestic* market, how can we expect to compete effectively in *world* markets?

The answer is, we can't.

But remember, healthy trade in manufactured goods is just another word for international industrial competitiveness.

A corollary connection is, if the Japanese *are* investing in a big way in new products and new product and process technologies in their own domestic market, why in the world don't they bring some of that investment over here?

The answer is, they do. More like the tortoise than the hare, but they do, and sometimes they even do it by acquisition, which is not an easy process for them.

There are cultural reasons for the Japanese opposition to mergers and acquisitions. In every organization, there is a hierarchy, reflecting the vertical structure of the society at large. *Tate shakai*, it is called. Literally, vertical society.

These institutional hierarchies give rise to internal cliques, or factions, called *habatsu*, that form around the men of merit and power. They're very informal; you won't find any *habatsu* on organizational charts. But they engender fierce loyalties that are direct throwbacks to Tokugawa, when the feudal lords, or *daimyo*, built up their domestic rivalries under the shogun and brought their local domains (which became prefectures after the Meiji Boys took over) under control.

So when you have one Japanese institution with its *habatsu* competing intensely against another, you don't get a lot of M & A work for the accountants or lawyers or investment bankers. The absence of a creative capital market helps, of course. But merging two Japanese organizations is more like trying to arrange a marriage between the Hatfields and the McCoys.

Once in a while, somebody gets overextended and has to be bailed out. This happened when C. Itoh "involuntarily" acquired Ataka & Co., back in 1974, under pressure from the Bank of Japan. The prospect of a major trading company going bust must have sent shivers up the spines of more Japanese government officials than there are Buddhist temples in Kyoto.

And occasionally there are "voluntary" mergers for purposes of curing what the Japanese call "excess competition." After the Occupation, the individual companies of the Mitsubishi Heavy Industries group got back together under their former *zaibatsu* umbrella. Fuji and Yawata merged in 1968 to become New Japan Steel, the world's largest steel company. And in 1971, the Dai-Ichi and Nippon Kangyo banks merged to form the Dai-Ichi Kangyo Bank, known as DKB, and now the biggest commercial bank in Japan.

Most Japanese investments in the U.S. market have been de novo, start-up situations otherwise known as greenfield projects. Take one green field. Borrow money, add plant and equipment, stir in a pinch of labor, and produce.

Sony did that with their TV tube plant in San Diego in 1972 and their videotape factory in Dothan, Alabama, breaking with the old export tradition. They also saw the *kanji* on the wall in the form of growing import barriers and voluntary export restraints. Mitsubishi Electric followed suit in Los Angeles in 1978, and Toshiba did the same in Lebanon, Tennessee; Sharp put up a plant in Memphis in 1979, and Hitachi went into Compton, California, shortly thereafter.

Also in the seventies, YKK established its U.S. manufacturing headquarters in Georgia, Kawasaki Heavy Industries started building motorcycles in Nebraska, and Honda initiated its operations in Ohio. Even Kikkoman Soy Sauce, which is not your usual hard goods manufacturing company, set up shop in Wisconsin to better supply the American market with *shoyu*. They didn't want to be too far away from the soybeans.

But some of the Japanese *zaibatsu* went after acquisitions as well.

In 1969, Mitsubishi Heavy Industries acquired the old Mooney Aircraft Company in San Angelo, Texas, and began making their YS-111 business jets there. Don't believe the Japanese aren't thinking about commercial jet aircraft as an industry priority for the 1990s.

In 1974, Matsushita bought up the old Quasar division of Motorola in Illinois and completely turned it around. Within two years of the acquisition, what had formerly been a rework rate of 90 percent had been reduced to 2 percent, and warranty claims had practically ceased to exist.

Sanyo bought the old Whirlpool division of RCA in Arkansas, in 1977, and converted it into *their* U.S. TV plant. Wacoal acquired Olga so they could make and sell properly proportioned bras in this market. (You don't have to be a genius to know that Japanese underwear won't fit American women.) While Nippon Kogaku, which makes the world's highest quality Nikon cameras, came by its American distributors, Ehrenreich Photo, in a stair-step transaction.

And in 1981, Mitsubishi Chemical Industries acquired three companies in the United States. All were market extension acquisitions— designed to help Mitsubishi expand into the American market by buying some existing market share rather than relying on exports as they had in the past.

Market share motivation. Qualitatively different from the profit motive. "Renounce desires and pursue profits," wrote the Zen master Suzuki Shozan in the seventeenth century, "but never enjoy profits. On the contrary, you should use your profits for the good of others."

Can you imagine the response at Baldwin-United and du Pont and U.S. Steel?

Market share.

"Rapid economic growth became a war to be won, the first total war in Japanese history for which all of the nation's resources were mobilized voluntarily," wrote Kozo Yamamura, an international economist who teaches at the University of Washington.

Professor Yamamura has written about MITI and he has written about Japan's recession cartels and he has written about the machine that maximizes market share. He has not let MITI escape altogether. "Japanese firms could take the long-term view," he once explained, "because MITI helped them minimize risks in a guided investment race."

Perhaps this was true back in the 1950s and 1960s, but not today. Also, many of our own high-tech companies benefitted from the Pentagon's guidance, paternalism, and R & D programs. That's our "Pentagon cushion."

So the "MITI cushion," as Yamamura calls it, may have been there to catch Mitsubishi Heavy Industries or Sumitomo Steel, but not Matsushita or Sony.

Maximizing market share (MMS) is not the same as profit maximizing strategy (PMS). (We must get a little technical here, so please be patient. Or you may skip ahead to page 165, if you wish.)

During a period of rapid economic growth, both MMS companies and PMS companies behave in the same way. This is because average unit costs are falling (the experience curve), so an individual firm can increase profit by increasing output. Therefore, when faced with decreasing long-run average unit costs of production, both MMS and PMS firms tend to behave similarly.

This is another way of saying that in periods of boom—rapid economic growth and expansion—American and Japanese companies perform in the same way. Both increase output because both are confident they can increase sales in a healthy economic environment.

But what happens when the long-term average unit costs of production are *increasing?*

In this case, Yamamura says that total output in an MMS company will be greater than that of a PMS company, and the consumers' surplus larger and the producer's surplus smaller than its counterpart under PMS.

This is another way of saying that when you maximize market share, you will outproduce a company that maximizes profit, generating both a greater supply of unsold goods and a lower rate of earnings.

So what do you do if your strategy is to maximize market share?

Cut prices and sell aggressively in your domestic market and try to find a way of expanding overseas.

Like market extension investments or product extension acquisitions.

It's another page out of Confucius' analects: "Work much, earn much, and spend little."

Some of our consulting firms learned this lesson well and spun their wheels trying to get America's manufacturing companies to learn it, too. They use what they call a Growth/Share Matrix, which looks something like this:

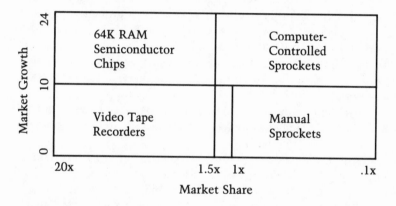

On the left-hand side, Market Growth. On the bottom, Relative Market Share, logarithmic, inverse directional. The matrix is divided into four quadrants.

If you have a product in the lower left-hand box, you have a product that has a high market share in a slow market. This is what the consultants call a cash cow. You don't have to do much with it, it just brings in lots of money.

If you have a product in the upper left-hand box, you have a product that has a high market share in a fast market. This is what the boys call a shooting star. The theory is you feed shooting stars with the loot you bring in from your cash cows.

If you have a product in the upper right-hand box, you have a low market share in a fast market. This is called a question mark. Can you increase your share faster than the market is growing? Will market growth outpace product growth? Or will it slow down suddenly and leave you with several boxcars of unsold inventory? CB radios come to mind here.

If you have any products in the lower right-hand box, you have a low market share in a slow market. These are called dogs and are part of the $82.6 billion of assets that were reshuffled during 1981.

The American experience has been rather spotty, on the whole, in all four quadrants. American companies (PMS types, mostly) tend to let their cash cows consume cash instead of throwing it off. They also have a tendency to put money on *all* their question marks, instead of feeding them selectively, so that what happens is that they may all turn out to be dogs. They take money away from the shooting stars instead of feeding them and making them grow faster. And the dogs can chew up company presidents who spend too much time trying to turn them around.

The Japanese experience, on the other hand, together with that of our own excellent companies as evidenced through the MMS style, has tended to have the following results.

They take money from their cash cows and selectively fund some of their question marks, knowing they won't hit the bull's-eye with all of them. They liquidate others. Thus, they try to move these targeted question marks into the shooting star quadrant and to bring some of their shooting stars down into the cash cow category to throw off more cash to fund more question marks to make more shooting stars. They tend to watch *market* growth rates and market *share* ratios much more carefully than reported profitability or margins.

And the dogs? They don't even get the time of day. They're liquidated as quickly as possible.

Neither was this point lost on the authors of *In Search of Excellence*. "The (truly) adaptive corporation has learned quickly to kill off the dumb mutations," they wrote, "and invest heavily in the ones that work." Which is another way of saying that our own excellent companies have themselves evolved over time through a kind of capitalistic Darwinism: they try, they make mistakes, but they nurture their successful mutations.

Maybe it's just that maximizing market share is closer to Zen than the profit motive is to Christianity. As Yamamoto Shichihei wrote, "In the past, some people said that the Japanese worked hard because they were poor. That was really not a causal relationship. If being poor made people work harder, a greater percentage of the world's population would be hard-working.

"No, we work hard because we believe in it. To do a good job and help one's company grow and prosper is what makes life worth living. Our worldly activity and achievement become part of a religious exercise. It turns into a kind of religious good. Of course, we do not have a priesthood in this religion of work, but in a sense, it is a priesthood of believers."

And, brother, do they believe in maximizing market share.

CHAPTER 18

DEAR SHAREHOLDER: MANAGING FROM A TO Z

We have unmistakable proof that throughout all past time, there has been a ceaseless devouring of the weak by the strong.

—Herbert Spencer, *First Principles*, 1861

"Perhaps we have been the victims of an extended period of superstitious learning, which must now be unlearned," American-born UCLA Professor William Ouchi wrote in his best-selling book about Japanese management called *Theory Z*. "For more than one hundred years, our nation [America] has surged forward under the momentum of the industrial revolution. If we take it as inevitable that the advent of factory production, of low-cost transportation and communication, and a few other innovations would bring a great increase in wealth in our nation, then the scene was set for superstitious learning. In essence, once these basic innovations were in place, our economy was destined to grow. No matter how well or how poorly we organized and managed our commercial enterprises, no matter what we did or failed to do, there would be growth, wealth, and success of an economic sort. In this setting, whatever beliefs developed about management were bound to be supported by success. Having 'learned' how to manage successfully, we have continued to perfect this approach. Only now, when most of the benefit of these innovations has been exhausted, are we forced to see that our paradigm of management never did contribute anything to that success."

William Ouchi was coming to town, and as I wanted to meet with him, I was rereading sections of his book. It can be embarrassing when you don't do your homework. Not long ago, when I was watching another author being interviewed on one of those somnolent TV talk shows, I was reminded of this fact rather tellingly. The writer had just published a new book on skydiving. "So tell me," the interviewer began, "when did you first develop an interest in skin diving?"

It was early February, and the Engineering Department at Princeton University had organized a Saturday seminar called "The Japanese Challenge to American Technology: Will We Meet It?" Professor Ouchi was scheduled to be the keynote speaker.

I say scheduled because the great snows came the night before and the following day about half the people didn't; but Bill Ouchi did, and I decided that was just further confirmation of the superiority of Z-type organizations.

Ouchi divides the world up into A-types and Z-types, which makes sense because America and Japan are practically poles apart on just about everything. A-type organizations, familiar to anyone who has worked for an American company in the last hundred years, are characterized by short-term employment policies (people are just another variable cost—when times get tough, get rid of them), rapid evaluation and promotion (otherwise known as fast-tracking), specialized career paths (once in sprockets, always in sprockets), explicit control mechanisms (everything laid out in manuals and policy books), individual decision making ("We've got to get Ralph to go along with this"), individual responsibility (it's his fault if it goes wrong), and segmented concern (that's not my department).

Z-type organizations, which are becoming more familiar to us now that Japanese products have wiped out American superiority in just about every industrial sector except puffed wheat and guided missiles, emphasize lifetime employment (labor is a fixed cost—when times get tough, pull some people off the assembly line and retrain them), slow evaluation and promotion (nenko joretsu, or advancement through seniority), nonspecialized career paths (everybody does time in sprockets as well as widgets, and exports, and personnel), implicit control mechanisms (learning through experience in an apprenticeship rather than by the numbers), collective decision making (internal rivalry that gradually gives way to consensus), collective responsibility (we must achieve our production targets for our chairman, for our company, for our country), and holistic concern (a closely knit society of people who know each other well).

Professor Ouchi had arrived but most of the others hadn't, so we spoke for a few moments before the proceedings began.

I asked him about his concept of superstitious learning.

He folded his arms across his chest and looked out across the snowdrifts. "People forget that we enjoyed a global monopoly in the 1950s and 1960s," he said softly. "No competition, anywhere. That's all a thing of the past. We have competitors now."

What about the electronics industry, I asked. Weren't we still in the lead?

"That's one of the sectors I've been looking at in some detail," he said. He pulled out a small pipe and began stuffing it with tobacco. "We've run the numbers for the leading firms in each country for the past three years. As a group, the Japanese are outperforming us financially. Their return on assets is now better than ours. Our average return on equity for that period was 12.4 percent, theirs was 17.4 percent. Our bank debt averaged 20 percent of total capital, the Japanese averaged 75 percent. Even the pattern of equity ownership is different. Over 85 percent of the shareholders in our industry are individuals; over 85 percent of theirs are banks, insurance companies, or other institutions within the corporate family."

He paused to light his pipe. "So that's another myth that's been exploded," he said between puffs. "We used to think of the Japanese as inferior in part because their *financial* performance wasn't up to snuff. They had market share and the work ethic and all those trading companies exporting everywhere, but their *numbers* looked worse than ours so we naturally thought the Japanese were no threat. Now their numbers are coming out better than ours. And if that doesn't make the financial analysts sit up and take note, nothing will."

I asked him a final question about superstitious learning. Would we get religion?

He shrugged his shoulders. "The jury's still out on that," he said. He puffed some more as he thought. "You've been to corporate conferences, haven't you?"

I nodded.

"Then you know how they usually schedule a few hours of tennis in the morning, followed by a short meeting, then a long lunch, then golf or tennis in the afternoon, followed by a second meeting, then cocktails and dinner and the same thing the next day. We have to remember when we're playing all that tennis and golf and drinking all those cocktails and eating all that wonderful midwestern beef that our Japanese counterparts are sitting around on Saturdays and Sundays in hard-backed chairs chalking their plans on the blackboard and developing the next phase of their strategy. I still don't think we realize how serious the competition is."

We have competitors now.

His words still echoed as he excused himself and withdrew into the auditorium.

Maybe it was something in the American culture, I thought, that prevented us from accepting *commercial* competition seriously. We take other forms of competition for granted; sports, for example. But commercial competition is something else. It's almost as though we have a divine right, a manifest destiny, a God-given privilege to be superior commercially.

Americans find it hard to acknowledge their shortcomings, which may be one reason hypocrisy is more prevalent here than in Asia. Perhaps it has something to do with our religious background. Protestantism and profits have gone hand in hand for years, but somehow the catechism doesn't quite allow us to take responsibility for our sins. We are sinners, to be sure, *but it's not our fault.* Amen. It's the Devil, or temptation, or the forces of evil, O Lord, but forgive us, for we know not what we do.

This may be why scapegoating is so much a part of our character. When the star tennis player loses a match, the linesman's at fault through poor calls. When the unions strike, it's management's fault for not paying them higher wages. When the U.S.-Japan trade balance gets out of whack, it's Japan's fault for either dumping exports in our market or closing their market to us.

And when American companies experience a down year and have to cut the dividend or report a loss, it's never the fault of management. In fact, nowhere is this tendency more evident than in the average American annual report, a repository of A-type behavior.

American Widgets & Sprockets, Inc.

Dear Shareholder:

This past year was not an easy one for your Company. Although sprocket sales increased for the thirty-fifth consecutive year, domestic market weaknesses combined with cheap foreign imports to put severe downward pressure on earnings, causing inventories to shrink, earnings per share to drop, and return on our assets and equity to fall below historic averages.

Your Management did everything in its power to prevent these adverse results from occurring, but we think you will agree that market circumstances simply intervened and prevented Management from doing its job:

    1. A lack of discipline in fiscal policies at the federal level has eroded confidence in our economy through irresponsible government spending that has escalated out of control.

    2. Disastrous monetary policies designed to fight inflation have instead weakened the dollar, driving interest rates to all-time highs.

    3. Rising labor dissatisfaction coupled with unproductive strikes protesting our generous wage and salary packages have soured union morale, making it more difficult for Management to conduct its corporate strategies effectively.

4. Government interference in your Company's right to decide its own corporate goals and objectives has increased for the sixteenth consecutive year. Nearly one fourth of our total staff is now engaged in compliance with federal, state, or local employment, education, occupational safety, and environmental standards without which we would be performing at historic peaks.

5. The worst weather in a century has kept our shipments down well below seasonal average, increasing inventories to dangerously high levels. Subarctic conditions prevailed in winter, heavy rains continued through an abnormally long spring, summer humidity was at an all-time high, and the autumn wind never stopped blowing. Your Company has never had to work under such adverse conditions.

6. Cheap Asian sprockets have flooded into the market throughout the entire year, creating untold confusion. Management has sued the Asian Sprocket Export Association in the International Trade Commission, seeking temporary relief through higher tariffs under a Section 201 ruling, but that petition was summarily dismissed by the government.

7. Floating exchange rates have continued to make it unprofitable for us to sell in overseas markets. Import quotas and nontariff barriers in other countries make it impossible for our sprockets to penetrate those markets effectively.

8. The National Sprocket Manufacturers' Association has sued your Company over allegations of price fixing and point-of-distribution monopoly in the U.S. market. Although Management firmly believes this lawsuit is totally without merit, it has spent much of its time preparing briefs and countersuits to protect shareholder interests.

In the absence of these debilitating circumstances, over which your Company had no control, Management would have been able to improve its operating performance and increase the annual dividend. Unfortunately, that was not the case.

However, in keeping with your Company's long tradition, the Annual Meeting will be held on the 15th of next month in Sprocket Tower. You are cordially invited to attend. Enclosed please find a Proxy Statement, which kindly complete and return, indicating acceptance or rejection of the following proposals:

1. To change the Company's auditors from a Big Eight firm to a local representative of H & R Block. This will better enable us to take full advantage of the Financial Accounting Standard Board's creative opinions on paper losses from foreign exchange translations and to exploit tax avoidance measures more aggressively.

2. To reinstate your Board of Directors in their current positions. The Chairman will receive a salary increase of 15.8 percent to

$485,553, and the President will be increased 14.7 percent to $370,680. Existing stock option plans, Directors' bonuses, pension benefits, profit sharing, and deferred additional compensation programs will continue in full force and effect for Directors and Senior Management, regardless of the Company's performance.

      3. To approve the Company's acquisition of Consolidated Beverages for the purpose of further corporate diversification. We can no longer depend on single-product stability in the future and must continue to diversify to protect your dividends.

      4. To change your Company's name from American Widgets & Sprockets, Inc., to ASI Corporation (with a new stock ticker symbol) that will more properly reflect your Company's dedication to product diversification and financial services.

    As Management looks ahead to the coming year, it faces the future with cautious optimism. Adversity is not behind us. The danger is always that a new Congress, looking for ways to raise federal revenues and reduce budget deficits, may take additional steps to enact legislation that will restrict our activities even further. We deeply deplore these tactics and urge all of you to oppose any new legislation covertly designed to lower earnings and dividends.

    A self-addressed, stamped postcard is enclosed to help you make your views known to Washington.

    On behalf of the Board of Directors and Senior Management, our thanks for your continued support and confidence.

                      Sincerely yours,

                      Ralph W. Johnson,
                      Chairman

    That's a typical A-type corporate annual report. When things go wrong, it's simply not our fault.

    The picture changes when you read some Z-type annual reports because they're practically polar opposites of the A-types. If anything, blame gets heaped on one's own shoulders in a great gesture of corporate guilt, and Z-type reports attack instead of defend management's performance against all those adverse, outside circumstances over which it has no control.

    So you find statements like the following.

    "Under the aforementioned adverse economic environment, the Company has strengthened its distribution network, reinforced its research and development capabilities, and introduced a variety of new products. Our new factory, equipped with the world's most advanced battery-making equipment, will be the first in Japan to mass produce maintenance-free automotive batteries with high-speed rotary expanded metal technique plates, further strengthening our superiority over our competitors."—A Japanese battery manufacturer.

"Creative workers using modern equipment assure the continuous high quality of products produced in the Company. Under the slogan 'Good Thinking, Good Products,' each employee submits ideas about his job through a Suggestion System, and all employees participate actively in QC Circles to find autonomous solutions to on-the-job problems."—A major automaker.

"Reasons for our huge increase in profitability include such improvements as more efficient production, increased productivity, higher operating levels, and reduced product cost. Our watchword will continue to be 'Technology is the driving force of corporate development.' Our research and development efforts will continue to receive considerable attention."—A major electronics manufacturer.

Nor is the magic of stellar performance contained in some Zen *koan* and limited to Japanese corporations. Our own excellent American companies exhibit the same tough standards, and the message is clear for all to read: we can do it, too.

"We continue to place great emphasis on our product-development programs, which we consider a fundamental strength of our company. An indication of the importance of this effort is the fact that more than half of 1982's orders came from products introduced during the most recent three years." —A major U.S. producer of precision electronic equipment.

"We benefited from a strong flow of new products, with products and services introduced within the last five years again accounting for over 25 percent of our total revenues." —A leading American manufacturer of industrial and consumer products.

"We intend to be the product leaders, to stay in the forefront of the industry in technology, reliability, quality, and value across our entire product line. We want to be not only the low-cost producer of the highest quality products...but also the low-cost developer, seller, and servicer." —A major U.S. computer manufacturer.

We can do it, too.

The same adverse conditions apply: poor weather, meddlesome governments, export quotas, erratic foreign exchange behavior, nontariff barriers, increasing competition. But that's what the game of trade is all about. Competition and domination. Exploit the competitor's weakness. Dominate his markets. Eliminate his uncompetitive products.

Competition. Domination. Elimination.

Honda Rimei put it all in perspective over two hundred years ago. Foreign trade is war.

CHAPTER 19

THE JAPANESE CHARACTER IS NOT ALL *KANJI*

Alternative mechanisms for dealing with dispute-resolution [other than law] work tolerably well in Japanese society because it has been a society of marked homogeneity. Japan was, and is, a society in which there has been a very strong and deeply ingrained sense of order. Unfortunately, however, the world community is not characterized by a high degree of homogeneity. [So] while the Japanese experience has much of relevance for those interested in rapid industrialization, it has its greatest relevance in showing us not how man can live under law, but how man can make a viable adjustment to a post-modern authoritarian order.

—Richard W. Rabinowitz, *Law and the Social Process in Japan*, 1964

A-types and Z-types. Polar opposites. Why? There is a veritable host of reasons.

For starters, we look down on the Japanese. Literally. We're *taller* than they are and, in our culture, we regard short people as inferior. When, for instance, was the last time we had a Real President under six feet? (Jimmy Carter doesn't count. Real Presidents don't wear cardigans, grow peanuts, and have brothers named Billy.)

We're individualists as well, so we also regard groupthink as inferior. The Japanese achieve their identity within the "family" (whether company or country), and regard our stark individualism as rather barbaric. Inevitably, cultural conflict is part of the reason we have been feuding with our Asian ally. And the list of these cultural differences is endless.

Back in 1906, Mr. Yamaguchi Shozo, manager of the Fujya Hotel at the foot of Mt. Fuji, became a little irritated at all the questions overseas visitors asked about Japanese customs and so, to protect himself from the most obvious of these, began printing answers on the backs of hotel menu cards to satisfy their curiosity.

In 1934, when he began to run out of space on the menus, he decided to publish a batch of these questions and answers, which he released in a volume called *We Japanese*. "It is often remarked that Japanese do things in ways directly opposite to those of 'foreigners,'" he wrote in a chapter called "Topsy-Turvydom." "But to the Japanese, foreign ways appear equally unaccountable. We wonder why foreigners do so many things topsy-turvy instead of doing them naturally, in the Japanese way."

Notice how in the first instance, the word *foreigner* appears in quotation marks as if to say "so-called." Politeness is a distinct Japanese cultural trait.

Notice also how Yamaguchi says foreigners do things backwards, instead of doing them "naturally, in the Japanese way." He could just as well have said "opposite" or "different" or "another way." But that's the beauty of cultural pride. We *all* believe the way we do things is natural, if not best. Cultural anthropologists have been reconfirming this point on desert islands and in mountain jungles ever since World War II.

But the differences! There are eleven pages of them. And when you think about these instances of "contrariety," as he calls them, you begin to see why the Washington bureaucrats throw their arms up in despair and call the postwar Meiji Boys crazy.

Japanese books begin at the back. The page is read vertically from right to left. Letters are written with name and address last, in inverse order: "Japan, Tokyo, Minato-ku (the ward), the district, the number, Smith, John, Mr." A man precedes a woman into a room. Cars drive on the left side of the street. Black is worn for weddings, white for funerals. Sweets are eaten before dinner. A carpenter's saw cuts by pulling, not by pushing. Gifts are never opened in the presence of the giver. Yes means no. No means yes. *Domo* means just about everything.

It's also easy to see how you can *misperceive* another culture by viewing it through your own backward lenses. For the Japanese, nothing could be more cockeyed than pushing a saw to cut wood, reading horizontally from left to right, or having yes mean yes.

When we look at Japanese institutions, we find more of the same contrasts. America has a political system in which politicians are dominant. You want something done in Washington, you lobby the pols: senators, congressmen, the executive branch. Our bureaucrats pack their bags when a new administration takes over. But in Japan, it's the bureaucracy that has all the power, whereas their politicians come and go like cherry blossoms in spring.

In our system, the single most influential career path for politics has been the law. (Statisticians may soon point out that former astronauts, professional football quarterbacks, and Hollywood actors are skewing the curve, but so far they're just exceptions that prove the rule.)

In Japan, the single most influential career path for politics is the bureaucracy. Back in 1970, 23 percent of the Japanese House of Representatives and 37 percent of the House of Councillors (their Senate) were ex-bureaucrats. In 1977, the corresponding figures were 27 percent and 35 percent.

Which means, in the topsy-turvy world of Japanese officialdom, if you want to get something done in Tokyo, you don't wander around the corridors of Parliament, you roam the halls of MITI or the Ministry of Finance. Cabinet bills originate exclusively within the ministries, not in the legislative branch. They are then passed to the ruling Liberal Democratic Party for its approval and introduction in the Diet. As a matter of course, ministerial officials are always present in the Diet to explain the proposed legislation.

George Packard, a scholar who has been concerned about the cultural perception gap between America and Japan, wrote an essay called "A Crisis in Understanding," which appeared about ten years ago in a small book titled *Discord in the Pacific*. He examined the many cultural differences between Japan and America, like an anthropologist on Easter Island scrutinizing the great stone statues.

"In our history books, Europe and America are still at the center of the universe," he wrote, "despite three land wars in Asia in the past half-century." Our traditional virtue of hard work becomes "fanaticism" when applied to the Japanese. Good manners become "hypocrisy." Rational economic policies become "industrial targeting" and "unfair trade practices." Tough competitors become "economic animals" and "little yellow people." We simply refuse to accept the Japanese as equals. Or they us.

Form = Substance

Misperception, that's what it is. But it can be formidable.

Like form and substance, for example. For us, substance is substance and form form. But for the Japanese, form is substance.

How's that again?

A good friend in Tokyo, Dick Rabinowitz, is a brilliant lawyer with over thirty years' experience in the Japanese market. He went to Tokyo shortly after completing his law degree at Harvard and now runs the largest and most prestigious law firm in Japan. He speaks and reads

Japanese fluently, by which I mean he knows all the covert and overt meanings of the word *domo*.

Some years ago, Dick wrote a book called *Law and the Social Process in Japan*, which was based on three lectures he had given to the Asiatic Society of Japan in 1964. "Anyone who has worked with the Japanese language is aware of the attraction of the ideographs," he said, "and where else but in a society in which ideographs are used could one hope to find schools for literate adults devoted to study of techniques for the visual rendering of the symbols for verbal expressions of one's own language?

"One only has to walk up the path to a temple such as Sambo-in on the outskirts of Kyoto to see the ideographs almost shouting out in their vigor from a screen standing in the entry hall to appreciate the strong and subtle forces continually at work to pull the perceiver away from the substantive content of the ideograph to the sheer beauty of its form."

When you write in Japanese, are you expressing an idea or are you painting a picture?

It doesn't matter. Form is substance.

The Japanese readily acknowledge this point. When President Nixon broke open diplomatic relations with Peking in 1972, he did it in great secrecy, not even informing Tokyo covertly. When the announcement was made, the Japanese were shocked that they had been bypassed, ignored. Nixon was shocked that the Japanese were shocked.

"A mature alliance," Nixon said afterward, "means seriously addressing the underlying causes, not the superficial public events."

A Japanese official replied that the underlying thought of Nixon's statement was that what matters is substance, not form. "But where face is involved, the form is as important and sometimes more important than the substance," he said.

It's tough. The concepts are *honne* and *tatamae*. *Honne* is actual intent, *tatamae* is principle. Principle takes precedence over actual intent. Because face is so important in Japan, sincerity doesn't mean telling someone the truth, it means avoiding hurting someone's feelings.

So American Widgets & Sprockets, Inc., would tell Tierra del Fuego that if they won't allow their sprockets in through the customs barriers with wooden components, they can lump it. Content. Matsushima Heavy Industries would say something like, we have substituted mountain aardvark tusk for wood, which we think is clearly superior in view of your honorable religion. Form. Matsushima probably *thinks* the local religion will never get Tierra del Fuego out of Christmas tree lights, dollar blouses, and sprockets, but they would never *say* it.

Form over substance.

The same was true when the Japanese surrendered in 1945. Lots of back-and-forth (or, as the Japanese would say, forth-and-back) about what to do with the emperor. Fortunately, we had a few experts around Washington in those days, such as Professors Edwin Reischauer and Hugh Borton, who could explain that form was as important as content. So the boys who wanted to get rid of the emperor lost out to those who said keep him on as a figurehead. They let him stay, and the Japanese did not fight to the last man defending their home islands.

Form *is* substance.

The same cultural juxtaposition is true with regard to general values. The Japanese value harmony, indirect or oblique reference, and consensus. We show a preference for confrontation, direct or precise reference, and individual action. The Japanese love and respect nature. We change it. We see a rushing river and we want to tame it. They see a rushing river and sit down to compose a poem.

In the 1950s, when Japan was just another underdeveloped country in the eyes of our political patriarchs, Professor Robert Bellah wrote a seminal book called *Tokugawa Religion: The Values of Pre-Industrial Japan*. One reason Japan was able to modernize its society so smoothly and so efficiently, the Professor tells us, is that the cultural values receptive to industrialization were already in place before the Meiji Boys took over. They *accepted* Western technology, *adapted* new systems and ideas to their own, *adjusted* their own beliefs to accommodate the new industrial ideologies.

"An industrial society may develop without a shift in basic value patterns," Bellah wrote, "but rather through a process in which economic values (performance, efficient production, and achievement) become very important in certain spheres, and the economy as a whole reaches a certain level of differentiation where it can develop freely and rationally with only minimal restrictions. Most Western industrial societies seem to illustrate this latter development. So does Japan."

Bellah characterizes Japanese basic values as particularistic or "political" in nature, rather than "economic." Which means that their central concerns are with collective goals rather than with production per se. "Controlling and being controlled are more important than 'doing,' and power is more important than wealth."

Thus, the particularistic values of Loyalty, Conformity, and Harmony have primacy in Japan, whereas our "universalistic" value system places priority on Freedom, Justice, and Truth.

"Japan alone of the non-Western nations was able to take over very rapidly what it needed of Western culture in order to transform itself into a modern industrial nation," Bellah observed. "Harmony, a willingness to compromise, and unaggressiveness were highly valued, whereas disputatiousness, contentiousness, overweening ambition, and other disruptive behavior was strongly disvalued. And in order to avoid friction, a great deal of everyday life was formalized. Close conformity to a multiplicity of detailed prescriptions for behavior tends to reduce all conflict to a minimum and ensure the smooth functioning of the collective life."

Can't you just see an American schoolchild pledging allegiance "to the Flag, and to the Republic, for which it stands, with Conformity and Harmony for all?"

Rabinowitz saw this same value reflected in the vagueness of the language, "the vagueness being attributed, at least in part, to linguistic devices conducive to diffuse and abstract statements. An inhibitant to clarity in communication is the oft-noted technique of dealing with any difficult problem through an intermediary. And directness in speech, in the sense of taking openly categorical stands, simply does not fit the pattern of Japanese life."

Ruth Benedict, in her classic book *The Chrysanthemum and the Sword*, viewed these particularistic values in terms of their impact on the development of self-discipline in Japan. "In the United States, technical and traditional methods of self-discipline are relatively undeveloped," she said. "The American assumption is that a man, having sized up what is possible in his personal life, will discipline himself, if that is necessary, to attain a chosen goal. Whether he does or not, depends on his ambition."

Not so with the Japanese, she found. "The Japanese assumption is that a boy taking his middle-school examinations, or a man playing in a *kendo* match, or a person merely living as an aristocrat, needs a self-training quite apart from learning the specific things that will be required of him when he is tested. The practice of self-discipline has a recognized place in life. Japanese of all classes judge themselves and others in terms of a whole set of concepts which depend upon their notion of generalized technical self-control and self-discipline."

Thus, the Japanese Army officer, who had been training his troops for nearly three days with only ten-minute breaks for sleep, could say, "They know how to sleep. They need training in how to stay awake."

"The will should be supreme over the almost infinitely teachable body," Miss Benedict concluded, "and the body itself does not have laws of well-being which a man ignores at his own cost."

Z-types. Harmony, loyalty, conformity, vagueness, principle.

Fu-Ryo-Mon-Ji. (Words are of no use.)

—Japanese proverb

As Rabinowitz observed, cultural values are strongly reflected in the language. Western languages are specific, direct, and content oriented. Japanese is vague, indirect, and emphasizes form over content.

If you've been to Japan, then you know the feeling. You stand on a streetcorner anywhere in Tokyo and you look around and you can't understand anything. Like a child in an adult's world, my wife used to say, as she would jerk my coat and ask what this character meant or how that character should be translated. Ideographs. God's great invention to confuse the Devil.

When I was living in Tokyo several years ago, there was a marvelous cartoon character, Sazae-san, that appeared in the *Asahi Shimbun* one day. It caught the Japanese language and culture in a kernel of Zen truth. Like the *koan* of one hand clapping.

Two men are seated on a park bench, Sazae-san and a stranger. The stranger pulls out a cigarette, turns to Sazae-san and says, "You got a match?"

Sazae-san shakes his head.

Then he reaches into his pocket, and pulls out his own cigarette.

Then he reaches into another pocket and pulls out a *lighter*.

In the final block, Sazae-san lights the cigarette, pockets the lighter, and stares at the stranger, who has a look of incredulity and total desperation on his face.

Sazae-san had answered the question precisely. He did not have a *match*.

Kunihiro Masao, my friend who earlier coined the Japanese cultural characteristic *zurui*, once wrote that sincerity in the Western sense means a frank expression of one's inner thoughts without mincing words and without considering the effects of one's words on the listener. "But in Japanese, this is being insincere," he said. "We Japanese are hesitant to give a frank and definitive expression of our feelings, not only out of consideration for the other person, but also to avoid being excluded from the group."

He reminded me once that the character *sei*, whose basic meaning is birth or life or existence has fifteen different readings and at least as many meanings. *Domo* can mean anything from "I'm sorry" to "Nice to see you again" to "Thank you." *Kekko* means "Yes, please, that will be fine," and "No, thank you, that's enough." Most foreigners wrack their brains learning how to use complicated expressions when *domo*, the most useful phrase of all, would probably suffice in nine out of ten situations.

When you ask a Japanese a question that contains a negative, such as, "You have no natural resources in Japan, do you?" the answer will be, "Yes, we have none." Yes means no.

Learning the *kanji* is the hardest part. There are *gaijin*—foreigners— who have spent a lifetime in Japan and still don't feel they've mastered the language. It's almost impossible to do without flash cards. Ultimately, a few thousand characters get burned into your memory, like cattle brands. And the flash cards get more dog-eared and worn than a well-used deck of Bicycles.

Kanji are also dangerous because the same character will have different pronunciations and different characters will have the same pronunciation. Like *komon* and *kōmon*.

Komon means advisor. *Kōmon* (long initial vowel) means anus.

So one day you're standing in a reception line for your company welcoming distinguished officials from the Ministry of Finance. If you're not very careful with your pronunciation, you may turn to a bureau chief and say, "Yamamoto-san, I would like to introduce you to the senior asshole from our head office in New York."

Or *korosu* and *orosu*.

Orosu means to let out or drop off, as in "Driver, let me off at the next corner, please."

Korosu means to kill or slaughter, as in "Driver, kill me at the next corner, please."

You might wonder what the cabdriver tells his wife that night about the foreigner who asked to be slaughtered on the streetcorner.

Or *ryokan*, which is the old, traditional Japanese inn, and *yōkan*, which is a yucky sweet bean paste made into little molds for dessert.

So when you arrive in a strange village for an overnight stay and ask the stationmaster, "Where is that yucky sweet bean paste called Yamanaka?" you won't wonder what he tells his wife about the foreigner when he gets home.

Jack Seward, who has been in Japan for many years, wrote a very funny (but very poignant) book in 1969 called *Japanese in Action*. In it, he coined an expression all foreigners who live and work in Japan should know: the Baka Valve. *Baka* is a word that means fool or simpleton. It is one of comparatively few Japanese swear words. (The Japanese do not swear, not because they don't have strong feelings, but because their culture does not value the outward expression of those feelings.)

The Baka Valve works as follows: Say you're a *gaijin* heading down the street looking for a particular address. You speak pretty good Japanese for a barbarian, and your Texas accent is disguised.

You approach an elderly Japanese man to ask directions, in Japanese, preceding your question with the proper verbal and physical gestures.

Now this Japanese gent will look at you and see that you're a foreigner, and his audio-receptor valve will automatically switch open to receive only foreign languages. The fact that you are speaking Japanese is irrelevant: you are a foreigner, therefore, you *must* be speaking a foreign language, which is all he hears.

He will stop, fumble for words, and then explain in broken English that he is sorry, he doesn't speak foreign languages, and excuse himself, leaving you to repeat the pattern with another stranger.

One of the virtues of Japanese, though, is its vagueness. "This was enunciated over a hundred years ago by Abe Masahiro," Seward wrote, "when he proposed to the Shogun what the government's attitude toward Commodore Perry should be: 'Our policy shall be to evade any definite answer to their request while at the same time maintaining a peaceful demeanor.'"

So you can see how our two cultures have been poised for some direct confrontation in trade negotiations. One language, direct and specific, sparring with a set of ideographs whose whole message to the world is that form is substance.

Bilateral negotiations means using linguistic intermediaries, otherwise known as interpreters. Because the whole process of intermediation is very familiar to the Japanese (arranged marriages, out-of-court dispute settlements, third-party compromise), they generally have fewer problems than we do. Because Americans always expect to deal in English and expect everybody else to do so, too, we have rarely been forced to cope with other cultures on their own terms as a condition of survival.

"When I go to Washington to see President Nixon," Prime Minister Satoh Eisaku reportedly said on the eve of those fractious textile talks in 1971, "our negotiations will be three parts talk and seven parts *haragei*." *Haragei* literally means "belly talk" in Japanese. It refers to the intimate or shared feelings of friends—reading each other's minds, so to speak.

Well, Nixon probably didn't do much mind reading when they got together. He is more likely to have stared speechlessly at the interpreter when he heard the Premier's poetic comments about *fu-ryo-mon-ji* (words are of no use) and *kuroi uma no kage* (shadows of a black horse). Come, Mr. President, your advisors should have told you that yes means no and form is substance.

So the Japanese and American negotiating styles are as different as their languages and their cultures and their contrasting ideologies and values. Could it be otherwise?

Negotiating Strategies

Japanese negotiating strategy has usually proceeded in three distinct phases: preliminary probing tactics, the bargaining stage, and the final phase.

Their preliminary tactics are usually defensive in nature, concerned with face and the other side's position, yet zealously pursuing Japan's own direct interests. Japanese negotiators establish a strong, inflexible base from which there is normally no fallback position. They refrain from early concessions, prefer behind-the-scenes maneuvering (back-door diplomacy), have a penchant for meticulous planning and a distaste for premature commitment. They will emphasize prefatory agreements and understandings that will be strongly pragmatic in nature and cautiously defensive, avoiding conflict, keeping all doors open, and ensuring that a final agreement is workable.

That's the preliminary phase.

A favorite Japanese tactic in the bargaining stage is the *atomawashi*, or delaying tactic. Often interpreted by Americans as failure or a breakdown in talks, it is welcomed by the Japanese who see it as an opportunity to rehuddle domestically to form a new consensus or to prepare new bargaining positions.

"It is only against the backdrop of Japanese domestic politics that one can understand why a Japanese negotiator will try to postpone an item until later when compromise seems inevitable," Michael Blaker wrote in "Probe, Push and Panic." "Most Japanese negotiators defer controversial items to the end simply because they are not authorized to concede. As initial Japanese bargaining decisions are reached only after herculean preliminary work, subsequent changes involving substantial concessions also require monumental effort. Delaying tactics are the nearly inescapable concomitant of rigid bargaining procedures, highly dedicated negotiators, and a deep-rooted fear of anything that smacks of capitulation to the other side."

Final-phase tactics include stubbornness, persistence, and a "stoic imperturbability" reflected as coolness under fire. The negotiator will avoid confrontation, often make a direct personal appeal, use time limits or refusals to proceed, and ice-blocking maneuvers. The overall thrust in the final stage is risk-aversion and avoidance of confrontation, as well as to ward off at all costs the impression that Japan is "weak, vulnerable, or inferior."

In the nineteenth century, Westerners tended to deal with the Japanese on basically Western terms and in Western languages, without significantly penetrating Japanese society. One account recalled:

> Out of both choice and necessity, Japanese tended to deal with foreigners in foreign tongues and according to foreign ways, abroad if possible, or at the shoreline. It was an unequal relationship characteristic of Western imperialism, but it survived into the 20th century despite the decline of the West in Asia. On the Japanese side, it survived not only because it met the strong need for autonomy and ethnic certitude, but also because it produced significant economic benefits. Not only could Japan retain control of its own domestic market, it could also follow and exploit foreign learning, while most foreigners were unable to monitor technological and other advances made in Japan. On the American side, it survived because all the political, economic and technical evidence for decades supported the gratifying belief that others, such as the Japanese, could learn much from [us] while [we] could learn nothing of consequence from them, and therefore had no need to gain a closer understanding of them.

After World War I, when Secretary of State Stimson was negotiating the London Naval Agreement that would assign relative sizes and strengths to the American, British, and Japanese navies, he penciled in some tonnage figures on the back of an envelope in an attempt to resolve the cruiser ratio problem in its final phase.

"If he had been Japanese," Tokyo negotiator Wakatsuki later remarked, "he would have used an abacus." He wasn't disagreeing with the numbers at that stage, only the style.

Form is substance.

"An awareness of impotence dominated Japanese thinking about negotiations [before the war]," Blaker wrote, "and produced two basic norms of diplomatic conduct: an abiding desire for freedom of action and an equally deep wish to avoid risk." That has held true not only for battleships and treaties but for beef and oranges as well.

Japanese negotiators often find themselves steering a difficult course through the Scylla of foreign governments urging more compromise and the Charybdis of domestic pressure demanding less. "Impressions are as important as actual achievements," Blaker observed. Why not? In politics, as we know, perception is reality.

But the essence of Japanese negotiating success is persistence and endurance and tenacity and patience. Or, in our local idiom, True Grit.

I often wonder how we prepare for negotiations with the Japanese. Perhaps Robert Strauss may have had an American Briefing Book for Beef and Oranges that looked something like this:

Preliminary Probing Tactics

1. Set preconditions.
2. Present artificially inflated or phony demands.
3. Manipulate public opinion to support these demands.
4. Offer meaningless concessions.
5. Make subsequent noncontingent concessions.

Bargaining Stage Strategy

1. Withdraw phony demands.
2. Make threats.
3. Create outside incidents as a distraction.
4. Break off, delay, or bluff.
5. Leak opponent's demands to the press.

Final Phase Tactics

1. Escalate demands.
2. Present counterdemands.
3. Present new drafts of previous agreements.
4. Repeat same positions.
5. Recall negotiator.
6. Change negotiator.
7. Gang up on opponent with other countries.

Topsy-Turvydom.

In our vernacular, it's the squeaky wheel that gets oiled. In Japanese, it's the nail standing up that gets hammered down. But to them, that doesn't mean attention. It means conformity.

CHAPTER 20

ZEN AND THE ART OF FLOATING CURRENCIES

"We've got cedars from Lebanon due at the sawmill in Oslo to be turned into shingles for the builder in Cape Cod. C.O.D. And then there's the peas."

"Peas?"

"That are on the high seas. We've got boatloads of peas that are on the high seas from Atlanta to Holland to pay for the tulips that were shipped to Geneva to pay for the cheese that must go to Vienna. M.I.F."

"M.I.F.?"

"Money in Front. The Hapsburgs are shaky."

"Milo."

"And don't forget the galvanized zinc in the warehouse at Flint...."

—Joseph Heller, *Catch-22*

A-types. Z-types. Form is substance. Perception is reality.

With all these contrasting ideologies, differences in national character, and divergent cultural values, one is often amazed that the United States and Japan still speak to each other, assuming they can agree on a common intermediary for translation.

The same might be said of their respective currencies. For when foreign goods are bought and sold, a common intermediary is needed to translate the value of one currency into the value of the other. That common intermediary is the market.

Old Willard out in Omaha is tickled pink to be selling his wheat to those little yellow people, for example, but what's he going to do with all that *yen?*

"George, I'm gonna buy me a new Cadillac this year. Payin' cash."

"How much?"

"Coupla billion yen."

"Say what?"

So when the Matsushima Trading Company is ready to pay Willard for his boatload of wheat, they call up the Matsushima Bank and tell them to wire the hairy barbarian about $8.3 million. Because the intermediary, called the foreign exchange market, tells both Matsushima and Willard that a dollar is worth about 240 yen at current rates.

Who decides the dollar is worth 240 yen?

The market.

Who is the market?

Well, you and me and Old Willard and Matsushima Trading and Mazda Motors and General Electric and Morgan Guaranty and Exxon and Elf Aquitaine and the Saudi Arabian Monetary Authority.

Anyone who needs to sell yen and buy dollars to pay for soybeans or winter wheat or anything else whose prices are denominated in U.S. currency. And anyone who needs to buy yen and sell dollars to pay for industrial robots or 256K semiconductor chips or anything else whose prices are denominated in Japanese yen.

The old Japanese money was called *mon*, or *ryo*, and it was round with a square hole in it. Then the Japanese started making their coins oblong in shape because this used less metal, but the square hole remained. During Tokugawa (1603–1868), the peasants took to cutting off small pieces to make change. The shogun disliked the idea. The peasantry didn't understand the government's explanations about how they were debasing the currency; but when the samurai chopped their heads off in punishment, they stopped making change this way.

Money had a tough time in the Tokugawa era. Not only were the coins getting bent out of shape, but the local *daimyo* in each fief were issuing their own clan notes, printed in red and black on rice paper from woodblocks just like the kind Hiroshige and Hokusai used for their famous views of Mt. Fuji and the old Tokaido Road. But because the *daimyo* had more power than the peasantry, they didn't stop when the shogun told them it wasn't such a good idea to have so much worthless money floating around.

In 1871, the Meiji Boys changed all that. The *ryo* became the yen and the government issued paper money through the national banks. Each bank printed its own notes. But counterfeiting was apparently so popular that the Japanese had to have their banknotes printed in Germany for a while. The Meiji Boys finally cleaned up the mess by creating the Bank of Japan in 1882 and burning all the old money.

In feudal times, money was backed by rice (in fact, rice was the more popular medium of exchange and measurement), but the Meiji Boys knew that foreigners would simply laugh when they said the yen was worth two *koku* of rice. So Japan joined the metal standard, which was silver at the time, until the switch was made to gold.

When the Pacific war ended, the yen was backed by chaos and ruin, so it was hard to determine a value. Joseph Dodge went to Tokyo during the Occupation to help design the Economic Stabilization Plan, part of which was aimed at pegging an appropriate value for the yen. When Dodge said the yen was worth 360 to the dollar, and nobody disagreed, that's what it became.

It stayed that way for nearly twenty-five years. Why? Because on the other side of the world, after the Atlantic War, international economists and monetary officials met at Bretton Woods to decide what to do about all those chaotic European currencies that had been so badly battered by Hitler's panzer divisions. And they decided that the U.S. dollar, by default, would be the world's reserve currency and the standard against which all other currencies would be measured. The dollar was also backed by gold, which made more sense than rice or wheat.

So a system of fixed foreign exchange rates was put into effect that remained until 1971. A dollar bought four deutsche marks in 1951 and 1957 and 1962 and 1969. It also bought 360 yen in those years, which was when the Japanese were running their chronic trade deficits.

But in the 1960s, we started fighting a war in Vietnam that took boatloads of dollars to finance and heated up domestic demand for foreign goods and dropped the international competitiveness of U.S. products in world markets. Multinationals were also siphoning dollars out to pay for their new overseas investments. So the greenback came under pressure, the Eurodollar was born, inflation soared, and Washington created an artist's palette of cosmetic controls to keep the dollar strong: the Office of Foreign Direct Investments, the Interest Equalization Tax, and the Voluntary Foreign Credit Restraint Program at the Fed.

In 1971, President Nixon devalued the dollar by 10 percent across the board, slapped a stiff surcharge on all imports, and unhooked the link to gold. Immediately, the currency markets were in turmoil, although they had expected as much because most central banks—those protectors of national currencies like the Banque de France and the Bank of England—had been net sellers of dollars since about 1969.

So the yen *revalued* to around 318, despite the best efforts of the Bank of Japan, as a more expensive yen meant more expensive Mazdas. By December 1972, when the rate had steadied at about 308, the international economists and monetary officials all got together again, this time in Washington, to change the system.

Fixed foreign exchange rates were simply too expensive to maintain and too inflexible. So a system of *floating* exchange rates was created and a fancy document called the Smithsonian Agreement was signed.

Under the fixed system, when currencies got "out of alignment," central banks—including our Federal Reserve Bank—were supposed to intervene by buying and selling to restore proper parities. Under the floating system, intervention was unnecessary because the market would constantly adjust the currency values for changes in comparative inflation, interest rates, balance of payments deficits, growths in money supply, and all those tricky things called "fundamentals," which are described in the papers each day.

The funny thing was that it worked for a while. Before the oil crisis in October 1973, Japan was still the Miracle Economy, growing twice as fast as everybody else, and the market floated the yen/dollar rate "up" to about 250. ("Up," because the yen was strengthening.) By December 1973, after the price of oil had increased fourfold, everybody thought Japan was going to hell in a handbasket because they had to import all that oil and had none of their own. So the market floated the yen/dollar rate "down" to 300.

But then the central banks saw they could artificially move their exchange rates one way or the other by buying or selling dollars in the market or by placing limits on what foreigners could do with their currency or by selling domestic bonds overseas denominated in another currency or by jawboning (administrative guidance, in Japanese) or by a dozen other tricks that created what the market called "dirty floating."

And foreign exchange rates frequently did not respond to the fundamentals. So the Europeans created the snake, or limited bands within which their currencies would float and without which the central banks would be required to intervene until agreement could be reached on new parities, if necessary.

This is all tough stuff for Old Willard sitting out there in Omaha who thinks this funny money isn't worth a hill of beans because all he wants is dollars. But like it or not, he has to realize that the price of dollars in the exchange market is dependent on more than just the cost of his fertilizer and the presence or absence of rain on his wheat.

America runs a chronic trade deficit, and the exchange market reacts by selling dollars. America starts running double-digit inflation rates, and the exchange market thinks Washington is no better than Tierra del Fuego, so it sells dollars. Or through its monetary policies, the Fed jacks up interest rates so high that foreigners want to buy dollars. Unemployed American automobile workers take a few potshots at passing Toyotas, and the exchange market buys yen. The Japanese sell more cars and video tape recorders and computer-controlled sprockets than anybody else, and the market buys more yen.

And this goes on twenty-four hours a day. Because when the market is closed in New York, it's open in London, and when it's closed in London, it's open in Tokyo.

When exchange rates are out of alignment, or misaligned, they have a negative effect on trade. If Willard sells his boatload of wheat to the Japanese at a rate of 240 yen to the dollar, he'll get his $8.3 million. But if the rate is 300 to 1, the Japanese may buy less wheat and eat more rice, so Old Willard can only sell half a boatload.

Now, if Willard wants to sell his Cadillac and buy a Nissan President because he wants to be the first on his block with a *big* Japanese car, he may pay $10,000 for it if the exchange rate is stable, say, 240/1. But if the rate drops to 200/1, the exporter has to increase his dollar prices to cover his higher yen exchange costs. Suddenly Old Willard is looking at a price tag of $11,700 for that same car, and the Cadillac prices become competitive again.

When a country runs chronic trade deficits, has historically high interest rate levels, a double-digit rate of inflation, high unemployment, low domestic demand, and erratic money supply growth, the exchange market says such a country should have a *weak* currency.

Countries that have usually had exclusive membership in this fraternity include Indonesia, India, Brazil, the Philippines, and Tierra del Fuego. Underdeveloped countries, or to be more polite, less developed countries. The LDCs. Weak currencies. Brazil traditionally devalued its cruzeiro almost daily.

The United States of America qualified for membership beginning about 1980. But with one significant difference: because the dollar was still the marker currency (like Saudi Arabian light oil is the marker crude), central banks and overseas investors and banana republics still kept the bulk of their reserve holdings in dollars.

So the United States had all the economic faults with none of the exchange rate benefits. Technically, the dollar should have been dramatically weaker in the markets, to help make U.S. exports more competitive and reduce the trade gap. But where else in the world could you get an 18 percent rate of return on your short-term investments without fear of a new crowd of generals taking over the government the next day? There was such a great demand for dollars in 1981 and 1982 that the yen weakened from around 211 to about 275 in less than a year, despite the largest bilateral trade surplus Japan had ever experienced with America. And a weaker yen meant even more competitive Japanese exports.

Now when the exchange rate is 275 to 1, and Japan is running a terrific trade surplus with the United States, the last thing you want is a weak yen. You want the price stickers on those Datsuns and Mazdas to reflect a higher dollar amount to compensate for a stronger yen and simultaneously make your domestic products more competitive. But the yen was weak. Not because of any inherent "fundamental" problems with the currency or with the Japanese economy or with Japanese inflation or interest rates or unemployment.

But because the dollar was so strong.

Back in the fall of 1978, the yen "rose" to an historic high of around 180 to the dollar. Japanese exports to the United States became more expensive, dollar exports to Japan became cheaper. Because the exchange rate alignment was right. When your wheels are out of alignment, your car wobbles. When exchange rates are out of alignment, the trade balance wobbles.

The average yen/dollar exchange rate for 1977 was 268. The average yen/dollar exchange rate for 1978 was 208, but it averaged 192 for the last six months of 1978 and under 210 for the first six months of 1979. The bilateral trade deficit in 1978 (reflecting the lag effect from 1977) was $11.6 billion. In 1979, reflecting the stronger yen rate, the trade deficit narrowed to $8.7 billion.

But in 1980, Jimmy Carter slapped on credit controls, our money supply skyrocketed, the second oil shock was in full gear, and dollar interest rates took off. That year, the average yen/dollar rate slipped back "down" to 225, and the bilateral deficit increased to $9.9 billion. In 1981, when the Reagan tax cuts, supply-side economics, and big federal budget deficits pushed the market into more uncertainty, the average exchange rate dropped to 230, and the bilateral deficit subsequently rose to $15.8 billion. In 1982, with an average exchange rate of 250, the bilateral deficit soared to an historic $18.6 billion and the fur started flying.

"Bilateral balances in themselves are neither a meaningful indicator of international competitive positions nor a sensible guide for policy," wrote C. Fred Bergsten in *Foreign Affairs* in the summer of 1982. Nor are currency swings the only policy tool available to fix the trade balance when it starts to wobble. But it's an important one, and when it is not available, the wobble gets harder to fix.

Beginning in 1981, most observers agree, the yen should have started strengthening from its 1980 average of 225, not weakening. "From its lows of late 1978 to its highs of August 1981 and April 1982," Bergsten wrote, "the dollar rose by nearly 40 percent against the yen. Meanwhile, Japanese inflation ran about 20 percentage points less than U.S. inflation. The price competitiveness of the United States in world trade, vis-à-vis Japan, thus deteriorated by *50 percent or more* within about three years."

Fred Bergsten was Assistant Secretary of the Treasury for Interna-

tional Affairs in the Carter administration. He is presently director of
the Institute of International Economics in Washington, another think
tank. He has written extensively on international economic problems
over the years, ranging from esoteric papers on exchange rate equilib-
rium to essays on the competitiveness of cheap imported footwear.

The real culprit of the U.S.-Japan trade deficit, in Bergsten's view,
is not Japan's "closed" market or "unfair" Japanese trading practices
like industry targeting, or nontariff barriers at the port in Yokohama.
It is the peculiar "policy mix" Washington has used over the past
several years, a combination of fiscal and monetary actions that have
produced abnormally high rates of inflation in this country, which have
increased dollar interest rate levels to record highs, and which have
caused massive foreign exchange flows into the dollar.

"The United States must simply tighten its fiscal stance over the
next several years by reducing the huge budget deficits which are inevitable under current policy," Bergsten concluded in his *Foreign Affairs* article. "The path to greater fiscal stability is clear: a stretch-out
in the buildup in our military expenditures, further judicious cuts in
nonmilitary expenditures (including entitlement programs), and primarily a rollback (or offset) of the massive tax cuts voted in 1981."

But as luck would have it, while the Washington bureaucrats were
legislating these huge budget deficits that put all the burden of fighting
inflation on monetary policy, the Japanese were pursuing a "policy
mix" that cauterized the wounds. Their policies represented polar opposites of ours: Tokyo emphasized a dramatic reduction of large budget
deficits, putting all the burden of rekindling their economy on monetary policy, which created very low yen interest rates and encouraged
capital outflows in search of higher yields.

Rimmer deVries is senior vice president in charge of international
economics at Morgan Guaranty, a brilliant international economist, a
crusty Dutchman, and an old friend.

I called Rimmer to talk about the misalignment between the dollar
and the yen, suggesting that maybe what we needed for these two
currencies was something like the European snake, now that the system of floating rates no longer seemed to have any correctional effect
on the yen/dollar rate. But because snakes are unlucky in Japan, maybe
we should call it an eel. Anyway, something to ensure more frequent
central bank intervention to realign the currency rates when they get
wobbly.

"Fixed versus floating is not the real issue here," Rimmer said in
his crusty voice. "The real issue is our policy mix. The Japanese have
a budget deficit now running at about 3.5 percent of GNP. Ours is 6.5

percent of GNP and growing. Plus the Japanese are still saving too much, and we are saving too little."

But to get the policy mix readjusted will take years, I said. Politicians are used to thinking in terms of days and weeks. You can't realign a wobbly trade balance in 1986 if you're running for reelection in 1984.

"I agree," the Dutchman said. "But simply realigning the exchange rates themselves won't do the whole job. Underlying policy has to reflect the broader issues. And the broader issues are very serious because an overvalued dollar is not good for the world."

We talked for a while about Nakasone bonds (Japanese government obligations denominated in dollars and underwritten in the U.S. market), savings rate differentials, and the divergent policy mixes. Rimmer's mind was on other things. Like debt restructuring in the LDCs, which threatened the stability of the international banking system as the oil crisis did ten years ago. He had a few words to say about the banks and some vinegary advice for the banana republics.

"Rimmer," I said. "You're still crusty."

"That's not fair," he said. "Somebody once wrote that about me, and I didn't like it."

"That's because you didn't take it as a compliment."

"You mean it's complimentary?"

"Absolutely," I said.

I told him politicians might be angry if they were called that, or preachers, maybe, but not brilliant Dutch economists.

He was right, of course. Simply realigning the exchange rates themselves wouldn't do the whole job. But it would help. Former German Chancellor Helmut Schmidt and President François Mitterand of France had both come out strongly, and publicly, in favor of establishing a new international monetary system based on flexible currency bands rather than continuing the Smithsonian system of floating rates. Other international economists were joining the groundswell.

So I still thought a dollar/yen "eel" corresponding to the European snake was a good idea. It would establish flexible bands within which the two currencies could fluctuate, and when they got outside those parameters, either the Fed or the Bank of Japan would intervene under set rules to realign them.

Besides, we all know how slippery eels are. So we wouldn't expect it to work flawlessly 100 percent of the time.

CHAPTER 21

SO WHY IS EVERYTHING GOING WRONG?

"Mrs. Carolyn Presky, you've Sold Out! Now let's see just what you've won on this, your third day on Hawaiian Sell-Out! Bob, what's Mrs. Presky's heap so far?"

"Right, Jack. So far, a complete broken set of color bars for Mrs. P's new home. Some level mountain skis and water rollers for that fun-filled open season. An unattached grid-five stand-upper heater, with a smoked window... and now—three hundred full pounds of Chef Antoine's Southern Fried Glymphs, toasted to golden perfection, then cubed, reheated and returned to water before you're ready, Mrs. Presky. And inside! Well, look at that, it's just as lovely, two shelves where none are needed, and look at that! Close the door and the light stays on!"

> —Second City TV, *Don't Crush That Dwarf, Hand Me the Pliers*

When unemployed American autoworkers start taking potshots at passing Japanese cars and when the workers who are left on the assembly lines weld beer cans to the chassis of American cars and when worker ranks are decimated on Fridays and Mondays because the recipe for company loyalty left out the ingredients for self-fulfillment and when worker productivity then begins to lag behind Tierra del Fuego's and when many of our children can no longer read and write and spell and when our global merchandise trade gap yawns wider and we blame it all on the Japanese, *something must be going wrong.*

Maybe somebody changed the rules of the game.

Used to be, you got up in the morning, ate breakfast with your wife and 2.3 kids, kissed the little woman goodbye, climbed in your Ford or Chevy station wagon, drove either to the train station for the 7:49 or straight to work, spent nine or ten hours at the office with the boys,

192

picked up a copy of the evening paper, and set off for home.

It was all so simple.

Inflation was low, interest rates were stable, mortgage rates were 3.5 percent, unemployment was unheard of, the federal budget was balanced, Ike was unintelligible but greatly loved, worker productivity was the highest in the world, American products were without equal in any market, our work ethic was the subject of profound respect and admiration, and the expanding American economy was a cornucopia of limitless wealth and affluence.

The future was ours. Because those were the rules.

Now, when you get up in the morning, maybe you kiss the woman or the man or nobody and maybe you have one kid or it's someone else's kid or no kids and maybe you feel like working today and maybe you don't. If you do, maybe you pile into your Datsun 280-Z or your Honda hatchback for the ride to work or maybe you stay at home and tap a few keys on your TRS-80 personal computer with the spiffy micromodem. In either case, you put in your six hours and call it a day. If you don't, maybe you smoke a little dope or maybe you sniff a little coke and read *People* magazine or maybe you write a little poetry or maybe you join the self-fulfillment group down at the local Unitarian church, and when you're done, you snap on the TV to groove with the Stars.

It's all so different.

Our inflation rate today is unpredictable, interest rates are stuck at levels you'd laugh at in Indonesia, mortgage rates have destroyed the home as the Last Great Investment, unemployment is giving young people in our cities a taste of what the Great Depression was like, our president is not a decorated general but a Hollywood Star, American productivity growth is at the bottom of the pile, Japanese products are pushing us out of every commercial market including our own, our work ethic is the subject of derision and scorn, and the contracting American economy looks less like a cornucopia than a conch shell.

The future is not ours.

Well, whose is it then? What happened to the rules?

Two years ago, this same question burned in the mind of Daniel Yankelovich, Harvard-educated president of Yankelovich, Skelly & White and one of America's most seasoned analysts of social trends and attitudes. It burned in his mind for so long and with such intensity that he finally set out to answer it.

His answer is contained in a brilliant book called *New Rules: Searching for Self-fulfillment in a World Turned Upside Down.* "The struggle for self-fulfillment in today's world is the leading edge of a genuine cultural revolution," Yankelovich writes. "It is moving our industrial civilization toward a new phase of human experience." He sees the giant tectonic plates of American culture shifting deep beneath the surface of the landscape.

Determination, self-denial, and sacrifice, which Yankelovich characterizes as part of the Old Experience, is giving way to relaxation, enjoyment of success, and what he calls the self-fulfillment quest— seeing the world through categories of thought borrowed from theories of self-help psychology. Americans are rewriting the giving/getting contract: no longer "getting" what they wanted out of Organizational life, they simply stopped "giving" to it, and instead began developing "an awesome array of hobbies and outside interests." EST. I'm OK, you're OK. Zen meditation. Yoga. The I-Ching. Left-side, right-side therapy. Metaphysical poetry. Transcendental meditation. Sufism.

"Americans began to test the system to see if it would yield the rewards of success (money, security, good jobs, recognition)," Yankelovich writes, "without exacting the penalty in self-denial that once accompanied these rewards. We are now choosing to live in ways that may not benefit our economy. The system presupposes that individuals will want to compete for the rewards society provides—good jobs, security, products, honors. *Cultural changes that weaken the urge to compete also weaken the economy.*" (My italics.)

Loss results from this self-centered lifestyle. Loss of jobs, loss of motivation, loss of respect for government and our institutions, loss of competitiveness, loss of markets. And the reaction to loss, in extreme cases, is what psychoanlysts call "the grief reaction." A parent or loved one dies, you feel grief. You lose a major market for your products, you feel grief. Your wife leaves you for another woman, you head for the mountains and grieve.

"As the process unfolds, one should expect to find in swift alternation expressions of anger, confusion, disbelief, denial, barely suppressed panic, scapegoating, grasping at straws, depression, exaggeration, fatalism, instability of attitudes, lack of realism and a Pollyanna wishful thinking that everything will turn out to be for the best, that nothing really has changed."

Scapegoating.

Lay it at the feet of the Japanese! They're the ones who are making us feel bad. They're the producers, we're just trying to consume.

"Producers are people who work hard, save, postpone their pleasure, develop discipline, concern themselves with efficiency, know how to husband their time and subordinate personal considerations to getting the job done," Daniel Bell wrote in *Cultural Contradictions of Capitalism*. "Ideal customers, however, do not postpone their satisfaction— they spend their time and energies consuming, not producing."

That's it. In a nutshell: *The Japanese sacrifice today for tomorrow. We sacrifice tomorrow for today.*

The Psychic Devaluation of the American Culture

Stephen Zimney is a group senior vice president at Yankelovich, Skelly & White. Youthful and energetic, he helps his boss track these social and attitudinal changes over time. I sat in his office one cold morning, talking about those shifting tectonic plates of culture.

"You have to remember," he said in clipped, precise tones, "that we have gone through three specific time warps in the last forty years. The first started right after the war and lasted until about 1962. It was a period of economic growth pure and simple, growth for growth's sake, the Organizational Man. America was number one militarily and industrially. We created the biggest middle class in the world, sacrificing our individual needs for something bigger—our families, our companies, our country. Nothing was unattainable. *We could do anything.*

"In the early 1960s," he went on, eyes darting, hands cutting the air, "we began moving away from a purely economic agenda to a predominantly social agenda. We had grown so fast we had left out the blacks and women, we were polluting the air, and we still had pockets of disease and poverty. So we said, let's fix it! Since we can do anything, there was no need to exclude blacks and women from the great social pie, there was no reason the air should be dirty, and if we threw more money at the sick and the poor, they could be fixed, too. There was no need for anybody not to have their share."

He paused for a moment to collect his thoughts, then continued.

"In the third phase, beginning in the 1970s, the adult portion of the country suddenly stopped, took a look around and said, 'Hey, we've worked hard to get where we are, and we've done well, so let's enjoy.' In the workplace, we said, 'Don't work so hard. Enjoy life for a change.' In the schools, we eased up on grades and electives and said, 'You don't want to study Latin? What *do* you want to study? The History of the Women's Movement? Why don't you take a major in it?' At home, we said, 'You don't love me anymore? So get lost.' We turned inward and started emphasizing personal growth, taking more time off, legislating entitlements in federal programs, getting divorced, spending money on leisure, living the full, rich life."

And these were the New Rules?

"We call it the New Agenda. And we're still adjusting to it. There has been a dramatic reduction in the classic American optimism. We're seeing limits to the American economic pie. We realize now the fix-it agenda didn't really work. We're having to manage our corporations through a series of gaps between systems of the organizations and new values in the work force. But the focus is still on the individual. That's why we have 137 different brands of shampoo in this country."

My thoughts suddenly shifted to Tokyo, where they have two brands of shampoo: one for oily hair, one for dry hair. The rest they export to the United States.

I asked Zimney whether his social-value measurements ever included Japan. As I spoke of the trade war, he reached into a desk drawer.

"This is a study we did in 1982," he said, handing me a crisp blue report. Its title reminded me of those presidential commissions that warn America about its deteriorating educational system. *Meeting Japan's Challenge: The Need for Leadership*, it was called.

"You want some glimpses into the future, take a look at page 10."

On page 10, I found two summary charts.

One was titled "Optimism That the United States Will Successfully Meet the Japanese Challenge." There were three leader segments: business, government, and experts. Only 24 percent across the board were very optimistic that we would do it. Less than *half* the business leaders were even somewhat optimistic that we would do it. In the financial community, that's known as cautious optimism. Very cautious.

The other chart was called "Comparative Impact of Key Elements of Industrial Competitiveness: United States and Japan." American business leaders, government leaders, and experts *all* agreed overwhelmingly that our business/government relations, business/labor relations, work ethic, short-term earnings emphasis, consumer psychology, entitlement policies, capital formation, savings rates, self-centeredness, government regulations, antitrust laws, tax laws, bureaucracy, defense spending, research and development, and product quality *diminished* American competitiveness. *And the responses were mostly in the eighty and ninety percentiles.*

On the other side of the chart, these same American leaders, responding to questions in the same categories regarding *Japanese* competitiveness, all responded overwhelmingly that they *enhanced* the Japanese side by the same lopsided majorities. Japan's business/government relations, business/labor relations, work ethic, producer psychology, capital formation policies, personal savings rates, government regulations, antitrust laws, tax laws, bureaucracy, R & D, and high product quality all worked in their favor.

Zimney shrugged his shoulders as I looked up, astounded. "Where's the old rah-rah-rah?" I asked. "We used to roll up our sleeves and give extra effort when things looked bad. You know, when the going gets tough, the tough get going."

I glanced back at the percentiles. They were as damning as they were unmistakeable. 82. 86. 88. 76. 91. 89.

"American leaders have been on their knees," he said. "What we seem to be witnessing is nothing more than the psychic devaluation of the American culture."

How ironic, I thought, as I prepared to leave. We of the free and boundless spirit had become shackled by rigid and pessimistic thinking, addicted to self-fulfillment and confrontation. The Japanese, governed by hierarchy and rigidity, had become free and spirited through harmony and consensus.

"Give us your loyalty," Japanese organizations said, "and we will make you feel like a human being."

"Give us a day's work," American organizations said, "and we will pay you $12.65 an hour."

A-types and Z-types.

Form is substance.

Superstitious thinking.

The wrong policy mix.

New Rules.

But the psychic devaluation of our culture?

The Productivity Dilemma

"Nothing of enduring cultural value is ever born without struggle, confusion, and contradiction," Alfred North Whitehead concluded. "Great ideas often enter reality in strange guises and with disgusting alliances."

The dramatic decline in American productivity beginning in the early 1970s has been well documented. Everybody agrees that growth in U.S. output during the last fifteen years has been among the slowest of the industrial countries of the world. Everybody also agrees that the Dean of Productivity Accounting in this country is Dr. Edward F. Denison, senior fellow emeritus of the Brookings Institution in Washington, D.C.

Retarded productivity growth is another one of those things that has gone wrong. What it means is, if the other guys are making more and better sprockets than we are, people are going to buy *their* sprockets and not ours. In other words, we lose product markets, including our own.

But what nobody can agree on is *why* our productivity growth has slowed.

So I went down to Washington to ask the Dean. And even he was unsure.

"What happened," he said to me over lunch, "is a mystery."

Now here was the Dean of Productivity Accounting in the United States saying that the reason for the decline in American worker output over the past two decades is a *mystery?* Here was a scholar who had written three books on American productivity in the past ten years who says that we really don't know why?

Well, as it turns out, it isn't that simple. Earlier, I had sat down with a copy of the Dean's most exhaustive work, *Accounting for Slower Economic Growth*, and looked at the factor inputs. There were *seventeen* suggested explanations, four relating to declines in advances in knowledge and thirteen pertaining to what the Dean calls miscellaneous output determinants. (Miscellaneous output determinants is a catchall category economists use. It excludes the more obvious productivity determinants, such as capital, equipment, and labor.)

So the Dean considered the general declines in advances in knowledge.

R & D expenditures were down. In 1964, we spent nearly 3 percent of GNP on R & D, by 1976 only 2.27 percent. But the overall impact on productivity decline was only 0.1 percent.

Decline of Yankee ingenuity. But the Dean found the remaining problems more difficult and stubborn to solve than in the past.

Decline in opportunities for major new advances. But these were discovered not to have any impact on recent figures.

Lag in application of knowledge and aging of capital. But even in an extreme vintage model of capital structures and equipment, he calculated the overall effect to be only 0.2 percent or less.

Not a lot of encouragement there. So the Dean turned to the miscellaneous output determinants.

Government red tape. Filling out forms: a favorite scapegoat. But the Dean found red tape to be a universal object of loathing and not a major contributor to the productivity decline.

Regulation and taxation. Business leaders felt they were spending more time interacting with government agencies and less with customers, competitors, and internal operations. Another traditional voodoo doll, which, like red tape, the Dean found simply impossible to quantify.

Regulation affecting delays in new products. Unquantifiable.

Regulation affecting misallocation of resources. The Dean found that efficiency is greatest when jobs and people are matched, and he suggested that a lot of matching had been eliminated through equal employment laws. (He was not suggesting that women go back to raising children.)

Effects of high tax rates. In 1966, the tax burden at all levels was

33 percent of national income, in 1978, 39.2 percent. In 1966, government outlays accounted for 34 percent of national income, 41 percent in 1978. But the Dean found these effects to be uncertain. In earlier periods of high and rising government expenditures, for example, there was no stagnation of productivity growth.

Higher capital gains rates. This biases distribution of investment away from more risky undertaking, but the Dean found the misallocation to be statistically insignificant.

Pollution and safety regulations. EPA and OSHA are favorite bogeys, but their effects are unmeasurable. Besides, the Dean said, the Japanese have spent greater sums for longer periods cleaning up their air and water, and their rates of productivity growth are still greater than ours.

"People don't want to work anymore." New Rules. The psychic devaluation of our culture. "Young people just don't work as hard as we did," the Dean heard people say. He couldn't measure the impact. But he did admit that an inability to do so was a serious gap in his calculations. This was a contribution, he said, but not a major cause.

Inflation. "That inflation impairs productivity seems certain," the Dean observed. But again, he couldn't *measure* it.

Lessening of competitive pressure. Less competition means inefficient firms and their managements are under less pressure to minimize costs and less likely to be displaced by those who can do better. But the Dean found no change in monopoly concentration in the competitive arena and, as we all know, foreign competition has become much more intense.

Rise in energy prices. To be sure, these affected price levels and the overall economy as a whole, but the Dean calculated their effect on productivity decline to be less than 0.1 percent.

Shift to a service economy. The Dean found the argument that opportunities to raise productivity were less in the service sector simply had no substance.

Errors in the data. Statistical errors in output measurement may have contributed something to observed productivity slowdown, the Dean admitted, but it was improbable that they contributed materially to it.

So we sat there, scratching our heads, the neophyte willing to accept any or all of the seventeen explanations as plausible causes of our productivity decline and the expert willing to accept none of them.

"Then how come the Japanese are passing us in productivity growth?" I asked. Every study you see confirms it, from the Harvard Business School to the American Productivity Center.

The Dean simply shrugged his shoulders. "Fear of the Japanese may have something to do with it," he said. "But if the Japanese are so smart, why aren't they outproducing us? Even if the *rate* of their productivity growth is higher, we still have the highest per capita output in the world."

WISC

That question finally jogged something in my memory. Something about the Japanese being so smart.

Often, when you try to remember something, it's best not to try. That's not a Confucian analect or a precept of Zen Buddhism; instead, it has something to do with synaptic gaps and the way the memory processes data.

So I didn't push it. But I couldn't put it out of my mind.

The next morning around 4:00, as I lay awake listening to the tree frogs chirping, it clicked into place like a *go* stone.

Intelligence. Standard deviations. Higher IQs.

That afternoon at the library I began to pore through the references.

Nature magazine had carried some articles on intelligence testing in Japan the previous year. One of these by an English psychologist, Richard Lynn, was called "IQ in Japan and the United States Shows a Growing Disparity."

"Evidence from 27 samples indicates that the mean IQ in Japan is higher than in the United States by around one-third to two-thirds of a standard deviation," Lynn wrote in calm, unemotional tones. He cited the basic categories for testing the Wechsler Intelligence Scale for Children—picture arrangement, object assembly, coding, mazes, block design, and digit span—with the block design subtest having been made slightly more difficult, thus making the test harder for the Japanese.

"Combining the results from the WISC with those of previous studies, we have IQ data for 27 Japanese cohorts spanning almost seven decades," Lynn observed. "The results suggest that the mean Japanese IQ has been rising relative to the American IQ during the twentieth century."

Other advanced Western nations, "such as Britain, France, Belgium, Germany, Australia, and New Zealand, all have mean IQs approximately the same as that in the United States," the Londonderry psychologist noted. "At 111, the mean IQ in Japan is the highest recorded for a national population by a considerable order of magnitude. Among the population as a whole, 77 percent of Japanese have a higher IQ than the average American or European. Since intelligence is a determinant of economic success, as it is of success in many other fields, the Japanese IQ advantage may have been a significant factor in Japan's outstandingly high rate of economic growth in the post–World War II period."

Lynn's statistics were there for the pros to analyze. But everybody knows we Westerners are the smartest in the world, so the critics started looking for explanations.

They didn't come up with seventeen, but they did formulate a bunch.

"A mixing of previously isolated peasant communities in the massive postwar urbanization, rapid economic growth and accompanying improvements in welfare, health, and education, and exposure to Western culture and ways of thought," wrote one *Nature* editor, "probably provide a large part of the explanation."

Of course. It's not the Japanese themselves, but what they have learned from *us* that makes them so smart! General MacArthur and the Occupation and the U.S. political and educational reforms and Quaker puffed wheat instead of soybeans and seaweed and all that beef and orange juice.

Improved nutrition, the editors continued, has accounted for the increase in physical size of the Japanese as well. They are taller and bigger than their prewar counterparts.

"Thus the popular, but erroneous, Japanese view that they have grown taller by adopting the habit of sitting on Western chairs rather than sitting with legs folded underneath the body on tatami mats," the magazine said. It also cited a traditional criticism of Japanese attention to rote learning. "Whether the difference in IQ represents a real difference in 'intelligence' or simply implies that the Japanese are better at taking tests, remains open to question. At present, there is little more to say than that."

Little more, indeed. We Westerners may be intelligent, but the Japanese are just 'intelligent,' whatever those inverted commas are supposed to mean. It's like saying, the Japanese don't really make better products, they're just better at *exporting* them. Well, the next thing we know the Japanese will not only dominate our product markets but also our TV quiz shows. And once that happens, Congress will undoubtedly pass legislation making it illegal for Asians to play Hollywood Squares.

Those Postindustrial Blues

"At the present rate, by the year 2000 the United States will be the world's leader in the production of hamburgers and ICBMs," said Dr. Chalmers Johnson of the University of California at Berkeley, author of *MITI and the Japanese Miracle.* "And the Japanese will be making everything in between."

You don't have to be quite as *zurui* to maintain global leadership in fast food and Minuteman missiles. Lots of underpaid, contented labor for the one and a fat federal checkbook for the other.

But when so many things start going wrong, the temptation is strong to look around for some cures.

Economists see the dramatic decline in our productivity growth, our weak capital formation, sagging personal savings rate, and high interest rates, and they write out lots of prescriptions.

The average postwar Japanese savings rate as a percentage of net disposable income has been around 18 percent. The Germans net about 12. In good years, we may average 6.

Thus, it is not an unreasonable expectation for us to increase our rate of savings, something most economists and the president have wanted us to do for some time. But every time we nudge the rate up to, say, 8 percent, the economy sags because people aren't spending, and the Council of Economic Advisers recommends policy measures to stimulate demand, so the rate slumps back to 6.

One well-known international economist has a simple recommendation: get the savings rate up. Way up.

"Given a 4 or 5 percent long-term real growth rate for the GNP," this friend told me recently, "a gross personal savings rate of around 25 percent of GNP seems necessary."

Twenty-five percent of GNP?

I don't want to tell you what sounds came out of Washington when he made that recommendation. "A more viable strategy for us is to keep a modern competitive basic manufacturing industry à la Japan," he went on, "even though its contribution to GNP and employment will gradually decrease. To do this, however, requires an increase in the gross savings rate and a targeted transfer of expanded capital resources to support modernization." Basic manufacturing industries include autos and steel. This strategy is not very likely when they are out buying oil companies.

The flip side of that coin is to get the Japanese to save less; that is, get them to consume more. Build an interstate highway system, for example, or a missile network or connect all their islands by big, expensive suspension bridges. Anything to get their savings rate down.

Well, you can imagine how such an argument would go over in Tokyo. In addition to arguing, correctly, questions of sovereignty (Would *we* want the Germans telling us how to fix our inflation?), the Japanese would have a few private guffaws as well.

"The Americans have had nothing but low productivity, high inflation, and poor product quality with their low savings rate," they would say, "and they want us to emulate that?"

Not very likely.

But neither is a gross savings rate in this country of 25 percent of GNP.

Scientists and engineers decry the abysmal number of technical graduates from our educational system each year, so their prescription is to spend more on education. The American Federation of Teachers would like higher salaries, but will they work longer hours?

We can't compete effectively in foreign markets if we're undereducated. Nearly 95 percent of Japanese teenagers now graduate from high school, compared with 74 percent in the United States. Nearly 90 percent of all Japanese junior high students go on to high school, and 30 percent of their high school graduates enter university.

Saburo and Noriko go to school 5½ days a week, 220 days a year. Dick and Jane go to school 5 days a week, but only 180 days a year. As a result, the Japanese have about four full years of education more than their American counterparts.

Among freshmen entering New Jersey public universities in 1982, nearly two thirds lacked proficiency in algebra, half could not solve simple math problems, and a third could not use the English language properly. Forty-three states suffered shortages of high school math teachers, and forty-two were short of physics teachers. And with half our population, the Japanese graduate over 30 percent more engineers than we do.

So when all these things are going wrong—the superstitious learning, the loss of our international industrial competitiveness, merchandise trade deficits, scapegoating the Japanese, the erosion of our work ethic, a low rate of personal savings and capital formation, a decline in our productivity growth, an excess of government regulations, serious education problems, the disappearance of some basic industries, and the psychic devaluation of our culture—something has to be done.

But what?

What can be done to get our resources out of fast foods and back into advanced industrial products? Is there a way we can prevent our country from becoming a second-class industrial power? And what happens if we don't?

PART IV

INDUSTRIAL POLICY. (WHAT?) INDUSTRIAL POLICY. (LOUDER, I CAN'T HEAR YOU.) INDUSTRIAL POLICY!

CHAPTER 22

HOW ON EARTH DID THE JAPANESE DO IT?

It was perhaps inevitable that the greatest freedom accorded under the new order of things should have been given in the direction of greatest danger. Though the Government cannot be said to have done much for any form of competition within the sphere of its own direct control, it has done even more than could have been reasonably expected on behalf of national industrial competition. Loans have been lavishly advanced, subsidies generously allowed, and, in spite of various panics and failures, the results have been prodigious. Within thirty years, the value of articles manufactured for export has risen from half a million to five hundred million yen.

—Lafcadio Hearn, *Japan: An Interpretation,* 1895

Industrial Strategy

We all know the myths. Japan's economic success today is due to (1) cheap wages and inhuman living conditions of its workers (they are economic animals who live in rabbit hutches); (2) "unfair" trade practices, such as predatory dumping and export drives; (3) that insidious collusion between government and industry known as Japan, Inc.; (4) restrictive administrative practices and those invisible nontariff barriers; and (5) a "closed" domestic market where foreigners find it easier to read *kanji* than to sell their wares.

But the foundation for Japan's modern economic success was laid by the Meiji oligarchs over a hundred years ago. They've spent the past century honing, sharpening, refining, polishing. The past century. We know this because we've done a little reading. But many of our commercial policymakers in Washington act as though they believe Japan's modern economic success is due entirely to these myths.

207

Professor Norman, whom we met back in Part II, was the first modern scholar to look critically at Japan's feudal age in terms of political exploitation, autocracy, and economic imbalance. Remember, Norman brought to light "that unique feature of Japanese industrialization: monopolistic and state control of strategic industries—*strategic* whether because of their connection with naval and military defense or because of their importance in export industries intended to compete against foreign products."

This policy of developing strategic industries, which the Meiji leaders began and which their successors refined over the years, had unfortunate consequences for the rest of the world. Because the emphasis on military defense as one strategic industry meant that by 1945 Japan had engaged in foreign military adventures and war in every decade of its modern era, with the exception of the 1880s. And the emphasis on exports as the other strategic industry meant that Japan had engaged in competitive foreign trade—economic warfare—in every decade of its modern era *including* the 1880s.

Simply put, it's called Industrial Policy.

"An indigenous Japanese term not to be found in the lexicon of Western economic terminology," Robert Ozaki wrote in *Japanese Views on Industrial Organization* in 1970. "It refers to a complex of those policies concerning protection of domestic industries, development of strategic industries, and adjustment of the economic structure in response to or in anticipation of internal and external changes which are formulated and pursued by MITI in the cause of the national interest."

Well, you knew it wouldn't take us long to get back to MITI. Because MITI has been instrumental in the orchestration and implementation of industrial policy in Japan. But not just since the war. Since Meiji.

It split off from the old Ministry of Agriculture and Commerce in 1925 at a time when economic conditions were changing throughout the world. The volume of foreign trade was beginning to shrink, protectionist walls sprang up in virtually every country including the United States, and the tectonic plates of the Great Depression had begun to shift.

Bureaucrats in the new Ministry of Commerce and Industry, MITI's predecessor, took a look at what was going on and said, "Hey, something isn't right." They saw the postwar boom fizzle into a long recession. They witnessed the unbridled growth of their *zaibatsu*, those huge industrial conglomerates. And they were pinched by a widening trade gap of their own.

So they wrote a lot of papers. Explanations. Maybe there was too much market competition, they said. Or maybe there was not enough government coordination. Or maybe Japan was simply fulfilling the

Marxist prophecy and was on its way toward replacing the Rising Sun with the Hammer and Sickle.

One of the new bureaucrats, a man named Yoshino Shinji, discovered that despite the huge power of Japan's *zaibatsu*, it was the small and medium-sized enterprises that accounted for the lion's share of jobs in the economy. He also found that the *zaibatsu* produced principally for the domestic market, whereas the smaller firms were the country's major exporters.

Also, he didn't like the way the bigger companies were gobbling up the smaller ones because that shifted not only the concentration in size, but also the direction away from exports. So in 1925, he and his colleagues pushed the MCI to sponsor two new laws that represented a first effort at refining industrial policy to respond to changing market conditions. One was called the Exporters Association Law, which helped create export unions along specific product lines among the smaller companies. The other was the Major Export Industries Association Law, which attempted to restrain excessive competition by organizing cartel-like arrangements wherein the member firms agreed to specified production volumes.

The basic strategy remained unchanged: exports are a top priority. And these two new laws were a first experimentation with tactics. They were controversial. They were opposed by the *zaibatsu*, of course. But they underlined the importance of the smaller, export-oriented firms who, if more effectively organized, could help Japan get out of its balance of payments deficits by expanding trade.

By 1927, the financial panic had hit Japan, and the depression was on its way. Banks collapsed, the big Suzuki combine went under, smaller firms found it harder to get loans, and the *zaibatsu* further increased their power and control. Needless to say, they were pleased. But the small and medium-sized companies howled.

Again, Yoshino and his MCI brethren sprang into action. They responded by setting up within MCI a Commerce and Industry Deliberation Council to bring everybody together to talk about all these negative things that were happening in the economy. Everybody. Not just the big boys, but the little fellows, too, along with representatives from labor; academia; other branches of national government, such as the Ministry of Home Affairs and the Ministry of Finance; local government; trade associations; exporters; importers; the manufacturing sector; the service sector; consumers; the news media; everybody.

In time, the Council persuaded MCI to sharpen its compilation of industrial statistics so that the Ministry could keep better track of economic developments. To orchestrate industrial mergers where excessive competition could, thus, be alleviated. To make more loan funds available to the smaller companies. And to improve its trade data and export subsidy programs.

For the first time, the term Industrial Rationalization came into use, and it has remained to this day. Yoshino said at the time, "We hung out the sign, then we had to figure out what it meant." *Sangyo gorika.* It became a kind of national buzzword or strategic motto, a rallying cry, like "Remember the Alamo" or "What's good for General Motors is good for the country" or "Dee-fense!"

Chalmers Johnson, whom we met earlier, has written extensively about MITI and knows the Ministry well. In *MITI and the Japanese Miracle*, he summarized the meaning and importance of Industrial Rationalization to the Japanese.

"Industrial Rationalization," he wrote, "means (1) the rationalization of enterprises, that is the adoption of new techniques of production, investment in new equipment and facilities, quality control, cost reduction, adoption of new management techniques, and the perfection of managerial control; (2) the rationalization of the environment of enterprises, including land and water transportation and industrial location; (3) the rationalization of whole industries, meaning the creation of a framework for all enterprises in an industry in which each can compete fairly or in which they can cooperate in a cartel-like arrangement of mutual assistance; and (4) the rationalization of the industrial structure itself in order to meet international competitive standards."

So here Yoshino and his colleagues were, creating a Commerce and Industry Deliberation Council way back in 1927 to try to get a handle on a rather shaky industrial economy. It was no easy task.

In 1929, the opposition government returned to power and decided to lift the gold embargo (which would put Japan back on the gold standard) and to link the country's international competitive ability to Yoshino's Industrial Rationalization. The gold decision was disastrous. It further deflated a wildly deflationary environment. By 1931, Japan had no alternative but to resort to its own Keynesian economic tactics to reflate, which it did by spending heavily on armaments. The unfortunate moral: if you can't export bicycles, make guns.

Yoshino's seniors created the Temporary Industrial Rationality Bureau within MCI and put Yoshino in charge. He drew up plans for, among others, the control of enterprises, improvements in industrial financing, product standardization, simplification of production processes, and subsidies to encourage production. He involved civilian industrial leadership in the activities of the bureau to get them to help MCI gain acceptance for its ideas within the broader business community and to solicit their support for such needed legislation as the Important Industries Control Law.

Yoshino, who later became vice minister of MCI because of his successes with Industrial Rationalization, singled out the German industrial model from among all the foreign systems he had studied at the time. "German industrial rationalization," he noted, "was devoted to technological innovation in industries, to the installation of the most up-to-date machines and equipment, and to generally increasing efficiency." It also used government trusts and organized cartels.

He began to see that excessive competition ought to be replaced by cooperation and that the purpose of business activities should be the attempt to lower costs, not to make profits.

"Modern industries attained their present development primarily through free competition," Yoshino said. "However, various evils of the capitalist order are gradually becoming apparent. Holding to absolute freedom will not rescue the industrial world from its present disturbances. Industry needs both a plan of comprehensive development *and* a measure of control. Concerning the idea of control, there are many complex explanations of it in terms of logical principles, but all one really needs to understand it is common sense."

Yoshino went out of his way to make sure people understood what he meant by "a measure of control." He was not referring to bureaucratic supervision of industry. He was referring to the creation by MCI of what he called "industrial order." The same kind of order and control that had characterized Japanese society for centuries, but applied now to industries. Order and hierarchy were uniquely Japanese and had their roots in the country's feudal past, principally the Tokugawa era, when the country had been closed to the rest of the world.

The Important Industries Control Law of 1931 enabled member firms in an industry to petition MCI to form a cartel. Two thirds of them had to agree a cartel was necessary, and MCI had to approve their request. In 1932, MCI asked for and got power to approve measures that would increase investments by cartel members (they had to ask first) and power to approve production cutbacks.

As Dr. Johnson observed, "All members of an industry were required to submit frequent reports on their investment plans and activities. It is in this law that we find the origins of the government's licensing and approval authority and of the practice of 'administrative guidance,' which together became the heart of postwar industrial policy."

However, a month after the new law came into effect, the Japanese army took Manchuria, and the country began marching to the sounds of a different drummer. The military elite assumed stronger political control. Heavy industrialization was the order of the day. And the *zaibatsu* took advantage of the new law by trying to amalgamate their economic control.

But here was the continuation of Japan's emphasis on higher value-added industries—strategic industries—as the core of its industrial policy formulation: the need to promote exports, the importance of a keen competitive ability in foreign trade, the overwhelming necessity to rationalize industry to take advantage of economies of scale. Petroleum refining took precedence over toys and handcrafts. Chemical combines became more important than textiles. And cement was accorded more weight than lumber.

That was the good news. The bad news was that those same industry sectors suited the militarists' needs as well.

Yet what this whole process did was to give Japan a head start down the learning curve. By replacing excessive competition with a form of self-control in industry. By finding a better criterion for corporate performance than short-term profitability. By attempting to gain a more competitive edge through effective cost cutting and economies of scale.

And the people who converted MCI to the wartime Ministry of Munitions to the postwar Ministry of International Trade and Industry were the same people who had guided Japan's industrial policy throughout the entire prewar era. All of MITI's vice ministers during the 1950s had entered the Ministry between 1929 and 1934. The civilian bureaucracy was characterized by nothing if not by continuity.

This historical continuity, notes Professor Johnson, is evidence that Japan's industrial policy is rooted in its "conscious institutional innovation." As he put it, "Economic crisis gave birth to industrial policy. That the Japanese solved their problems more effectively during the postwar period than during the 1930s is greater testimony to their ability to profit from experience than to any fundamental change in the situation they faced. From this perspective, the early years of industrial policy were a period of indispensable gestation in the evolution and perfection of a genuine Japanese institutional invention, the industrial policy of the developmental state."

The prewar model sputtered and lurched. And the wartime model got sidetracked. But the postwar model. . . .

As they say in Detroit, unfuckingbelievable.

Tactical Tools

"The Japanese not only sin against the rules of market economics," the *New Republic* said last year. "They convert sin into productive virtue. By our own highest standards, they must be doing something right."

Well, Herbert Norman would say they've been doing something right since about 1872. And Chalmers Johnson would say they've been doing something right since about 1927. And if the postwar evidence is anything to go by, we'd *all* say they've been doing something right since about 1949.

Which is when MITI as we know it was born.

MITI was purposefully given a broad and powerful charter. Together with the Ministry of Finance, it controls and orchestrates Japan's industrial policy. MITI has specific responsibility to (1) shape the structure of industry and adjust dislocations, (2) guide industrial production and development, (3) direct Japan's foreign trade and its commercial relations, (4) ensure an adequate supply of raw materials and energy, and (5) manage specific sectors, such as small business, patents, and technology.

As Dr. Johnson put it, MITI applies the government's industrial policy based on "such standards as income elasticity of demand, comparative costs of production, labor absorptive power, environmental concerns, investment effects on related industries, and export prospects. The heart of the policy is the selection of the strategic industries to be developed or converted to other lines of work." In a way, it is almost like a government-owned think tank as far as its intellectual scope and resources go, but, of course, it has the full faith and power of the government itself.

As you would imagine, MITI does not accept the conventional wisdom that market forces alone will create the desired effect. So it helps the market along, and it has several tactical tools in its kit that it has made, borrowed, or copied for this purpose. These policy tools are *protective, developmental, and interventionist* in nature. Like the playbook of a professional football team: defense, special teams, and offense.

When MITI's defense takes the field, it protects—infant-industry sectors mostly—by imposing tariffs, import controls, preferential taxes, foreign exchange controls, and limits on foreign investment in those sectors.

The special teams emphasize development, or what MITI calls "nurturing," of special situations. This is accomplished through low-interest loans to targeted industries, subsidies, special depreciation measures, research and development funding, cartels, and foreign technology licensing.

When the offense takes over, MITI intervenes using a stick-and-carrot approach: withholding approvals in cases where client companies are obstinate, licensing plant and equipment investment for strategic industries, rewarding cooperative companies by making government funds available—all by authority of its broad charter under the enabling legislation or by means of its unique administrative guidance.

The closest thing we have to administrative guidance is jawboning. But administrative guidance is more than that. Although it may not have the *force* of law, it has the *effect* of law. It refers to the discretionary authority the Japanese bureaucracy has in administering legislation, which is always created purposefully broad. This consists of suggestions, hints, threats, directives, and innuendoes that influence action in the desired direction.

Say MITI thinks increased investment in fast-food chains is not part of the Japanese government's strategic industrial policy goals. Not a lot of added value in fast-food. But say you're a foreigner with one hamburger joint and you want to establish a second one.

Before you can order the ground beef, MITI is on the phone.

"Mr. Smith? We don't think another hamburger stand is such a good idea."

You argue. It helps unemployment. It helps increase beef imports. Maybe it even helps increase the size of the Japanese stomach.

"But Smith-san, you don't understand. Fast-food is not a strategic industry."

You go ahead anyway. Market forces are more important than government direction and control, right? But when you get ready to remit your profits back home, all of a sudden you find your Japanese bank won't convert your yen into dollars. And neither will anybody else. You're stuck. Everybody got the message but you.

Administrative guidance. Carrots for those who cooperate, sticks for those who don't.

Now, before my friends in Kasumigaseki cite me for inaccuracies, I should say that these are the tools MITI has *historically* used to implement industrial policy, especially during the high-growth era from the end of the war to the early 1970s. Some of these policy tools are irrelevant today, such as foreign exchange controls, which were superseded by a new banking law in December 1980. Not all of them are tolerated any longer, such as import quotas on manufactured goods, which have gradually been eliminated. But most of them, in one form or another, have helped MITI achieve more winning seasons over the years than any other industrial team in the world league.

If Professor Norman were alive today and able to compare the Japanese economic machine of the 1980s with its predecessor of a century earlier, I suspect he would merely nod and say, "*Naruhodo.*"

Naruhodo is another Japanese word with countless meanings, such as "to be sure" or "indeed" or "really."

But the myths continue to prevail over the realities. And the realities are so apparent it's hard to see how they have become so misconstrued.

MITI's own structure enhances its policy-implementation role. The minister's secretariat and four key bureaus coordinate policy across industry lines: the Industrial Policy Bureau, International Trade Policy, International Trade Administration, and Industrial Location and Environmental Protection. The Industrial Structure Council, an outgrowth of the old Commerce and Industry Deliberation Council, is attached to the Industrial Policy Bureau. Three bureaus—Basic Industries, Machinery and Information Industries, and Consumer Products Industries—develop and implement general policy. And nine regional bureaus throughout the country sort out conflicts between national policy and local interest—employment, plant siting, training—and help develop MITI's broad industrial data base.

MITI's career bureaucrats are the government elite. *MITI and MOF each recruit more graduates from Tokyo University each year than any other ministry.* It's as though the Dallas Cowboys and the Pittsburgh Steelers got the top draft choices, year after year after year.

In addition to the general account budget, MITI had access to the government's Fiscal Investment Loan Program, known as FILP. FILP is an off-budget source, administered by MOF and funded through citizens' savings in the Japanese postal system and national pensions. FILP is almost half as large as the general account budget and represents an additional source of funds for specified projects. About half of its funds go into policy-implementation financing, such as providing capital to the Japan Development Bank (JDB). The rest goes into public investments and distributions to local governments. Revenues from these investments, in turn, pay the interest on postal system savings and national pensions that created the capital to begin with.

The JDB was created in 1951 to succeed the Reconstruction Finance Corporation, which was set up during the Occupation. It gives long-term, low-interest loans to targeted industries. Private financial institutions watch very carefully what the JDB does and to whom it lends because they are not far behind with their own money.

So you have MITI orchestrating industrial policy; MOF orchestrating monetary and fiscal policy; funding through the general account budget and FILP and JDB (and the Export-Import Bank, which helps finance strategic exports); support from the private banking sector (13 city banks, 3 long-term lending banks, 7 trust banks, 63 regional banks, 71 mutual loan and savings banks, and 959 credit associations or corporations working together like one big hydrocarbon molecule)—and assistance from private organizations, like the Keidanren (the Federation of Economic Organizations, Japan's Business Roundtable), which represents the big boys; the Shoko Kaigisho (a Chamber of Commerce and

Industry), which represents the little fellows; the Keizai Doyukai, a private Committee for Economic Development; and the Nikkeiren (the Federation of Employers Associations); the Trade Associations (which do not lobby but work together with MITI to formulate broad policy issues for the industries they represent)—and the recession or export cartels formed through the 1978 Structurally Depressed Industries Law (whose forefather was the Important Industries Control Law of 1931); the Agency of Industrial Technology, which maintains sixteen centers around the country to spur research in key sectors, like high performance jet engines and computer chips; corporate tax incentives for technology development; tax-deferral reserves for overseas market development and exchange rate fluctuations; and bicycle racing tax revenues, which can be used in a small way to help fund some of the targeted industry sectors.

Whew!

But bicycle racing?

Bicycle racing.

Anything and everything that supports industrial policy. Because it's in the national interest. MITI says, in effect, "Hell, we Japanese can't make ICBMs, so we might as well cut loose on industrial policy."

Three Simple and Obvious Ideas

In 1978, Ira Magaziner and Thomas Hout, who spent many years in Japan working for the Boston Consulting Group, were concerned that not enough people knew about Japan's industrial policy, let alone even what industrial policy *was*. So they wrote a small book called, appropriately enough, *Japanese Industrial Policy*. It's only a hundred pages long. But it's very *zurui*. And it's also been about as ignored as Professor Norman's book and Dr. Johnson's book, all of which unfortunately are hard to find on local book racks.

"The economics of Japan's industrial policy are straightforward," the authors began:

> The objective is to help raise the real income of the population by assisting the shift of resources to the applications in which they can be most productive. The guiding force and discipline in this policy is that of international comparative advantage. Simply stated, this means that in an open economy a country's real industrial wage can rise sustainably over time only if its labor and capital flow toward increasingly higher value-added, higher productivity businesses; the country's industry is then likely to become internationally cost-competitive in these businesses. The quality of Japanese industrial performance rests on the ability

of both Japanese government and Japanese companies to operate successfully in this way.

There are three main elements in Japanese industrial development:

(1) Recognition of the country's need to develop a highly competitive manufacturing sector,

(2) The deliberate restructuring of industry over time toward higher value-added, higher-productivity industries, and

(3) Aggressive domestic and international business strategies.

These are three fairly simple and obvious ideas. Individually, they are unremarkable. Together, however, they explain very effectively the dynamic of Japanese performance.

You need no reminders as to what those higher value-added industries are. You see their products around you all the time. Automobiles. Steel. TVs. Video tape recorders. 64K RAM computer chips.

In the early 1950s, nearly a third of Japan's exports still consisted of fibers and textiles. Another 20 percent was sundries, and only 14 percent was in machinery and equipment.

By the mid-1960s, however, machinery and equipment was the leading category of Japanese exports, accounting for nearly 40 percent. Next was metals (steel) and metal products, with 26 percent. Fibers and textiles had dropped to less than 10 percent.

International comparative advantage. Highly competitive manufacturing sector. Higher value-added, higher productivity businesses. Deliberate restructuring of industry. Aggressive strategies.

It's as though every other country in the world was pursuing an industrial strategy based on the old football philosophy of Woody Hayes: three yards and a cloud of dust.

Then along comes this strange team that doesn't *run* with the ball, they *throw* it. Everybody laughs at first. Nobody understands. Until they see how many points this new team scores. This of course leads to much yelling about how unfair it is for them to throw the ball and how the rules ought to be changed to stop them from throwing it. Or else, God forbid, this inequitable balance will be perpetuated.

All because America and others never understood the concept of industrial policy.

On Harmony and Death

We should learn from advanced countries, not only what to do, but also what not to do, and if we look at the terrible problems of industrialization, the terrible problems of class conflict, and the poverty and degradation of the proletariat that are being brought about by industrialization in Europe,

*we should take a lesson from that and make sure that we
put in place the machinery that will stop this and persuade
our industrialists to adopt management patterns that will
prevent class conflict.*

—*Koto Shoko Shingikai* (Higher
Commission for Commerce and
Industry), 1890

One of my Washington friends, who's a hairy barbarian and proud
of it, sees MITI as the penultimate cheerleader.

In fact, MITI is more than just a cheerleader. It's the entire coaching
staff of the team.

Sometimes we get the impression that the execution of all this
industrial policy in Japan is right out of *Life with Father*: neat, and
orderly, and harmonious, and everybody agreeing with everybody else,
because Father knows best.

That's the *result*.

But getting there is a cat fight. Harmony is a great cultural value in
Japan. No argument there. But *achieving* harmony is not all rice pud-
ding. Harmony in Japanese culture masks a lot of conflict, and that
conflict is translated into social rivalry, and that social rivalry is translated into industrial competition.

Harmony is just the tip of the iceberg. All that messy stuff is hidden
underneath. Just as when you look at Mt. Fuji and see this poetic
snowcapped mountain which, underneath, is a defunct volcano. Which
is why Japanese society can be characterized as a pyramid, a kind of
Andy Warhol Mt. Fuji: harmony on the surface doesn't reveal all that
conflict, rivalry, and competition below.

So just because MITI is the coaching staff doesn't mean the players
all agree with the coach's strategy and tactics for industrial policy.

Before the game, at halftime, and during time-outs, there is great
dissension: conflict, rivalry, and competition.

But when the team is on the field, there is great coordination, consensus, and harmony. Teamwork.

Nor does the coach always get it right: sometimes he calls a pass
play and the quarterback gets sacked.

In the 1950s, MITI had this novel idea to merge all the Japanese
automakers into three main groups. You can imagine what Honda and
Toyota and Nissan thought about that. They fought it hard and enlisted
all the support they could get, including some of the other elites at
MOF. And MITI backed down. Today they're glad they did. (Here they

would say they fought a strategy of winning by losing, but the point is not lost.)

Or petrochemicals, in the early 1960s, when MITI thought it would be terrific to have all this domestic refining capacity to crack that cheap crude oil. This spurred a considerable excess capacity by the time OPEC jacked up the price of crude, and the coach wasn't too happy.

Or a more recent case of MITI against the Ministry of Posts and Tele-communications, who fought MITI's brainchild to form consolidated R & D centers to speed key information and telecommunications re-search. Nippon Telephone and Telegraph wanted to go its own way. The Post Office lost that one. But it was a tough fight.

So even though the team loses a few, it has still put together a long string of winning seasons.

Naitoh Masahisa, MITI's New York special representative in the late 1970s, once wrote the following:

"In the U.S.," he said, "industrial structure is simply an expression of the aggregate of all industrial activities occurring at any given time; it is described and expressed statistically. It is seldom perceived as a set of objectives or specific targets. But in Japan, the process is more systematic."

Mr. Naitoh characterized industries as growing much like humans do: first, an infant stage, then a high-growth stage, then maturity, and finally senescence. "Japanese industries traditionally receive protec-tion from competition during their infant stages. Then they maintain the high-growth stage as long as possible. But when they arrive at the senescent stage, they accept 'death' relatively easily. The opposite is true of American companies: they resist death fiercely, and it is during the mature stage of their life cycle that their demand for protection becomes most pronounced."

One thinks immediately of Detroit and Pittsburgh. But our indus-trial philosophy seems to be closely related to our social philosophy. As a Christian culture, we resist personal death as fiercely as our in-dustries resist corporate death. Buddhism accepts death tranquilly, as just another stage of life.

Mr. Naitoh also recognized the strategic aspects of development:

From the end of the war until the mid-1950s, both government and private enterprise in Japan concentrated on fostering such basic industries as steel and coal. These heavy industries were viewed as strategic ele-ments in the effort to revive a war-devastated economy and to lay the foundations for sustained industrial growth in the future. From the 1950s to the 1960s, this focus was broadened to include other heavy industries, such as automobiles, industrial machinery, and electronics. These industries were singled out because they realized large economies of scale, their impact on other industries was considerable, their capacity for manpower absorption was large, and their elasticity of income to demand was high. Japanese corporations depended heavily on external financing, and a steady supply of investment capital was available, thanks to the high savings rate and the banking system. As a result, the Japanese economy maintained high levels of fixed investment, which permitted a considerable expansion of capacity and encouraged the adoption of the newest production technologies in steel, electronics and other, higher value-added industries.

You certainly can't argue with results.

Between 1960 and 1980, for example, machinery as a percentage of Japan's total exports to the United States increased from 17 percent to 68 percent, whereas textiles and fibers fell from 26 percent to 3 percent. But the *structure* of American exports to Japan remained relatively unchanged: raw materials (grain, coal, ore) and fuels from 8 percent to 20 percent, and manufactures from 33 percent to 37 percent.

When Mr. Naitoh returned to Tokyo, he became director of the petrochemicals division of the Basic Industries Bureau. One of Japan's senescent industries.

Our team understands industrial structure as merely a statistical aggregate.

Why are we having trouble coming to grips with industrial policy?

CHAPTER 23

GOOD OLD AMERICAN PLURALISM: FIVE EXPERTS AND SIX DEFINITIONS OF INDUSTRIAL POLICY

And so these men of Hindustan,
  Disputed loud and long,
Each in his own opinion
  Exceeding stiff and strong,
Though each was partly in the right
And all were in the wrong.

So, oft in theologic wars,
  The disputants, I ween,
Rail on in utter ignorance
  Of what each other mean,
And prate about an elephant
  Not one of them has seen.

  —John Godfrey Saxe, "The Blind Men
  and the Elephant"

From Sunrise to Sunset

Washington has think tanks. Brookings. Carnegie. The Institute for International Economics.

New York has talk tanks. The Lehrman Institute. The Japan Society. The Council on Foreign Relations.

Percy Bidwell did his work on tariffs for the Council on Foreign Relations back in the 1930s. Fifty years later another economist, William Diebold, did some work on industrial policy for the Council as part of their 1980s Project, chaired a year's worth of seminars on the subject, and then published a three-hundred-page treatise called *Industrial Policy as an International Issue.*

He did this at a time when American businessmen and politicians were becoming increasingly agitated at the loss of world market share

221

to the Japanese. This was in the late 1970s, about the time of the second oil crisis, when voluntary export restraints had finally been reached on Japanese steel, when Washington was pressuring Tokyo to buy more beef and oranges, and when Datsuns and Toyotas had started to roll into this country in large numbers.

Detroit was still producing its big cars, and Pittsburgh was getting out of steel. America wasn't interested in *basic* industries anymore, everyone was into hamburgers and fast-food franchises and health care. Over 70 percent of the American economy was now in services.

So newspaper and magazine editors around the country began lamenting the demise of America's smokestack industries—focusing on autos and steel—and calling for the United States to *reindustrialize.* That's a word we've heard a lot about recently.

Business Week did a long cover story called "The Reindustrialization of America." The *Atlantic* featured a lengthy article called "American Industry: What Ails It, How to Save It." And the *National Journal* ran its own cover issue called "Reindustrialization: Economic Panacea or Political Mirage?"

The gist of these "early" alarms was, as James Fallows put it in his *Atlantic* piece, "something has gone wrong with our industrial base," and what is needed is "a greater emphasis on production in the pantheon of social values."

The *National Journal* said that reindustrialization does not imply a return to basic industries but rather to a strong infrastructure and capital goods sector, higher investment, and more innovation. In other words, don't try to recapture the cutting edge in autos and steel, put the money into high technology—bioengineering and telecommunications and computers.

This could be a giant plus, some people argued. We'll buy our cars and steel from the Japanese, and they'll buy their soybeans and maize from us. That way we get to keep the Mazdas *and* the blue skies because we can export all our pollution as well. *Isseki nicho.* Two birds with one stone.

But hold on, others said. We need steel to build ICBMs and Minuteman missiles, and the automobile companies make all those tanks and half-tracks, so we have to keep *some* productive capacity in these industries. We've just got to make these industries "lean and mean."

They are called basic industries because they are fundamental— they form our industrial base, create millions of jobs, and produce a lot of votes. They are also called smokestack industries for obvious reasons, and sunset industries because they are mature (or, as Mr. Naitoh would say, senescent). And they are sinking slowly in the west.

Reindustrialization as a political rallying cry tended to die out after the 1980 elections. Because one of President Reagan's platform issues was "government." We had too much of it, he said, and we needed to get it off our backs. Which meant, in effect, let the market decide. If market forces decided America should be in health care and fast-food rather than autos and steel, well, the market knows best.

President Reagan also attracted the "supply-siders," those economists who work the other side of the street and draw tax curves on cocktail napkins. Instead of designing fiscal policy to influence *demand* in the economy, as Keynesians had done through all that deficit spending for the past fifty years, the supply-siders designed policy to influence *supply*. They reasoned that with lower taxes, more money would be freed up for investment and the sunset industries would become more productive because of all the new plant and equipment they could buy. General Motors could tool up aggressively to produce smaller, fuel-efficient cars, for example, and the steel industry could now get into basic oxygen furnaces instead of oil.

But the auto companies continued to make those large cars, and U.S. Steel bought Marathon rather than new plant and equipment. So people began to talk about *industrial policy* instead of *reindustrialization*.

"All countries take a variety of measures," William Diebold wrote, "to shape the structure of their domestic economies, to determine the long-run use of resources, and to affect the distribution of gains from economic growth—though many countries do not have comprehensive and consistent industrial policies."

Diebold suggested that the word *policy* would imply "deliberate, thought-out, systematic, and more or less consistent lines of action." But with one eye on Washington, he said: "That would ignore the largest part of what governments do in the field of industrial policy, where ad hoc, unsystematic, and sometimes inconsistent measures are far more common than their opposite."

He looked at the three basic measures of industrial policy (the defense, the special teams, and the offense) and then surveyed a number of countries and their deliberate (as in Japan) or unsystematic (as in America) policies.

"Japan's effort," he wrote, "dates from the end of the American occupation in 1952." Well, neither Herbert Norman nor Chalmers Johnson showed up in his bibliography, so he was off by either twenty-five or eighty years. Yet his was the first major attempt to bring together the various pieces of the industrial policy puzzle and to examine the whole realm of policy measures: tax and depreciation incentives, export subsidies, industry protection, research and development, production cartels, government procurement, regulation, financing, planning, and relief.

At the same time, probably because of the spate of books on Japanese management techniques and the explosion of Japanese products in our market, people began to take a closer look at what MITI was doing to see if America's free-market forces might not benefit from an occasional nudge or push. Unemployment can make a lot of otherwise unpalatable medicine taste pretty good.

So by 1982, industrial policy had become Washington's new buzzword. The *National Journal* ran a new cover issue called "In Search of an Industrial Policy." *Harper's Magazine* asked, "Can Creeping Socialism Cure Creaking Capitalism?" And the Office of Technology Assessment in Congress released a paper called "Industrial Policy: Where Do We Go from Here?"

Felix Rohatyn, the former chairman of New York's Municipal Assistance Corporation, wanted a new Reconstruction Finance Corporation. Frank Weil, former undersecretary for trade in the Carter administration, called for the creation of a Federal Industrial Coordination Board, modeled on the Federal Reserve Bank. Lester Thurow, MIT economist, wanted a National Investment Committee. Robert Reich, former Federal Trade Commission official, wanted the government to shift national resources into high technology and help workers in sunset industries train for jobs in sunrise industries by issuing them training vouchers. The Hudson Institute called for the creation of a National Industrial Council that would do for industry what the National Security Council does for defense.

Suddenly, everybody had discovered industrial policy. But nobody really knew exactly what it was.

Picking Winners and Losers

"Industrial policies are effective when they support what private industry wants to do anyway," John Alic was saying over lunch early last year. John was the author of the Office of Technology Assessment's paper on industrial policy that he had given as a speech in the spring of 1982 at a conference in Chicago.

"And there's no doubt America's policies are more ad hoc than anybody else's."

I asked him why.

"We have a problem, any problem, and the response is always the same. Political activists lobby for support, some narrow legislation gets passed, and everybody sits back and says, well, we've solved *that* problem, what do we do next? So you have a national industrial policy in this country that is based partly on inadvertence and partly on the political clout of the industry that is looking for solutions to its problems."

John is a mechanical engineer by training and uses terms like control algorithms, X-ray lithography, and direct electron-beam slicing, just as we might use words like front-wheel drive, personal computer, and microwave oven. He is very tall, and very bright.

"Aggregate economic policymaking—your standard monetary and fiscal policy—is inadequate to the current problems of advanced industrial economies. They're like two sides of a triangle. The third is industrial policy."

I told him I wasn't very optimistic about our developing a hybrid industrial policy in this country. We had no MITI, let alone any bureaucratic elite. We had an administration committed to free-market forces. And somehow, a concerted, organized, orchestrated industrial policy went against the grain of American pluralism. We seem to thrive on doing things ad hoc.

"There's a lot of pressure to imitate the Japanese," John said. "In management, in education—they graduate twice the per capita number of electrical engineers we do—in industrial policy. But cultural transplants won't work. We need to strengthen our analytical capabilities before we can do anything else. When the Chrysler case came up a couple of years ago, we had tons of analysis on emission standards and traffic safety but nothing on the competitive dynamics of the global automobile industry. We need throughout government more sector-specific, disaggregated analysis—rather than focusing on the broad categories which you get through the aggregate approach."

Disaggregation is to aggregation as a Honda motorbike is to "manufactured goods." We lump electronic computers and bulldozers and motorbikes into "manufactured goods."

Aggregated analysis says, I wonder how our manufactured goods are doing compared to their manufactured goods. And we get distorted results because one industry sector, like computers, which may be doing well, disguises another industry sector, like machine tools, which may be on its knees, although the *aggregate* for the industry overall may not look too bad.

Disaggregated, or sector-specific, analysis says, I wonder how our motorbikes are doing compared to their motorbikes. Or, I wonder how our Harley Davidson 280cc dirt bikes are doing compared to their Honda 280cc dirt bikes. You get "no response" in that category because Harley Davidson stopped making motorcycles under 1000cc displacement years ago. So you have to ask, I wonder how our Harley Davidson Super Chief Black Hawk 2000cc Road Monsters are doing compared to their Honda 2000cc Jetstream Challengers. And you find out that Harley is losing its shirt, so you petition the ITC for import relief in the form of higher tariffs.

What about a new federal agency for industrial policy, I asked.

John frowned.

"We need to ask what the appropriate federal role is in the longer term before we rattle around creating any new agencies," he said. "We need to take a hard look at education, at human resources, at innovation—hell, we're still looking for inventor-heroes, while industrial competitiveness and the underlying technological innovations are much more broadly based. We need to figure out a way to get both capital investment and the savings rate up. We need to ask whether the so-called sunrise industries really need more investment incentives than they already have. We need to reexamine our antitrust laws in the light of global competition. And we need to look at technology diffusion. In the past, it's all been one way—out."

In his speech on industrial policy, John had said, "The United States is an underdeveloped country when it comes to getting useful, proven technologies transferred to business and industry. Other countries are successfully experimenting with institutional mechanisms through which government can speed technology diffusion. Japan's cooperative R & D programs come to mind. By comparison, the infrastructure in the United States looks weak. And no more than 20 percent of the technical literature originating in Japan is now indexed, abstracted, or otherwise made available to engineers and scientists in the United States. Given the excellence of Japanese technology, shouldn't we be making a greater effort to learn from these sources?"

There were two problems about learning from Japan, I said. One was there are no Nobel Prizes in process technology. The other was the Japanese language.

He laughed. "I just got back from a conference on science and technology at MIT," he said. "We've got scientists who are linguistic illiterates and Japanese specialists who are technological illiterates. So there's not much hope for our guys to read statistical abstracts on fifth-generation computers in Japanese. Plus we're addicted to pure research, not applied technology. Figuring out the secrets of the universe is just more important to us than building a better lawnmower."

John's comment reminded me of Thomas Edison's definition of genius: 1 percent inspiration and 99 percent perspiration. Critics of Japan's industrial policy and lack of inventive ability point out how few Nobel Prizes the Japanese have won, as if the innovation of transverse-mounted front-wheel drive technology is somehow inferior to the discovery of Z-particles and quarks. We've been sitting around waiting for creative inspiration in the pure sciences to hit and getting rewarded with Nobel Prizes when it did, whereas the Japanese were doing all the perspiring, getting no prizes, and on their way to becoming one of the wealthiest nations in the world.

The MIT conference on technology was not the only one at which the Japanese attracted attention last year. The Solid State Circuits Conference discussed the next generation of integrated chip technology. There were ninety-six papers presented: forty-nine from the United States, forty from Japan, six from Europe, and one from Israel. The top three contributors were Fujitsu with ten, Hitachi with nine, and NEC seven. The best we could muster was six each from Intel and Berkeley and five each from Bell Labs, IBM, and TI. Of six papers on the 256K dynamic RAM chip, five were from Japan.

I asked John if he had any thoughts on MITI and whether we ought to copy their organizational format.

"MITI doesn't *plan* the Japanese economy, as you know," he said. "It's more a vehicle for consciousness raising in the country as a whole— reaching consensus, resolving conflict, building a common data base. We can't create a MITI overnight, and I'd hate to see us try. But that's viewing industrial policy from an arbitrarily narrow perspective. Government planning or government management is not the way to go. MITI exhorts and guides and directs, but it stops short of second-guessing. It doesn't pick winners."

Picking winners.

I gave some thought that afternoon to the process of picking winners and losers. Critics of industrial policy (who are those on the other side of the street arguing for free-market forces) look at MITI's development of strategic industries, or sectoral targeting, and say, "Aha. They're in the business of picking winners and losers. And do we want some government bureaucrats in Washington doing *that?*"

It's as if industrial policy were to be decided in Atlantic City or Las Vegas.

"George, let's put $25 billion on double-O green."

"What about the red?"

"Yeah, that looks good. $10 billion on 17 red."

Picking winners and losers is a dubious game anyway. Nobody does it, not even the market. It just seems that way. To be sure, MITI's Industrial Structure Council—whose constituency is the market— says something like, "Knowledge-intensive industries represent another step up the value-added ladder. That's the general direction we want to take because the less developed countries are breathing down our backs in shipbuilding and steel, so we may not be competitive in those industries much longer. We need a strategy to remain competitive in world markets. It's in our national interest to create one."

Formulating competitive strategies is a lot different than picking winners and losers. The Department of Commerce did an analytical exercise not long ago and came up with automobiles as a winner. (Somehow, that sounds like Commerce.) While former chairman of the Council of Economic Advisers Charles Schulze studied a list of the twenty industries that were the fastest growing during the 1970s—yesterday's winners. Some of them are still winners today—small cars, computers, and semiconductors. But others turned into losers—vacuum cleaners, construction glass, and tufted carpets. The industry with the highest productivity gains was poultry rearing.

Eleanor Hadley is an economist who knows Japan well. She was a graduate student in Tokyo in the 1930s, returned during the Occupation as a trustbuster, and spent some years in Washington with the GAO. She wrote a landmark book in 1970 called *Antitrust in Japan*, in which she analyzed both the prewar and postwar Japanese experience with industrial conglomerates, oligopolies, and competitive behavior.

In the fall of 1982, Ms. Hadley wrote a short article called "Industrial Policy for Competitiveness" in MITI's *Journal of Japanese Trade and Industry*. Because she was then teaching in Washington, I met with her on one of my trips to talk about industrial policy.

"Oh, you mean picking winners and losers," she said with a wry smile. "The present administration is irrevocably committed to the magic of the market. And the market is after profits wherever profits are to be found, irrespective of national borders or industry distinctions. Paper profits are just as meaningful as production profits."

I asked her where that left us with industrial policy—the market couldn't designate *strategic* industries, only nations could do that.

"That's part of MITI's genius," she said. "Strategic industries are part of Japan's national interest. In formulating an industrial policy, they would rather be the chaser than the chased. We need to do a little chasing ourselves. And the place to start is with a national economic inventory."

I suddenly had visions of Price Waterhouse taking charge of America's strategic industries.

"We need to take stock of our strengths and weaknesses—the age of plant and equipment in our key industries, the extent to which our best manufacturing processes are used in those industries, where our labor-management relations are the most successful. We can't formulate strategy until and unless we have a more reliable data base."

Ms. Hadley wants to centralize her national economic inventory within an existing federal function, she said. Preferably outside the bureaucracy to keep it away from political influence. Her choice would be the Joint Economic Committee in Congress. Not Price Waterhouse.

So John Alic would like to develop disaggregated, sector-specific industry analysis as a first step toward a more organized industrial policy, and Eleanor Hadley wants to see a national economic inventory.

Industrial policy is, thus, a little like Mona Lisa's smile: what you see depends on where you stand.

Neither John Alic nor Eleanor Hadley have political ambitions, however, so they're more concerned with substance than with style.

The RFC

But Felix Rohatyn, who favors a new Reconstruction Finance Corporation, might also like to be in charge of it. And Frank Weil, who has recommended creating a new Federal Industrial Coordination Board, wouldn't mind being its chairman.

Rohatyn first detailed his ideas in the *New York Review of Books* in March 1981. He was basically concerned with the dramatic loss of population in the Northeast and its migration to the Sun Belt. Pittsburgh had shut down a lot of steel mill operations. The workers were unemployed. Some left for Texas. Many stayed and went on welfare.

The burdens were twofold: how to revive the basic industries and how to alleviate the social strains.

Enter the RFC. The United States needs nothing less than a second Industrial Revolution.

"What we have to do," Rohatyn wrote, "is to turn the losers into winners, restructure our basic industries to make them competitive, and use whatever government resources are necessary to do the job.

"What is needed, first, is an industrial policy committed to restructuring basic U.S. industries, to enable them to take their place as healthy competitors in the world markets; and second, a regional policy whose aim will be to maintain the U.S. as a country in which all geographical areas (and thereby all classes and races) share the burdens as well as the benefits this country has to offer."

Rohatyn agrees America needs a competitive steel industry because our national defense depends on it and a competitive auto industry because it still accounts for one out of every eight jobs. His RFC would provide capital that the basic industries either don't have or can't get, and it would make capital contributions conditional on both wage concessions from unions and management changes that would increase productivity.

That's the industrial side. Sticks and carrots.

On the regional side, Rohatyn's RFC would provide long-term, low-interest loans to depressed municipalities to help them rebuild infrastructure, improve schools, and tighten budgets. Funding for the regions would also be conditional on participation by the private sector—reform would be a joint process.

All Rohatyn needs to do this is a capital account of $5 billion and congressional authority to lend up to five times that amount. No single industrial or regional project could get more than 50 percent of its funds from the RFC, so on a $50 billion deal, for example, half would have to come from the private sector. The RFC's bonds would be guaranteed by Uncle Sam.

"The old liberalism has proven itself incapable of coping with our present problems," Rohatyn concluded. "We need an active partnership between business, labor, and government to strike the kind of bargains—whether on energy policy, regional policy, or industrial policy—that an advanced Western democracy requires to function, and that, in one form or another, have been made for years in Europe and Japan."

But would the RFC establish a disaggregated data base? And who would control the money? And how powerful should it be?

The FICB

"Knowledge, money, power. Those are the three ingredients you need in any industrial policy," Frank Weil was saying to me as we sat in his office on Pennsylvania Avenue. He ticked the items off on his fingers and then made a fist.

"That, and a long-term orientation," he said. "Industrial policy has to be insulated from normal short-term political pressures. Plus it has to have autonomy."

I asked him how he would make his industrial policy autonomous.

"By creating a separate institution modeled on the Fed," he said, handing me a copy of his paper. It was a thirty-page article written for Georgetown University's *Law and Policy in International Business* and titled "U.S. Industrial Policy: A Case for and Outline of a Federal Industrial Coordination Board."

Only a lawyer could have written it, I later discovered, as there were 115 footnotes in the first ten pages, 271 overall. But, as one would also expect, the analysis was thorough.

Weil started with the admission that industrial policy in America had been pretty much an uncoordinated, ad hoc affair, through "tax laws, regional development plans, government procurement, trade policies, health and safety regulations, public works programs, and government-sponsored research and development." It all began, of course, in 1792, with Alexander Hamilton's *Report on Manufactures*, which argued for infant-industry protectionism. But even then, pluralism reigned supreme.

Weil proceeded to document industrial policies at work in other countries: Japan has one, orchestrated by MITI; France has one, and it's called State Control; Germany has one, organized through the Ministry of Research and Technology; England has one (well, sort of), under the rubric of the National Economic Development Council. We seem to be the only advanced industrial nation without one.

So he believes we need a Federal Industrial Coordination Board to pull it all together, help the country speak with one voice, institutionalize the collecting of information, establish standards and goals, "with carefully defined powers to manage incentives and disincentives to encourage private corporations to move toward those goals, and to negotiate the complicated tradeoffs among the competing interested parties. Specifically, it would be empowered to collect information, convene hearings, coordinate international trade policies, intervene in certain federal, state and local regulatory proceedings, provide loans and guarantees for research and development, modernization, or expansion, and manage changing levels of certain tax incentives and disincentives."

Broad powers, just like the Federal Reserve Bank. And, not unlike the Fed, Weil's FICB would be sited in Washington with six regional Feds called Regional Industrial Development Corporations. The industrial Fed would have nine full-time salaried members serving staggered ten-year terms, a chairman and a vice chairman to serve five-year terms, and a $5 billion authorization for loans and loan-guarantee assistance. After ten years, it would automatically cease to exist unless renewed by Congress.

But would an industrial Fed be any less subject to political influence than a financial Fed? And would its policies and objectives be any more effective? And would it orchestrate the development of strategic industries the way the Fed manages interest rates and the money supply? Close your eyes and imagine the FICB's equivalents of M-1 and M-2: I-1 and I-2, where I-1 would represent nonfarm, nonresidence business output and I-2 would include I-1 plus hamburgers and ICBMs.

Frank Weil now has a private law practice in Washington. But he was undersecretary of commerce for trade administration in the last Democratic administration. He knows the Democrats have become converts to industrial policy, just as Richard Nixon finally became a believer in Keynesian economics. And he expects the Democrats to regain power in 1984.

"I'm betting my time and money on it."

So you can begin to see the difference.

Japanese industrial policy, from its origins in the 1870s, through the period of experimentation in the 1920s to the postwar Economic Miracle, was based on the simple concept of economic nationalism.

American industrial policy, to the extent it is being conceived, seems to be based on our standard concept of political pluralism. Or, as the Republicans might say, if industrial policy didn't exist, the Democrats would have to invent it.

More Definitions

Not everyone's industrial policy is as institutionally oriented as Rohatyn's or Weil's. Robert Reich, the former Federal Trade Commission official who now teaches at Harvard, has written two books on the subject. His latest is called *The Next American Frontier*.

"A rational industrial policy," Reich believes, "must accomplish two interrelated objectives. First, it must strive to integrate the full range of targeted government policies—procurement, research and development, trade, antitrust, tax credits, and subsidies—into a coherent strategy for encouraging the development of internationally competitive businesses. Second, it must seek to facilitate the movement of capital and labor into businesses that permit higher value added per employee. In these ways, industrial policy should complement the strategic decisions of U.S. firms."

Reich has no new federal department or agency in mind to run America's industrial policy, nor does he envisage a new marble building in Washington to house it. Rather, he would work through existing institutions, which is politically realistic, but he would introduce new tactical tools, such as transitional vouchers to ease adjustment from sunset industries, such as autos and steel, to sunrise industries, such as semiconductors and fiber optics. He would require advance notice of plant shutdowns and would encourage regional assistance programs, along with measures to correct market imperfections (such as R & D), measures to encourage productive investment (such as high-risk lending), and measures to coordinate government policies (such as antitrust and trade policy).

In short, Reich says, "The United States needs a political forum capable of generating large-scale compromise and adaptation—a national bargaining arena for allocating the burdens and benefits of major adjustment strategies." But some feel that forum is already there, in the form of our political system. Don't we have elections at regular intervals to decide the issues? And if industrial policy is an issue, won't it be on the ballot in some way next November?

In late 1981, the U.S. Department of State, the U.S. Department of Commerce, and the Office of the USTR commissioned the Hudson Institute to analyze Japanese industrial policy and government-support measures to industry with a view toward drawing implications for U.S. policymakers and private firms. Their report was published in October 1982 under the rather long, government-commissioned title *Japanese Industrial Development Policies in the 1980s: Implications for U.S. Trade and Investment.*

"In contrast to Japan," the report found, "the U.S. does not even have an industrial policy in the sense of an explicit and coordinated set of government policies aimed at industrial development, and the issue of whether it should have one is currently a subject of considerable discussion."

The Hudson analysts argued that the effects of Japanese industrial policy were difficult to quantify in any event—segregating the warp of policy effects from the woof of macroeconomic behavior was like separating whites from yolks after you have already scrambled the eggs. And, "although some aspects of Japanese practice, notably the importance given to articulating clear goals and then to formulating consistent policies in search of such goals" were worth emulating, they cautioned against accepting Japanese industrial policy wholesale. But they admitted that "efforts that are likely to be most effective in improving overall U.S. competitiveness vis-à-vis Japan are those that can and should be made primarily within the U.S. itself."

So they called for the establishment of an organization comparable to the National Security Council that would perform the policy-coordinating role that MITI plays so well, to "institutionalize some kind of economic policy coordination that incorporates both macro and micro considerations, integrates domestic and international effects, and has sufficient authority to do the job."

But we know the NSC depends on the personality of its leader. Under Kissinger, it replaced the State Department as formulator of U.S. foreign policy. Under less dominant individuals, people tend to forget it exists. Would a National Industrial Council be any different? Under a Rohatyn or a Weil, it could conceivably make the Department of Commerce irrelevant. Under a career Department of Commerce bureaucrat, people would ignore it. And where would be the source of its power?

The best part of the Hudson story came after their report was released. Some Commerce bureaucrats were secretly hoping that the

report would detail some of those doubtful or illegal Japanese government policy practices, and these findings could then be used to put
pressure on the Japanese to cease such practices. Ammunition for more
Jap-bashing. Like a Bible of sins.

When that didn't happen, and the Hudson analysts concluded we
needed to do our own homework rather than criticize the Japanese,
the Commerce bureaucrats tried to get them to change their conclusion.

DOC/DOT/DOTI/DIT/DITI/DOODAH

That rather cryptic collection of Morse Code sounds is what you
get when you put together the various recommendations to reorganize
the Department of Commerce and make it into a more "coherent and
coordinated" body. Washington has played with such configurations
as a Department of Trade, a Department of Trade and Industry, a Department of International Trade, and a Department of International
Trade and Industry. Doodah is what one needs to make the line scan.

The conventional wisdom says, Commerce is ineffective. Let's shuffle the boxes around and make it more relevant. That will give us what
we need. Take one part International Economic Policy out of Treasury,
one part International Affairs out of State, two parts Export Subsidies
out of Agriculture, a pinch of International Trade out of the Pentagon,
and mix thoroughly with the Office of the USTR. Result: a bigger and
better pie.

So Senator Roth of Delaware proposed a DOTI in 1979. And in 1982,
Senator Moynihan of New York proposed a DITI. And in 1983, President Reagan suggested a DOT that would meld USTR into Commerce.

There's only one thing wrong with that approach. Turf. Nobody
wants to give up what he already has (a fundamental principle of bureaucratic infighting, and probably a corollary to one of Parkinson's
laws). The motivation is to build on strength where strength can be
found. But if that's the case, then Commerce ought to be melded into
USTR rather than vice versa. The problem there is that you can't fit
35,000 people into space occupied by 130.

Excuse me, did you say 35,000 people?

The Department of Commerce started in 1903 as the Department
of Commerce and Labor, then split off from Labor in 1913 to lend a
helping hand to the business community. "The many components of
Commerce seem unrelated at first glance," said Secretary Baldrige in
his 1981 report *Serving the Nation*. They seem unrelated at second and
third glance, too.

Commerce has lots of responsibilities. But you have to look hard to find any that bear the slightest relation to industrial policy or to the development of strategic industries.

It houses the National Bureau of Standards, which provides science and industry with accurate and uniform physical (nonmetric) measurements for length, mass, time, volume, temperature, and light.

It houses the National Oceanic and Atmospheric Administration, which serves to improve our understanding of the earth's environment and its oceanic life and to ensure wise use of the oceans. When you dial the National Weather Service, you listen to the voice of a Commerce bureaucrat.

It houses the National Technical Information Service, which acts to develop our productivity and innovational goals.

It houses the Patent and Trademark Office, which processes applications for patents, and the Bureau of Economic Analysis, "to provide a clear picture of the U.S. economy," and the Bureau of Industrial Economics, which engages in industrial forecasting, and the Minority Business Development Agency, which develops national programs for minority businesses, and the National Telecommunications and Information Administration, which formulates positive support policies, and the Bureau of the Census, which counts our population, and the U.S. Travel and Tourism Administration, which counts our tourists.

Commerce also houses the Economic Development Administration, which focuses on long-term economic development and job creation in depressed areas, and Economic Affairs, which coordinates economic policy for the department. The International Trade Administration, which serves to promote trade, was added in 1980 "to strengthen the international trade and investment position of the United States."

It used to have responsibility for the National Fire Prevention and Control Administration until that was withdrawn in 1974 to become part of the Federal Emergency Management Agency. There are now nearly *sixty* independent federal agencies and government corporations.

The mammoth marble building was built in 1932, occupies eight acres of what used to be the Tiber Creek bed, and looks like a bank: unfunctional pillars, tall ceilings, and long, wide hallways with no people. The census clock sits in the main lobby, ticking away as it counts our population (a birth every ten seconds), and there is a modern aquarium in the basement with forty-eight display tanks that contain fish, frogs, turtles, and other aquatic life common to our waters.

This, ladies and gentlemen, is the modern American MITI.

A ministry without a mission, as one of my Treasury friends calls it. Not that counting babies and keeping track of tourists aren't relevant government functions. But the Department of Commerce?

No wonder politicians get infatuated with reorganization plans. MITI is out there, developing strategies to keep Japan competitive in the international marketplace and formulating tactics to push its industries farther up the value-added ladder, whereas Commerce gives you a number to dial for the weather and tells you how many inches there are in a foot (to six significant figures).

"Bureaucrats," said my Treasury friend wistfully. "They're like women. Can't live with 'em, can't live without 'em."

There is a precedent, of course. In 1980, Jimmy Carter created the Department of Energy, and his administration spent its first year moving organizational boxes around.

Not that we had a coherent, coordinated energy *policy*, mind you, but we had an Energy *Department*. I used to see all these esoteric energy papers sitting around on library shelves written by DOE.

But DOE is now being disbanded, and the boxes are being shuffled again. Where are most of them going?

You guessed it. To the Department of Commerce.

CHAPTER 24

FIRST-CLASS HAMBURGERS FROM A SECOND-CLASS INDUSTRIAL POWER

Then, too, ideals of beauty differ from land to land. We Anglo-Saxons consider ourselves a handsome race. But what are we still, in the eyes of the majority of the Japanese people, but a set of big, red, hairy barbarians with green eyes?

—Basil Hall Chamberlain, 1895

Well, it all boils down to choice. The Japanese, through discipline and not a little self-denial, have chosen industrial policy and a conscious strategy of higher value-added sectoral development that has vaulted them into global preeminence in manufactured goods exports, national industrial strength, and product quality. As Alexandre Dumas the Elder would say, Nothing succeeds like success.

The hairy barbarians, through evaporation of their work ethic and an addiction to self-fulfillment, have chosen a philosophy of *que cera cera*, embracing those free-market forces, which has made us number one in fast-foods, soybeans, and Minuteman missiles but has eroded our industrial base. Or, as Rudyard Kipling wrote in *The Lesson*, we have forty million reasons for failure but not a single excuse.

Conscious choice.

The Hudson Institute report summed it up for the pessimists. "If the Japanese prefer to maintain a higher rate of economic growth for a longer period of time, and to seek this goal through policies that maintain a higher level of investment than other advanced industrial countries—and if the Japanese follow this course in the full knowledge that they live less well in the short term than their counterparts elsewhere—there is little that other governments can do to compensate for any international trade effects created by this choice."

One of my Japanese friends was more succinct.

"You want to know the real reason we'll prevail in the long run?" he asked me one day over a little raw fish and sake.

I nodded.

"We don't believe in God."

It was true. The Japanese have no religious rites on Sunday, nor professional football games either, to distract them from their national economic priorities. And sumo wrestling, that national sport which pits those massive wrestlers against each other with such intense competitive rivalry, is almost imbued with a patriotic pride of the sort we only feel when we hear our national anthem. Neither do the Japanese have any meaningless mottos about God on their currency. Their lives seem to be caught up in a contemporary version of economic nationalism, a kind of common purpose and drive we understand only when we're fighting military wars and exhorting Rosie the Riveter to hammer 'em in for democracy.

It's uncomfortable to watch our relative standard of living decline. We may still have the highest absolute standard of living in the world, as measured by the number of swimming pools or the percentage of homes with central air conditioning or our per capita income, but how does that translate into a *relative* standard that says our cars are inferior, our steel is increasingly priced out of the market, and nobody wants to buy our machine tools anymore?

Zero-Sum Games

Foreign trade may well be a zero-sum game. Zero-sum games are where there are only winners and losers. Honda Rimei, the nineteenth-century philosopher of Tokugawa Japan, understood that 150 years ago. Foreign trade is a war in which each party seeks to extract wealth from the other, remember?

Football is a zero-sum game. Ask Tom Landry. Baseball is a zero-sum game. Pete Rose knows that. Tennis is a zero-sum game. John McEnroe has known that since he was about nine years old. We seem to understand the concepts of winning and losing in athletic competition much better than we understand them in economic competition.

Sumo is also a zero-sum game. One against one. One winner and one loser. Very easy to see. No tricks, no concealed weapons, nothing up my sleeve. Me against you. And only one of us will win.

"We are confronted with a fundamental question," MIT economist and Rhodes scholar Lester Thurow wrote in *The Zero-Sum Society*. "If we were to raise investment from 10 percent of GNP to the 15 percent level of West Germany or to the 20 percent level of Japan, who would be willing to give up 5 or 10 percent of the GNP? More investment, speedier disinvestment, more process R & D—they all pose the fundamental zero-sum distributional question. Someone's income will have to go down and these losses are going to be substantial. For those that lose, the existence of even larger social gains are irrelevant. They are only interested in preventing their losses."

So there is a basic irony in the two philosophical approaches, East and West.

The Japanese have a fundamental position of respect for nature. They are noninterventionists. They see nature as something to be admired and respected. They approach it with a spirit of humility. They want to exist in *harmony* with it. But when it comes to markets, which are man-made to begin with, they have an equally fundamental understanding that markets are imperfect and that intervention may sometimes be necessary to keep them moving in the desired direction.

We Americans have a fundamental position of disregard for nature. We are basically interventionists. We see nature as something to be changed, manipulated, maneuvered, to bring us additional advantage. We approach it with a spirit of challenge. We want to *master* it. But when it comes to markets, which are man-made, we have an equally fundamental understanding that they are somehow perfect and that intervention may upset the precarious balance of invisible powers.

If the Japanese had taken the same position with respect to markets that they take with nature, they would still be exporting Christmas tree ornaments, dollar blouses, and cheap toys.

If we Americans were to take the same position with respect to markets that we take with nature, we might find our international industrial competitiveness is in fact dynamic, not static.

Well, we're at least toying around with institutional reforms like RFCs and FICBs and NICs in an attempt to get a handle on things. There are so many concepts of industrial policy floating around that you need a national bargaining arena just to sort them all out. Television is our national arena. But it has yet to exploit its power in bringing industrial policy as an issue to the citizenry.

Targeting

So concepts of industrial policy have begun to pop up like broadleaf weeds, but there is by no means a consensus on what industrial policy is or what it should do or even that it is a good thing.

Some critics focus on one aspect of industrial policy and pronounce it unhealthy.

"The most insidious kind of unfairness," said one Department of Commerce bureaucrat, "is protecting certain industries until they become robust."

True, infant-industry protection is one component of Japan's historical industrial policy. Most international economists have justified it as almost the only kind of allowable protectionism. Give the kid a little elbow room so he can grow up to compete with the big boys. Well, we all know how Alexander Hamilton felt about it. But there's not a lot of support in Washington these days for infant-industry protection. Maybe it's because they think we don't have a lot of infant industries around to protect anymore. But fiber optics is an infant industry. As is bioengineering. And 256K integrated circuitry.

Another subject for criticism is industry targeting—selecting specific industry sectors for favorable development and trade priority. A cornerstone of Japan's industrial policy since the Meiji Boys first started learning the game a century ago.

"We must reduce the economic costs which Japan's industrial policies sometimes impose on U.S. companies," Lionel Olmer, undersecretary of commerce for international trade, wrote in late 1982. "The technological race does not need to be a zero-sum game."

Mr. Olmer is representative of Commerce bureaucrats who said back in the 1960s that the problem with Japan was its "unfair" trade practices. In the 1970s, they said it was market access—Japan's market was "closed" to U.S. goods. And by the 1980s, the problem had become industry targeting. We keep telling the Japanese they simply have to stop.

Industry targeting has itself become such a target of criticism and scorn that the Department of Commerce has tried to get the Japanese to cease their practice of it, Congress has started to worry, and the Semiconductor Industry Association has commissioned a Washington law firm to study the problem.

Now the development of strategic industries—targeting, in other words—has been a priority in Japan for at least a century. So when Japan singles out the computer industry as a target for the 1980s and 1990s, that should come as no surprise, right?

Well, industry targeting was discovered by Washington toward the end of the 1970s. By this time, MITI had begun issuing its periodic "visions" (white papers), in English, so even we could follow what the Japanese were planning to do. In 1971, Yoshino-san's successors released a long report called "Trade and Industrial Policy for the 1970s." In 1975, they wrote "Japan's Industrial Policy: A Long-Range Vision." And in 1980, MITI laid out its plans for world conquest in a little-noticed document called "MITI's Vision of International Trade and

Industry Policies for the 1980s." In Tokyo, these scripts can be purchased at any corner newsstand.

MITI has no crystal ball. But its Industrial Structure Council met and met and met to discuss national commercial priorities for the decade ahead: Will the world be friendly or unfriendly? Will growth rates be high or low? What should we do about diversifying our sources of energy? What new strategic industries ought we to be promoting? What is our *strategy?*

The 1980 "vision" included a section on high technology that targeted computers and information technology as national priorities. The handwriting was there for all of us to read.

By fall 1980, Congress had heard enough about the implications of MITI's visions that the Subcommittee on Trade of the Committee on Ways and Means commissioned its own analytical report: *High Technology and Japanese Industrial Policy: A Strategy for U.S. Policymakers.* By this time, Japan's VLSI project had successfully ended. VLSI is high-tech shorthand for very large-scale integration and refers to new generations of semiconductor technology. Silicon chips, they had determined, would be the crude oil of the 1990s.

When the first silicon chip was developed, in the early 1960s, it was called the 1K. One thousand bits of data capable of being stored on a chip of silicon no larger than a little fingernail. The next generation was a 2K. Then a 4K. Then a 16K. (They jump geometrically when they grow, for reasons known only to binary theoreticians and children educated in digital math.)

The 16K was called LSI—large-scale integration. Its offspring, the 64K, was the VLSI, which the Japanese targeted. The 64K RAM chip has the same computing power of the first Univac. So all that power, which once would have filled a living room, now fits on your fingernail and has become the industry standard. The Japanese have about a 75 percent *global* market share in these chips. And they are on the threshold of commercializing the 256K random access memory chip before Washington can say "industrial policy."

How did they come so far so fast?

The congressional report laid it all out.

"MITI attempted to rationalize the industry and promote collaboration by selective exemptions to the antitrust laws," Congress wrote. "And by subsidies allocated to the development of targeted technologies.

"The Government extended financial benefits to the industry through preferential government procurement, credit allocation, and tax incentives. Tax incentives included special depreciation for productive facilities, special depreciation for purchasers, tax credits for R & D, special tax provisions relating to computer leasing, tax breaks for the software industry including a deferral, tax credits for the expenses of training information processing engineers, special depreciation for users, and various tax incentives to promote the export of high technology products."

Familiar tactics, as Japan's targeted technologies were the contemporary equivalent of their 1872 strategic industries plan.

But industry targeting was somehow "unfair." Insidious. It didn't seem right that a foreign government should "intervene" that way, to skew the odds so heavily in its favor that free-market forces never even had a chance. Criticism grew rancorous. Our private companies are competing against the Japanese government, people howled.

Of course, it could have been worse. The Japanese could have taken a page out of the French text and simply nationalized their high-technology industries. That wouldn't have been unfair because it's a good old barbarian practice called socialism. But the Japanese liked their way better. It had worked for over a hundred years.

So our Semiconductor Industry Association commissioned a Washington law firm to study the problem. If U.S. firms were losing global market share to the Japanese through this insidious technique called industry targeting, then a modern-day Paul Revere had to tap out a warning on his TRS-80 and get the message to the home folk. Its report, *The Effect of Government Targeting on World Semiconductor Competition: A Case History of Japanese Industrial Strategy and Its Costs for America*, was published in early 1983.

"In the mid-1970s," the SIA said, "the Japanese government set a long range goal—world leadership in the high technology industries. The development of Japan's semiconductor industry was a central element of this program."

You start to conjure up images of smoke-filled rooms, lots of green tea, blackboards, and chalk.

"Accordingly, the Japanese Ministry of International Trade and Industry *targeted* [their emphasis] Japan's semiconductor firms for accelerated growth," the SIA report went on. "MITI took a series of major steps to ensure that Japan's leading semiconductor firms would achieve marketplace and technological preeminence."

Well, as we know, it's really no different than what the Japanese have been doing time and time again, from dollar blouses to automobiles to steel. Why should we be any more concerned about these little pieces of silicon? Let the SIA answer that question.

"Loss or even serious injury to the U.S. semiconductor industry would be profoundly damaging to this country. Our industrial base, and indeed, our future as an industrial power, increasingly depend on semiconductor technology. Semiconductors form the basic memory and logic elements of computers. They are revolutionizing such diverse fields as telecommunications, automobiles, industrial robotics, aviation, security systems, genetics, medicine, and virtually all segments of the consumer electronics and information-processing industries. They have pervasive military and space applications; they have made possible, for example, the development of precision-guided 'smart' weapons and Cruise missiles. In a very real sense, our national security rests on these devices."

Basically, there's nothing wrong with shooting for high-volume production in these little things, according to the SIA. In fact, you *need* high-volume production to ride the experience curve and to get your unit costs down. Which happens very quickly. In the early 1960s, you could buy a 2K chip for about fifty bucks. Now you can get a 64K for less than ten.

So "a competitive strategy aiming at volume production does not violate the rules of the international trading system," the SIA concluded. "Indeed, U.S. semiconductor firms themselves employ such a strategy. However, the Japanese have added a crucial element to the equation—government targeting. Government targeting entails a series of government measures that are designed to ensure volume advantage for Japanese firms and that fundamentally distort free market competition."

The solution?

Stop it.

The SIA said, "The U.S. government should announce as U.S. policy that foreign industrial targeting practices will not be allowed...."

So recently the Department of Commerce has been trying to talk MITI out of targeting strategic industries. They might have better luck trying to get the Japanese to stop using chopsticks.

Some people secretly hope Japan might be struck by another massive earthquake, like the one in 1923. To slow them down or, at least, to stop their industrial targeting practices for a while.

I asked a Japanese friend about that one day. A friend who was bemused by all the attention *In Search of Excellence* had gotten in this country because he, as did many Japanese, thought *all* their companies were on a par with our excellent ones.

"That would be terrific," he said.

"Terrific?" I replied.

"Sure," he said. "It would force us to work even harder. The way things are going now, it would hardly be a diversion."

Houdaille

Houdaille Industries, Inc., went Commerce and the SIA one better.

Houdaille makes machine tools. Machine tools are machines that help machines make machines. Computer-assisted drilling equipment, for example, that cuts and shapes the fittings for internal combustion engines. Like everything else in the world, America used to be number one in machine tools. No longer.

Today, over a third of U.S. machine tools are more than twenty years old, the highest percentage in any advanced industrial nation. In Japan, less than 20 percent of their machine tools are that old, and nearly two thirds are not even ten years old. America also has fewer numerically controlled machine tools in place than anyone else. Numerically controlled machine tools are to everyday ordinary machine tools as your TRS-80 is to pencil and paper.

Machine tools are crucial to our future, along with computers and industrial robots and all those advanced technological devices that help us make things smaller and better and faster. They use lots of integrated circuits. They are called "productivity enhancing." We like them.

So do the Japanese. And you think they didn't target machine tools as a strategic industry?

They targeted them so well that Houdaille Industries, Inc., blew the whistle. Said machine tool targeting was unfair. Said the Japanese government created a cartel of machine tool makers. Said the Japanese had given them outlandish R & D grants and tax breaks. Said they had used revenues from bicycle racing to help finance them.

Bicycle racing?

Yes, but only to the extent of $100 million.

$100 million?

Maybe that's not only unfair, Houdaille thought, maybe it's illegal. So *they* hired a Washington law firm that, after several months of reading footnotes, found an obscure clause in the federal tax code that gives the president power to deny U.S. investment tax credits to American companies that buy Japanese machine tools if the Japanese are using unfair trade practices.

"This could be the ideal surgical instrument in the president's hands," the lawyers said, rubbing their hands with a litigant's glee.

So in late 1982, Houdaille petitioned the president to use his legislated powers to deny tax credits to anyone caught buying a Japanese machine tool and to limit Japanese machine tools to 17.5 percent of the U.S. market. This will show "how pernicious industrial targeting policies of the Japanese really are," they said.

Pernicious. Insidious. Unfair.

President Reagan turned them down. And rightly. He feared retaliation by other countries, for one thing, and he found, again, that the Japanese simply made better machine tools and marketed them more aggressively than their American counterparts. Plus, he concluded, MITI's policies had heightened domestic Japanese competition over the years and their R & D approach did not violate *Japanese* law.

But it was also hard to make a case against Japanese machine tool makers when the American industry got significant government assistance as well. The Department of Defense gives around $200 million a year to help train manufacturing engineers (part of that Pentagon cushion we read about earlier), and the National Science Foundation grants $150 million annually to fund a manufacturing-technology program specifically for the machine tool industry. That's different, you see. Those are regular government programs, not Lotto receipts.

Yet Houdaille can still file a 201 with the ITC and try to seek relief from import injury. And if that fails, a 301. Machine tool imports now have nearly a third of the total American market, compared with only about a 10 percent share in 1980. But in the numerically controlled machine tool sector, imports have a 50 percent market share, and half of those come from Japan.

U.S. companies began buying Japanese machine tools for the same reason you might buy a Sony or drive a Honda. The price is better. The workmanship is often better. And the service is better and faster.

The American machine tool industry is fragmented and disorganized, with nearly 1300 small manufacturers in the business. They do not market aggressively, have been slow to invest in state-of-the-art technology, and have not expanded production capacity to keep pace with foreign competition, according to a Department of Commerce report.

In 1981, our own National Machine Tool Builders Association found "to its surprise" that Japan's machine tool industry was investing without special tax gimmicks. A delegation that had visited Tokyo concluded in its report: "The strong competition from the Japanese is primarily the result of the willingness of management to invest heavily in its future, market its products aggressively throughout the world, work doggedly toward long-term goals, and pay an unusual amount of attention to the training and motivation of its workforce."

The machine tool case was similar to semiconductors, which was similar to automobiles, which was similar to steel—with the game plan right out of Mr. Yoshino's office in 1927.

Encouragement and financing of a strategic industrial sector. Reaction to economic forces in anticipation of change. Infant industry protection.

Offense. Defense. The special teams.

Or, as other analysts have construed it—

> *Calculation*: the formulation of an industrial strategy.
>
> *Domination*: the concentration of competitive power in a handful of industries on the cutting edge.
>
> *Elimination*: capitalistic Darwinism, survival of the fittest.

A zero-sum game.

Our Past Is Not Our Potential

America adopted a free trade policy right after World War II. How did that happen? We have all been taught that wars do not solve anything, so we fail to notice that our postwar policy might be related to the fact that our potential competitors had been smashed to ruins, mostly by American bombers mostly mass-produced by auto factories nurtured by a 45% ad valorem tariff. Only the mature reader can recall what authority the U.S. had in 1945. As masters of the world, Americans decreed free trade. Much of our current economic difficulties, as our political and strategic problems, derive from the erosion of that extraordinary position.

—B. Bruce-Briggs,
Hudson Institute, 1983

By 1980, America had created the greatest fast-food revolution known to man as our industrial society moved into its postindustrial phase and the service sector grabbed a 70 percent share of GNP.

Three industries—fast-food restaurants, health care, and business services—accounted for more than 40 percent of all new jobs created between 1973 and 1980. The increase in employment in fast-food restaurants alone was greater than *total* employment in the automobile and steel industries combined. And total employment in these three service industries had become greater than all employment in the entire range of basic industries: construction, machinery, electric and electronic equipment, motor vehicles, aircraft, shipbuilding, chemicals and chemical products, and scientific and other instruments.

You know what the largest job producer in America today is? Retail sales. The Bureau of Labor Statistics showed nearly three million people employed as sales clerks in 1980. Then come janitors. And then come secretaries.

In the Top 20, one has to look hard to find anybody *making* anything anymore. Construction helpers and carpenters, well down on the list, are the first to appear. Nurses' aides, office clerks, waiters and waitresses, truck drivers, cashiers, typists, bookkeepers, and accountants dominate the list.

And the fastest growing job segments? The BLS Top 20 reads like a page out of George Orwell. Paralegal personnel, data processing mechanics, physical therapists. Fast-food workers, tax preparers, correction officials. Travel agents. Economists. Psychiatric aides. Insurance claims examiners. Somehow, bankers missed the cut, possibly because they're being replaced by automated teller machines.

No wonder labor leader Lane Kirkland is so upset. "What are we going to do?" he asked. "Put all our kids to work in Burger Kings or taking in each other's laundry?"

Well, that's the way we're heading, like it or not. The "post" postindustrial society. Economists have been preparing us for it since the hula hoop made its debut in 1955. We don't produce any longer, we *consume*. We consume fast-food, and then we consume diet books. So why is everybody's favorite economic index still industrial production and not service output?

But surely, you say, there must be a solution. Some way to stop the slide from postindustrial to second-rate industrial. After all, isn't this basically the same crowd that won two world wars, created the most awesome nuclear force in history, and put a man on the moon?

It depends on whether you are an optimist or a pessimist.

The optimist says the glass is half full. We may be a postindustrial society getting slapped around by the Japanese, but by God, they're on their way, too. Once they stop saving so much, quit working so hard, get out of production and into consumption, they'll be just like us: overweight and undernourished. It's inevitable. After all, Korea and Singapore and Taiwan are all gearing up to take production in basic industries away from Japan as the Japanese experience their own declining industrial base.

The pessimist says the glass is half empty. The reason the Japanese save so much and work so hard and stick with industrial production is that they have game plans and strategies that enable them to do so.

They *sacrifice*, just like we used to do before and during the war. So they're not about to eat frozen dinners or play golf every week or relax any of that Zen-inspired discipline that has brought them where they are today. Nor are we likely to rev up our own industrial policy and play the game by their rules. If we were going to do that, we would have started getting serious years ago when the Arabs discovered that oil was a weapon as well as a lubricant. It's inevitable. The twenty-first century is theirs. For them, it's a matter of national survival.

Conventional wisdom says, not to worry. In the long run, market forces will have a leveling effect on everybody, including the Japanese. But, as Keynes said, in the long run we're all dead. So unconventional wisdom says, worry. In the short run, the guys who goose up market forces stand a better chance of surviving.

Money and Politics

Well, if merchandise trade deficits can be traced back to a decline in our international industrial competitiveness, then the absence of a coherent American industrial policy can be traced back to money.

That's a little convoluted, so let's try it again. If greed (as a motivating influence) has fueled the American corporate machine in the postwar era, with a corresponding drop in product quality, export prowess, and global market share, then greed (as a cultural force) may have had a similar influence on the American political machine.

Because we have been such a wealthy society, we have had a great fondness for financial solutions to our problems. If people aren't happy at work, we offer them more money. If they aren't working at all, we simply *throw* money at them. If companies aren't working, we shuffle their financial assets around. If government agencies aren't working, we shuffle their organizational boxes around. And if the political machine isn't working, we simply shuffle the money around.

Industrial policy is inherently a bipartisan, apolitical issue. It reflects the national interest in the form of coherent industrial strategies. But we Americans seem to treat it just as we do welfare and taxes: if you're a Democrat, you're for it. If you're a Republican, you're against it. And if you're a political action committee, you put your money where the special interest groups are, regardless of national priorities.

So all this talk about RFCs and FICBs and NICs tends to miss the point. Industrial policy in America begins and ends with political action committees. As a friend in Washington put it, we either have to declare PACs unconstitutional or we have to get the industrial policy advocates to use them as a Trojan horse.

Because there seems to be no other way to get the attention of Congress.

"Politicians are forced to respond less and less to their constituents and more and more to the interests with the money," Elizabeth Drew wrote in *Politics and Money.* "The interest groups have displaced the congressional committee system: they write the bills and they sign up so many co-sponsors that the committee system is irrelevant."

What do PACs promise? One congressman put it bluntly: "Access. Access. That's the name of the game. They meet with the leadership and with the chairmen of the committees. We don't sell legislation; we sell the opportunity to be heard."

Representative Dan Rostenkowski, Democrat of Illinois, was even more blunt. "As we leave Washington, word of our impotence will precede us," he said on the eve of a recent congressional recess, Congress having failed yet again to come to grips with the mounting federal deficit. "We have put special interests on notice that we can be pushed around. We have confessed to an already doubting nation that we are ruled by political fear rather than economic courage."

Industrial policy advocates do not have access. But PACs do. There are bank PACs and company PACs and industry PACs and association PACs and local PACs and regional PACs and national PACs. There is even a BIPAC—Business-Industry Political Action Committee—and a Six PAC—the Beer Industry's Political Action Committee. There is hard money and there is soft money and there are limitations on how much money—hard or soft—you can give to any one candidate, but if you give through the PACs you can circumvent them all.

We pay for this access in the declining quality of our politicians, Ms. Drew wrote, and in the rising public cynicism.

Until the problem of money is dealt with, it is unrealistic to expect the political process to improve in any other respect. It is not relevant whether every candidate who spends more than his opponent wins—though in races that are otherwise close, this tends to be the case. What matters is what the chasing of money does to the candidates, and to the victors' subsequent behavior. The candidates' desperation for money and the interests' desire to affect public policy provide a mutual opportunity. The issue is not how much is spent on elections but the way the money is obtained. The argument made by some that the amount spent on campaigns is not particularly bothersome, because it comes to less than is spent on, say, advertising cola, or purchasing hair-care products, misses the point stunningly. The point is what *raising* money, not simply spending it, does to the political process. It is not just that the legislative product is bent or stymied. It is not just that well-armed interests have a head start over the rest of the citizenry—or that often it is not even a contest. It is not just that citizens without organized economic power pay the bill for the success of those with organized economic power. It is not even relevant which interests happen to be winning. What is relevant is what the whole thing is doing to the democratic process. What is at stake is the idea of representative government, the soul of this country.

Political action committees don't just corrupt the system by focusing everyone's attention on money and the power it has. They prevent the system from developing the kind of public consensus that is necessary before *any* major issue, such as industrial policy, can be addressed in the national interest.

Because in the absence of that consensus, industrial policy will remain a political issue, which it is not. And because the Democrats have embraced it, they may make industrial policy a plank in their political platform, just as Jimmy Carter did with a Department of Energy in 1980. And if the Democrats win, we'll get a kind of "industrial policy" that may last four years, unless of course they get reelected, in which case it may last eight.

Walter Mondale, who is now considered the Democratic party's front-running candidate for president in 1984, has already endorsed policies that stress the need to spur economic growth and corporate investment through the traditional patchwork pattern of changes in the personal income tax system and a more stimulative monetary policy. These are nothing more than measures that have been conceived and reworked by both parties in the past.

A fundamental misperception of postwar politics is that Democrats are somehow different from Republicans. In fact, both parties are for higher (lower) taxes and bigger (smaller) federal deficits and more (less) defense spending, as is convenient for them.

But industrial policy is not the individual idea of one man or the political idea of one party or the intellectual idea of the East Coast Establishment.

Industrial policy is simply another name for economic nationalism.

So what we may have to do is to help the concept of economic nationalism find its way into our national consciousness instead of trying to politicize what is essentially an apolitical issue.

This will not be easy to do. We are attached to the primacy of the political process. Our political values, such as equality and peace and freedom, take precedence over our economic values, such as performance and added value and growth.

What we need to ignite it is a national buzzword. A rallying cry.

Like, Sputnik.

We are facing another Sputnik now—a Japanese Sputnik.

—David Nitzan, Director, Industrial Robotics, Stanford Research Institute

On October 5, 1957, when the Russians put 184 pounds of electronic gear 560 miles into space, travelling at 18,000 miles per hour and making 15 orbits a day, Rear Admiral Rawson Bennett, chief of naval operations, said the first Soviet space satellite "was a hunk of iron almost anybody could launch."

Well, then, why couldn't we launch ours first?

The Admiral wasn't alone in reacting with scorn and disbelief. Bill Holaday, special assistant to the secretary of defense for guided missiles, said the launching of Sputnik was not evidence of Soviet technological superiority in missile and rocket development.

All right, but the less developed countries thought it was. And the shocked Japanese ambassador to the United States said that the Soviet feat "punctured Japan's faith in U.S. scientific superiority."

Sputnik was nine times heavier than the contemplated American satellite, which weighed only twenty-one pounds. It was a first. Moscow taunted Washington for not being first in spite of America's highly advertised collection of German rocket experts.

American leaders were astonished.

They were more than astonished.

They were scared.

Within a *month* of the Sputnik shock, we had pulled ourselves together.

On October 7, Senators Symington and Jackson said that Sputnik was indeed evidence of Soviet superiority in the long-range missile field.

On October 16, Dean Somers described the effect on U.S. defense spending as a "controlled panic."

On October 17, the Pentagon announced new space projects to recapture the initiative from the Soviet Union and regain American prestige.

On October 18, A. I. Berg warned the Russians not to underrate the United States and the *New York Times* praised the Eisenhower administration for moving from complacency to action. Eisenhower was a Republican.

On October 23, former President Truman decried the panic over Sputnik and voiced his serious concern over our inability to develop a missile capable of launching an artificial satellite. Truman was a Democrat.

On October 24, Sputnik officially became a campaign issue in the 1958 off-year elections; and the following day, Dr. Nathan Pusey, president of Harvard, linked the Sputnik feat to the Soviet stress on technical education.

Sputnik had become a national buzzword, etched in the public consciousness like acid on glass.

Before long, we had a coherent, concerted, coordinated, and (would you believe) bipartisan policy to recapture the lead in the space race. We passed the National Defense Education Act, to put more stress on science and engineering in our schools. We enacted tax and depreciation legislation to encourage American business to invest in space technology because it had become a *strategic* industry. And we created the National Aeronautics and Space Administration to orchestrate the federal government's role, and we ultimately put a man on the moon. NASA also became a household word.

All because Sputnik was viewed as a threat, and that Russian satellite helped us develop a consensus and a national strategy to counter that threat.

But the Japanese are our political allies. So when they make better cars and higher quality steel and more advanced electronic products, we don't even perceive them as a challenge. It's just unfair trade practices and closed markets and insidious industrial targeting. We're not really doing anything wrong, just drifting along with the free-market tide to our postindustrial island in the sea. It's the Japanese who are at fault.

Can you imagine the public outcry in 1957 if our political leaders had told us not to worry? Sputnik is nothing more than the product of a centrally planned economy that is characterized by inefficiency and imbalance. Central market economies depend on government intervention, but free-market forces will enable us to surpass the Communist threat and launch our own artificial satellite in good time.

The Japanese may be our political allies. But they are also our most formidable commercial competitors. The problem is, we don't view politics and commerce as ideological equals, so we don't perceive a commercial challenge the same way we perceive a political threat.

But remember what William Gladstone said: "Nations do not have permanent enemies, nor do they have permanent friends. They have only permanent interests." Is it in our permanent interest as a nation to see any country, including Japan, achieve such a degree of industrial superiority that America may be relegated to the status of a second-rate industrial power?

"The [erroneous] American assumption," Adam Smith wrote not long ago, "is that future Japanese will be just like present Japanese: polite, agreeable, golf-loving baseball fans. They put on white lab coats and make tape cassette players the size of your thumbnail. But money and economic activity have their own momentum, and if the glory is coming from missile frigates, that's not the same mentality that makes microwave ovens. Maybe future Japanese will be more independent and less agreeable. If the Japanese start making F-15s, the F-15 may come out lighter, smaller, and half the price. *Then* where do our customers go?"

But, you say, the Japanese don't make F-15s. They make transverse-mounted front-wheel drive engines and automatic-reverse mini video tape recorders and high-speed electronic computers. Well, all those nifty commercial products, which Japan now dominates, revolve increasingly around one tiny ingredient: the random access memory chip. And they do, in fact, make F-15s, but not for export. By licensing American technology, for their self-defense forces. And while our defense industry is relatively diffused, the bulk of Japan's is concentrated in the power of three major corporations. Sort of like having our own military-industrial complex controlled by Lockheed, Raytheon, and General Motors.

"The United States needs to realize that its economic problems result from fundamental weaknesses in its own society and not from Japan's economic strength," Isaac Shapiro wrote in "The Risen Sun: Japanese Gaullism?" a few years back. "The solution does not lie in pressure and protectionism, but rather in remedial steps to eliminate the internal causes for the U.S. economic decline."

The reason we don't perceive a Japanese commercial threat is the same reason we didn't perceive a Russian rocket threat until October 5, 1957. We have no national buzzword.

National buzzwords are mostly short, with two or three syllables. Sputnik. Marshall Plan. Pearl Harbor.

When you try to coin a national buzzword that symbolizes the Japanese commercial challenge, it's not easy. It has to burn into the public consciousness.

But that's where it must start. Not with finger pointing and scapegoating and name calling. We already have our share of industrial Rear Admirals. America needs a rallying cry.

We're astonished at the Japanese economic achievements, but we're not humble enough to take them seriously. Once we do, the strategy-formulation process will start soon enough. The problem is, all the ideas being generated now come under the rubric of tactics, not strategy.

Industrial cities like Pittsburgh and Detroit turn into depressed economic areas, and we formulate Reconstruction Finance Corporations to turn them around. Tactics.

Basic industries like autos and steel turn into declining industries with high unemployment and poor product quality, so we formulate Federal Industrial Coordination Boards to revitalize them. Tactics.

High-tech industries like semiconductors and fiber optics compete with low-tech industries like fast-foods and shampoo for capital, so we formulate National Industrial Councils and National Investment Committees to referee. More tactics.

Unemployed, blue-collar workers need training to become employed, white-collar workers, so we formulate Transitional Vouchers to speed and ease the process. Still, just tactics.

Nothing is wrong with any of these ideas. They all have merit. But they are all tactical, not strategic.

So let's put ourselves in the wooden sandals of the Meiji Boys a hundred years ago to see if we can get a feeling for how the process goes.

First, they started with a buzzword, a rallying cry. *Strategic industries*. More than two or three syllables, but then Japanese is that kind of language.

Then, they developed a strategy. *Exports and national defense*. Everything connected with those strategic industries got priority attention. If you wanted aggressive federal tax credits for a fast-food franchise in Yokohama in the 1880s, you were out of luck.

And finally, they worked out the tactics. This took a long time, but they eventually got them refined and honed. You know what they are. Tax credits and special depreciation policies, research and development grants, assistance for declining industries, enhancements for the smaller exporters, trial-and-error experimentation with higher value-added sectors, government procurement, proceeds from bicycle racing, VLSI projects, special subsidies, infant-industry protection, overseas market development reserves, Industrial Structure Councils, industry targeting. All under the rubric "Industrial Policy." All under the coordination, coherent guidance, and watchful eye of MITI.

One reason we're having so much difficulty coming to terms with the definition of a slippery concept like industrial policy is that we're starting with the tactics and trying to work back to a strategy. It's like Tom Landry experimenting during the week with lots of those sophisticated halfback-reverse and pass-option and flea-flicker plays without formulating a game plan. There is nothing wrong with flea-flickers. They're great plays. But they are only one part of the game plan.

So we start with a national buzzword. Trade War.

Everybody's been tiptoeing around the term since that first thin-tired Raleigh bicycle made its appearance in the American market in the early 1950s. We have been fighting a trade war, except only our most formidable foreign commercial competitors know it. We need some kind of rallying cry.

Next we develop a strategy. That's the hardest part because we're so pluralistic it's not easy to agree on what that strategy should be. But we ought to try, and probably the best way is to get the president to appear on national TV (because that's our preferred forum), take some prime time from "Hill Street Blues" or "Family Feud" or "Dallas," and announce the formation of one of those Blue Ribbon panels called the Industrial Policy Commission.

Now last July, President Reagan created a small committee comprising a few leading businessmen to study our international industrial competitiveness. This Commission on Industrial Competitiveness is an important first step, and represents an historical opportunity. "We cannot afford to consider competitiveness a partisan issue," said John Young, president of Hewlett-Packard and chairman of the Commission. "Our continuing success in world markets will require the best efforts of all of us—and then some. We need to realize that we all have more interests in common than we might have presumed. It's time to recognize and build on those shared interests." But the Commission is only a first step.

Because an Industrial Policy Commission would be a large and unwieldy body composed not only of representatives from American business (conglomerates, Fortune 500 companies, and partnerships), but also private associations (the Business Council, the Business Roundtable, the National Association of Manufacturers), basic industries (autos, mining, steel), high-tech industries (computers, semiconductors, biotechnology), low-tech industries (fast-foods, health care, leisure), labor (AFL-CIO, the Teamsters, ILGWU), education (the presidents of Harvard, Grinnell, and the University of Texas), consumers (Common Cause, Consumers Union), lawyers (the ABA, the ACLU, and some prominent national attorneys), accountants (from the Big Eight as well as from smaller, regional firms), science and technology (NSF, MIT, Cal Tech), the business schools (Harvard, Stanford, Columbia), minorities (a black, a woman, an Hispanic-American), the Church (ministers, priests, and rabbis), local government (a few governors, and maybe some mayors), the press (the *Times*, the *Wall Street Journal*, *Harper's Magazine* or the *Atlantic*), think tanks (Brookings, Carnegie, SRI), talk tanks (the Council on Foreign Relations, the Japan Society, some regional Councils on Foreign Affairs), exporters (Boeing, Caterpillar Tractor, the grain companies), importers (energy companies, foreign car dealers, wine distributors), and even special interest groups (the American Association of Broadcasters, the National Machine Tool Builders Association, but please, no political action committees).

Unwieldy might not be the half of it. But because we are such a pluralistic society, our national consensus cannot be reached without meaningful participation from our principal interest groups. Yoshino Shinji realized this, too, over fifty years ago with his Industry Deliberation Council, which itself was certainly no overnight success, and the Council had to cope with all that competition, rivalry, and conflict to achieve some semblance of harmony for Japan's industrial policy.

And just as our own excellent companies are characterized by a philosophy of experimentation and adaptation, is there any reason our own *government* can't learn from their experience? "Do it, try it, fix it," is the watchword. What do we lose by experimenting? What do we gain by doing nothing? It's not a matter of imitating the Japanese; it's learning from our own best experience.

So there would be far too many people for regular group meetings, of course, because our Industrial Policy Commission would have more than a hundred people overall. But, organized properly, the IPC through its board could designate working committees or task force groups (another characteristic of our best-run companies) in seven priority, or strategic, sectors: Basic Industries; High-Technology Industries; Consumer and Service Industries; Regional Dislocation and Industrial Relocation; International Trade Policy; Government Coordination (Education, Tax, and Departmental Reorganization); and Overall Industrial Policy (Research, Industrial Structure, Financing). And the working committees would crunch the numbers and grind out the analyses and create the data base that would represent a first attempt at formulating a national strategy.

The IPC would report to the president, and it would have to be insulated from the short-term pressures of domestic politics. Its mandate would be to come up with a strategy formulation for an American Industrial Policy within two years. That strategy would revolve around economic nationalism and would target our industrial priorities from the vantage point of our overall national interest.

Then it could begin devising tactics: what tax incentives would be necessary to stimulate production and to curb consumption; what priorities should be set for government procurement; what role special depreciation should play, and for what industries; how should our research and development efforts be strengthened, and funded; what curriculum changes in the American educational system are necessary, and how should they be funded; what industrial sectors should be targeted for special treatment; how can exports be strengthened and an export mentality encouraged; how can the savings rate and gross capital formation be increased; what assistance is necessary to help declining industries adjust; what special industries might be eligible for protection in infancy; what regulations should be required to stem the drain of our proprietary technology—and a host of related tactical tools that could be devised over time in anticipation of, not as a reaction to, changes in the international economic environment. Tactics that would help ease the pain of transition we are currently experiencing.

And maybe some of these tactics would include specific tax measures to stimulate investment and production and to curb consumption—such as elimination of capital gains taxes and double taxation on dividends, and raising the ceiling on tax-free interest income (as has been recommended through investment accounts whose proceeds would be taxed when withdrawn but be free of tax when reinvested), and slapping some stiff consumption taxes on goods whose production may not be in the national interest, like gas guzzlers. Overall, appropriate sticks and carrots.

And maybe these tactics might include painful measures to boost the savings rate and gross capital formation dramatically, with incentives to invest in strategic sectors—such as the value-added, knowledge-intensive industries—and disincentives to discourage investment in hamburgers and hair care.

And maybe the IPC would recommend more interventionist tactics by the Fed, with or without an "eel," to protect the dollar from becoming artificially strong in the exchange markets, to enhance the price competitiveness of U.S. exports, and to gauge more accurately the international effects of exchange rate behavior on our domestic money supply.

And maybe these tactics should include setting limitations on merger and acquisition activity in our domestic market, to deflect some of that able legal, banking, and accounting talent into more productive areas—into the strategic sectors. Or impose limitations on foreign acquisitions of American companies in designated strategic industries, such as biotechnology and fiber optics. Or encourage relaxation of restrictions on joint R & D activity in those designated sectors, as has been recently accomplished in the semiconductor industry, to strengthen it against foreign competition.

And maybe, just maybe, the whole process of experimenting with a national industrial policy might lift us out of the era of politically inspired, ad hoc, and patchwork policies that have characterized our postwar economic behavior into an era of stability, consistency, and broad strategic policy consensus.

Once the IPC completes its assignment and makes its report to the president, it would be reformulated into an Industrial Policy Council. (This has the added advantage of keeping the same acronym.) And the Industrial Policy Council would be organized along the lines of the National Security Council, which has a remarkably simple structure: chaired by the president, its statutory members would be the vice-president, the secretary of Commerce, and the U.S. trade representative. It would have representative advisers from the State Department, from the Pentagon, and from Agriculture. The statutory function of the IPC would be to advise the president with respect to the integration, coordination, and implementation of our national industrial policy. Although this function could conceivably be carried out by a restructured Department of Commerce, political realities would suggest that moving those DOC boxes around isn't going to accomplish very much. And as with the NSC, the IPC would be insulated from domestic political pressures by chartering it to survive irrespective of the administration that created it.

Stability, consistency, policy consensus. The Japanese are not the only ones capable of such accomplishments.

We can do it, too. But the evidence isn't very encouraging, and the longer we wait, the harder it may become to take those remedial steps. We might be surprised at what we can accomplish in this more intensely competitive era if we respond properly by putting the same energy and brainpower and resources into commercial competition that we have traditionally put into our national defense.

Or we can also let the market decide. Free-market forces, free trade, free lunch. Well, if there is no such thing as a free lunch, there may be no such thing as free-market forces or free trade.

"The classical theory of free trade was based on what economists called 'factor endowments,' a nation's natural advantages," said the *New Republic*. "But the theory doesn't fit a world of learning curves, economies of scale, and floating exchange rates. And it certainly doesn't deal with the fact that much 'comparative advantage' today is created not by markets but by government action."

Which is simply recognizing that most advanced industrial nations regard economic nationalism as a fundamental part of their overall foreign and economic policies. What's good for their companies, they reason, is good for the country. We often confuse our national interest with our corporate interests. And our traditional policy mix—fiscal policy and monetary policy—is but two sides of the triangle. Industrial policy could be the third.

Why? Because the game of international commercial competition may well be a zero-sum game. The Japanese have understood that far better than we. And our attempts to get the Japanese to stop industrial targeting or to eliminate their Industrial Structure Council or to dismantle their century-old industrial policy are simply shortsighted and flawed.

The Japanese are just too *zurui*. Even if they agreed to stop industrial targeting, for example, which is like saying we shall stop being pluralistic and adversarial, they will just devise something else to take its place. That is in the nature of the beast.

And because Japan is now a capital-abundant country, venture capital fever and entrepreneurism are building. Used to be, venture capital was the privileged domain of the United States, just like everything else. The real competition in the years ahead will be in sectors where we have heretofore never been challenged: our inventiveness, our creativity, our entrepreneurial spirit. Sony and Matsushita and Honda and a host of other quality Japanese firms are not only postwar phenomena but also creations of individuals who are strongly entrepreneurial in nature.

Where the market is, of course, MITI is not far behind. Yoshino's successors have recognized this entrepreneurial trend by establishing a Venture Equity Corporation (VEC) under the Agency of Industrial Science and Technology. Tiny fissures in the vaunted lifetime employment system have emerged, evidenced by recent corporate spinoffs and managerial bail-outs. All the major Japanese investment banks have established venture capital arms, and the Ministry of Finance has relaxed listing requirements for its over-the-counter market to encourage more private companies to go public in the future. More than *zurui*, it's smart thinking.

So we can stand by and watch our once-proud, quintessentially American industries continue to topple like tenpins while we wait for those free-market forces to rally and prop them up again. Or we can create a game plan ourselves—first a buzzword, then a national strategy, and then some thoughtful tactics—that will enable us to compete more effectively with everybody else.

We can do it, too. The examples are there, from our own best-run firms.

If we don't, then we stand a very good chance of becoming a first-class military power with a second-class industrial base. And it won't take the rest of the world very long to figure out how that zero-sum game will end. The precarious debt overhang in the less developed countries is too crucial to our own survival for us to allow that to happen.

"Maybe it takes a crisis for America to flex its muscles," Jared Taylor, author of *Shadows of the Rising Sun*, wrote last year. "If so, the crisis is gathering. Our supremacy is being threatened in one field after another, and we are slowly waking up to the challenge. We should not be whimpering about unfair competition or running to Uncle Sam for protection. We should be working, investing, innovating, taking risks, and thinking big. America is still number one, [but] it is up to us to keep it that way."

From semiconductors to machine tools to automobiles to steel, America is now only number two. So from here on out, we'll have to be smarter and try harder ourselves.

Which means that we have to formulate a new national strategy, just like the Meiji oligarchs did in 1872.

And just as we did with Sputnik in 1957.

On a quiet spring day not long ago, I was about to step out of a cab at Horyu-ji, near Nara, in western Japan, the site of Buddhism's most famous temple. The oldest wooden structures in the world. A National Treasure.

I had asked the driver what he thought about *boeki senso*.

"Trade war?" he asked. "*Maa,*" he said as he counted out my change. The five-yen coins still have that little square hole in the center.

"*Shikata ga nai,*" he said, shrugging his shoulders.

It's inevitable.

LIST OF ABBREVIATIONS

ABA	American Bar Association	IPC	Industrial Policy Commission (or Council)
ACLU	American Civil Liberties Union	ITC	International Trade Commission
ASP	American selling price	JDB	Japan Development Bank
BIPAC	Business-Industry Political Action Committee	LDC	less developed countries
		LDP	Liberal Democratic Party
BLS	Bureau of Labor Statistics	LSI	large-scale integration
CAP	Common Agriculture Policy	M&A	mergers and acquisitions
		MAC	Ministry of Agriculture & Commerce
CEO	chief executive officer		
DKB	Dai-Ichi Kangyo Bank	MCI	Ministry of Commerce and Industry
DOE	Department of Energy		
DOT	Department of Transportation	MFA	Ministry of Foreign Affairs
EEC	European Economic Community	MITI	Ministry of International Trade and Industry
EPA	Environmental Protection Agency	MMS	maximizing market share
		MOF	Ministry of Finance
FDA	Food and Drug Administration	MPT	Ministry of Posts and Telecommunications
FICB	Federal Industrial Coordination Board	NASA	National Aeronautics and Space Administration
FILP	Fiscal Investment Loan Program	NATO	North Atlantic Treaty Organization
GAO	General Accounting Office	NEC	Nippon Electric Corporation
GATT	General Agreement on Tariffs and Trade	NSC	National Security Council
ICBM	intercontinental ballistic missile	NSF	National Science Foundation
IEI	International Economic Indicators	NTB	nontariff barriers
IMF	International Monetary Fund	NTT	Nippon Telephone and Telegraph

OECD	Organization for Economic Cooperation and Development	ROI	return on investment
		SIA	Semiconductor Industry Association
OECF	Overseas Economic Cooperation Fund	STR	special trade representative
OMA	Orderly Marketing Agreement	TPM	trigger price mechanism
		UAW	United Auto Workers
OPEC	Organization of Petroleum Exporting Countries	USTR	U.S. Trade Representative
		USW	United Steel Workers
OSHA	Occupational Safety and Health Administration	VER	voluntary export restraint
PAC	political action committee	VLSI	very large-scale integration
PMS	profit maximizing strategy	VTR	video tape recorder
		WISC	Wechsler Intelligence Scale for Children
QC	quality control, or quality circles	YSW	Yankelovich, Skelly & White
R&D	research and development		
RFC	Reconstruction Finance Corporation		

APPENDIX:
BILATERAL ECONOMIC, TRADE, AND INVESTMENT STATISTICS

Table 1

MERCHANDISE TRADE EXPORTS, UNITED STATES, 1982
($ Million, FAS value basis)

CATEGORY	AMOUNT	TO JAPAN
Food & Live Animals	23,953	3,944
Beverages & Tobacco	3,026	400
Crude Materials (Excl. Fuels)	19,248	4,055
Mineral Fuels & Lubricants	12,729	2,441
Oils & Fats (Animal & Veg.)	1,541	83
Chemicals & Related Products	19,891	2,530
Manufactured Goods	16,739	1,320
Machinery & Transport Equip.	87,148	4,090
Misc. Manufactured Articles	15,961	1,410
All other Goods, N.E.C.	6,925	96
Total Merchandise Exports	212,275	20,369

SOURCE: U.S. Department of Commerce, Bureau of the Census, Foreign Trade Division. *Highlights of U.S. Export and Import Trade*, FT 990, December 1982.

Table 2
MERCHANDISE TRADE IMPORTS, UNITED STATES, 1982
($ million, CIF value basis)

CATEGORY	AMOUNT	FROM JAPAN
Food & Live Animals	15,731	301
Beverages & Tobacco	3,666	19
Crude Materials (Excl. Fuels)	9,302	62
Mineral Fuels & Lubricants	67,657	23
Oils & Fats (Animal & Veg.)	446	6
Chemicals & Related Products	9,935	937
Manufactured Goods	35,048	7,348
Machinery & Transport Equip.	75,723	27,169
Misc. Manufactured Articles	29,631	3,641
All Other Goods, N.E.C.	7,798	425
Total Merchandise Imports	254,885	39,931

SOURCE: U.S. Department of Commerce, Bureau of the Census,
Foreign Trade Division. *Highlights of U.S. Export and
Import Trade*, FT 990, December 1982.

Table 3
MERCHANDISE TRADE EXPORTS, JAPAN, 1982
($ million, FOB value basis)

CATEGORY	AMOUNT	TO U.S.
Food & Live Animals	1,270	301
Beverages & Tobacco	131	19
Crude Materials (Excl. Fuels)	1,159	62
Mineral Fuels & Lubricants	411	23
Oils & Fats (Animal & Veg.)	88	6
Chemicals & Related Products	6,365	937
Manufactured Goods	31,100	7,348
Machinery & Transport Equip.	78,069	27,169
Misc. Manufactured Articles	18,723	3,641
All Other Goods, N.E.C.	1,516	425
Total Merchandise Exports	138,831	39,931

SOURCE: Government of Japan, Ministry of Finance, 1982 *Sta-
tistics*. U. S. Department of Commerce, Bureau of the
Census, Foreign Trade Division. *Highlights of U.S.
Export and Import Trade*, FT 990, December 1982.

Table 4
MERCHANDISE TRADE IMPORTS, JAPAN, 1982
($ million, CIF value basis)

CATEGORY	AMOUNT	FROM U.S.
Food & Live Animals	13,745	3,944
Beverages & Tobacco	830	400
Crude Materials (Excl. Fuels)	18,636	4,055
Mineral Fuels & Lubricants	65,618	2,441
Oils & Fats (Animal & Veg.)	275	83
Chemicals & Related Products	6,824	2,530
Manufactured Goods	9,848	1,320
Machinery & Transport Equip.	8,181	4,090
Misc. Manufactured Articles	5,398	1,410
All Other Goods, N.E.C.	2,576	96
Total Merchandise Imports	131,931	20,369

SOURCE: Government of Japan, Ministry of Finance, 1982 *Statistics.* U. S. Department of Commerce, Bureau of the Census, Foreign Trade Division. *Highlights of U.S. Export and Import Trade*, FT 990, December 1982.

Table 5
DISPOSABLE PERSONAL INCOME, SAVINGS, AND
RATIO OF SAVINGS TO INCOME

	Ratio of Savings to Disposable Personal Income (Percent)		
Year	U.S.	Japan	Germany
1970	8.0	18.2	14.6
1976	6.9	22.4	14.7
1979	5.9	18.6	14.4
1980	5.8	19.4	14.6
1981	6.4	19.4	15.3
1982	6.5	20.6	14.7

SOURCE: U.S. Department of Commerce (USDOC), International Trade Administration (ITA). *International Economic Indicators (IEI).*

Table 6
GROSS FIXED CAPITAL FORMATION

Year	Ratio of Gross Fixed Capital Formation to GNP (Percent)		
	U.S.	Japan	Germany
1970	17.4	35.6	25.5
1976	17.0	31.3	20.1
1979	19.5	32.1	21.8
1980	18.3	32.0	22.8
1981	17.7	31.0	22.0
1982	16.7	29.6	20.4

SOURCE: USDOC, ITA. *IEI.*

Table 7
BALANCE OF MERCHANDISE TRADE ($ BILLION)
(Exports FOB, Imports CIF)

Year	U.S.	Japan
1970	− 0.2	0.4
1976	− 17.3	2.4
1977	− 39.2	9.7
1978	− 42.4	18.2
1979	− 40.4	− 7.7
1980	− 36.4	− 10.7
1981	− 39.7	8.7
1982	− 42.7	6.9
1983 (est.)	− 70.0	19.7

SOURCE: USDOC, ITA. *IEI.*

Table 8
SHARES OF FREE-WORLD EXPORTS (PERCENT)

Year	U.S.	Japan
1970	15.4	6.9
1976	12.8	7.4
1977	11.9	7.9
1979	12.2	6.9
1981	13.0	8.4
1982	12.8	8.4

SOURCE: USDOC, ITA. *IEI.*

Table 9
DIRECT INVESTMENT ABROAD
(Net capital outflows, $ million)

Year	U.S.	Japan
1970	7,590	355
1976	11,949	1,991
1977	11,890	1,645
1978	16,056	2,371
1979	25,222	2,898
1980	19,238	2,385
1981	8,691	4,894
1982	−2,198	4,517

SOURCE: USDOC, ITA. *IEI.*

Table 10
FOREIGN DIRECT INVESTMENT
(Net capital inflows, $ million)

Year	U.S.	Japan
1970	1,464	94
1976	4,347	113
1977	3,728	21
1978	7,897	8
1979	11,877	239
1980	13,666	278
1981	21,301	189
1982	9,424	439

SOURCE: USDOC, ITA. *IEI.*

Table 11
RATIO OF MANUFACTURING TO TOTAL EMPLOYMENT

Year	U.S.	Japan
1970	24.6	27.0
1976	21.4	25.5
1977	21.4	25.1
1978	21.3	24.5
1979	21.3	24.3
1980	20.4	24.7
1981	20.1	24.8
1982	18.9	24.5

SOURCE: USDOC, ITA. *IEI*.

Table 12
OUTPUT PER MAN-HOUR (MANUFACTURING PRODUCTIVITY)

Year	U.S.	Japan
1967	75.4	41.9
1970	79.2	61.4
1976	97.7	93.3
1977	100.0	100.0
1978	100.9	107.9
1979	101.5	117.4
1980	101.7	125.4
1981	104.5	129.1
1982	103.6	129.4

SOURCE: USDOC, ITA. *IEI*.

NOTES

References to daily newspapers are abbreviated as *NYT* (*New York Times*) and *WSJ* (*Wall Street Journal*). All other citations are given as to author and primary source, full details of which are listed in the accompanying Bibliography.

PART I: THE SEEDS OF WAR

CHAPTER 1: THOSE LITTLE YELLOW PEOPLE

pp. 3–4 Mondale: *NYT*, 10/13/82.

p. 4 Danforth: press release from the senator's office, 6/11/81. See also *WSJ*, 3/17/83, "Congressional Anger on Free Trade Could Lead to Changes."

p. 4 Dingell: *NYT*, 3/27/82. See also *WSJ*, 2/17/83, "U.S. Mulling Tougher Trade Policy."

pp. 4–5 America's omnipotence: see Ouchi, *Theory Z*, pp. 187–188.

p. 5 See Chamberlain, *Things Japanese*, p. 249.

p. 6 Merchandise trade deficits: see U.S. Department of Commerce, *Survey of Current Business*, various issues.

p. 6 Export Trading Company Act: see *Congressional Record*, 7/27/82.

p. 7 Manufactured goods exports, global market shares: see Carlson et al., *The Economic Importance of Exports to the United States*.

pp. 9–10 Purists will note that the bill was technically called Hawley-Smoot. Everybody today reverses the order.

pp. 9–11 Charles P. Kindleberger: personal interview with the author, February 1983.

pp. 11–12 See Snider, *International Economics*, pp. 308–318.

p. 13 See Kantrow, *Survival Strategies for American Industry*, pp. 2–3.

CHAPTER 2: DOWNSIZING THE AMERICAN DREAM

p. 14 Mr. Amaya quoted in *Journal of Japanese Trade and Industry*, January 1982, pp. 22–27.

pp. 14–15 OPEC: cited in Adam Smith, *Paper Money*, pp. 144ff.

p. 15 Auto statistics: see Fuller, *Note on the World Auto Industry in Transition*.

p. 15 See Kraft, "Annals of Industry," *New Yorker*, 5/5/80.

p. 16 Auto statistics: see Fuller.

pp. 16–17 Auto statistics: see *Journal of Japanese Trade and Industry*, January 1982.

p. 17 ITC: *NYT*, 11/11/80.

pp. 17–19 Auto statistics: see Fuller.

pp. 19–21 Japanese auto statistics: see Abernathy, *Testimony Before the Subcommittee on Industrial Growth and Productivity*, 1/27/81.

p. 21 Potshots at passing Toyotas and sledgehammers to Datsuns: CBS Evening News, "Anti-Japanese Sentiment," 1/31/83.

pp. 21–22 Dingell: *NYT*, 3/27/82.

p. 22 Senator Gore: cited in a personal interview with Mr. Gotoh Mitsuya, Vice President, International Affairs, Nissan Motor Co., Ltd., Tokyo, January 1983.

pp. 22–23 Voluntary Export Restraints: *NYT*, 5/6/81. "I love it," one importer was quoted as saying. "It's the law of supply and demand. It means more money. People know what they want. They're buying quality, and they'll pay the price."

pp. 23–24 VER extension: NYT, 11/2/83.

p. 23 Bilateral trade deficits: see U.S. Department of Commerce, *Survey of Current Business*, for the years in question.

pp. 24–27 See Johnson, *MITI and the Japanese Miracle*, pp. 289–290. See also Amaya, "Who's Being Unfair?" *Japan Times*, 11/9/80. Personal interview with Mr. Amaya, November 1980.

CHAPTER 3: THE MEN IN MAROON

p. 28 Takahashi quote: cited in Miyoshi, *As We Saw Them*.

pp. 31–39 Personal tour by the author of the Zama assembly plant, Nissan Motor Co., Ltd., January 1983. GM assembly plant visit in the United States, February 1983.

CHAPTER 4: WHEN STEEL REIGNED SUPREME

p. 41 Bidwell quote: cited in Bidwell, *The Invisible Tariff*.

pp. 41–42 Section 201: Trade Act of 1974 and personal interview with the ITC, Washington, D.C., March 1983.

p. 42 Section 301: Trade Act of 1974 and personal interview with the ITC, Washington, D.C., March 1983.

pp. 42–43 See Patrick and Sato, "The Political Economy of U.S.-Japan Trade in Steel," cited in *Report of the Japan-U.S. Economic Relations Group*, January 1981. See also *Journal of Japanese Trade and Industry* (Steel Issue), November 1982.

pp. 46–47 See Magaziner and Reich, *Minding America's Business*, pp. 155–168.

CHAPTER 5: A BIKE IS A BIKE IS A BIKE

p. 48 Japanese Bicycle Industry Association quote: cited in *Business Japan*, December 1982, p. 71.

pp. 48–51 See Bidwell, *What the Tariff Means to American Industries*, pp. 68–88. See also *WSJ*, 3/29/83, "U.S. Pasta Makers Are Angry at the Italians, Saying Cut-Rate Imports Are Stealing Sales." It's the same old story all over again. American pasta makers complain about cheap Italian pasta imports, saying Rome subsidizes pasta (while Washington subsidizes wheat). The Americans also complain that Italian pasta is filthier than domestic pasta, but FDA tests routinely show foreign pasta is well within U.S. guidelines: 225 insect fragments and 4.5 rodent hairs per 225 grams.

CHAPTER 6: FROM XENOPHOBIC TO ZURUI

p. 52 Japanese Imperial Navy Song, sung periodically by the author and some of his Japanese friends on visits to the right bars in Ginza, downtown Tokyo. You don't have to remember all the lyrics as long as you get the refrain right: it's a reference to the famous seven-day workweek.

pp. 53–55 See Sansom, *Japan: A Short Cultural History*, and Norman, *Origins of the Modern Japanese State*.

pp. 56–58 Personal interview with Mr. Kunihiro Masao, Tokyo, January 1983.

CHAPTER 7: RICH COUNTRY, STRONG ARMY

pp. 59–62 See Norman, *Origins of the Modern Japanese State*, especially

Chapter 4, "Early Industrialization," pp. 211–242, for an excellent account of the strategic industries concept.

p. 63 Fujita quote: cited in Miyoshi, *As We Saw Them*, p. 95.

pp. 63–65 Personal interview with Mr. Kakimizu Koichi, OECF, Tokyo, January 1983.

PART II: THE TACTICS OF TRADE WARS

CHAPTER 8: FOOD FIGHT!

pp. 69–70 MITI: see Johnson, *MITI and the Japanese Miracle*, pp. 28–34. See also *NYT*, 5/17/83.

p. 71 Merchandise trade deficits: Japanese Ministry of Finance Statistics.

p. 71 Bilateral trade figures: U.S. Department of Commerce, *Survey of Current Business*, for the relevant years.

p. 71 Kodama quote: cited in Storry, *Japan and the Decline of the West in Asia*.

pp. 71–73 Food statistics: see Sanderson, *Irritants in U.S.-Japanese Agricultural Relations*.

pp. 73–77 Sato and Curran, "Agricultural Trade: The Case of Beef and Citrus," in Destler et al., *Coping with U.S.-Japanese Conflicts*. See also Lappé, *Diet for a Small Planet*, for an account of American dietary overreliance on beef, pp. 7–30. Also, *WSJ*, 1/5/82, and "Inside Japan's 'Open' Market," *Fortune*, 10/5/81.

pp. 77–79 Tobacco complaints: see U.S. House of Representatives, Committee on Foreign Affairs, *United States–Japan Relations*. See also *NYT*, 10/25/81, "How the U.S. Struck Out in Trade with Japan," for a summary of the famous baseball bat case. Washington bureaucrats also chose to single out aluminum baseball bats as another symbol of Japan's "closed" market. And they set out to teach the Japanese another lesson: the *kinzoku batto* issue was an example of how the United States chooses a meaningless product sector for its object lessons. Metal bat exports were perhaps $10 to $15 million a year until little Taro whacked a home run in Tokyo in the late 1970s. The ball went over the fence, but the bat hit a spectator in the head: it flew out of the batter's hands because the rubber grip came unglued. So MITI (Product Standards) and MOF (Customs Bureau) and the Japanese Consumer Protection Agency all got involved in the dispute, which centered around the Baseball League Seal of Approval (denied to American bats that behaved like unguided missiles), the S-Mark (Safety Seal), and unit inspections at the port rather than in lots at the factory. Negotiations dragged on with Commerce and the USTR for over eighteen months until a settlement was finally reached in February 1983. A similar case, but no cause célèbre, was the California company that wanted to export sake to Japan. MOF reportedly leaned on importers not to distribute the hairy barbarians' wine, denying them tax concessions if they did. It's a little like the coals to Newcastle analogy. One doesn't recall Mitsubishi gearing up to export cow chips, or chili, to Texas.

p. 78 Tobacco exports: see U.S. Department of Commerce, *Highlights of U.S. Export and Import Trade*, for the relevant years.

p. 79 *WSJ*, 9/30/82 and 5/15/83, and "Japan Blows Smoke," *Fortune*, 2/21/83. See also *WSJ*, 4/26/83, "The Yen to Smoke," for a Japanese rebuttal.

pp. 79–82 Think tanks: personal interview with Dr. Fred Sanderson, Guest Scholar, Brookings Institution, Washington, D.C., January 1983.

pp. 82–85 Zenchu: personal interview with Mr. Iwamochi Shizuma, Chairman, Zenchu, Tokyo, January 1983.

CHAPTER 9: R2D2 AND THE POLITICS OF HIGH TECH

p. 86 Senator Mangum quote: cited in Miyoshi, *As We Saw Them.*

pp. 86–90 NTT: see Curran, Timothy J., "The NTT Case," in Destler, et al., *Coping with U.S.-Japanese Conflicts*, which formed much of the background for this chapter. The author is also grateful to Dr. Curran for his personal observations and comments on the NTT negotiations.

p. 89 See Drew, "Equations," *New Yorker*, 5/7/79.

pp. 90–92 Personal interview with Dr. Okita Saburo, Chairman, *Naigai Seisaku Kenkyukai*, Tokyo, January 1983.

p. 93 Hagusa quote: *WSJ*, 4/29/83.

pp. 94–95 See Drew, "Equations," *New Yorker*, 5/7/79. See also *NYT*, 10/29/82, "Bashing Japan Isn't the Answer."

pp. 95–96 See Hoffmann, "The American Style," *Foreign Affairs*, January 1968.

CHAPTER 10: VISIBLE AND INVISIBLE TARIFFS

p. 97 Hasegawa quote: *NYT*, 4/17/83, "Peeling Away Japan's Trade Barriers."

pp. 97–99 See Bidwell, *The Invisible Tariff*, and Baldwin, *Non-Tariff Distortions of International Trade*. See also Hemmendinger, *Non-Tariff Barriers of the United States.*

pp. 99–100 The Battle of Poitiers: see *NYT*, 4/29/83. The French assigned the case customs code number 732. Charles Martel, a French general also known as Charlie the Hammer, stopped the Moorish army from taking over Europe in A.D. 732.

pp. 100–03 Personal interview with Dr. Robert E. Baldwin, Professor of Economics, University of Wisconsin, April 1983.

CHAPTER 11: THE VIEW FROM MT. FUJI

p. 104 Hotta quote: cited in Miyoshi, *As We Saw Them.*

pp. 104–06 See Johnson, *MITI and the Japanese Miracle*, pp. 28–34. See also, *NYT*, 5/18/83.

pp. 106–09 See U.S.-Japan Trade Study Group, *Japan: Obstacles and Opportunities*. Case studies cited based on the author's personal experience in Japan. See also *Mainichi Daily News*, 1/19–21/82. "U.S.-Japan Trade Relations: Background and Policy Analysis."

p. 109 See Johnson, *MITI and the Japanese Miracle*, p. 13.

CHAPTER 12: OF POTS AND KETTLES: AMERICAN HYPOCRISY

pp. 110–13 See Lloyd, *Tariffs*. See also Hemmendinger, *Non-Tariff Barriers of the United States*, and the *Guardian*, 12/13/81, "Fear and Resentment at Japan's Success."

pp. 114–15 See Trollope, *Domestic Manners of the Americans.*

CHAPTER 13: MANUAL TYPEWRITERS IN THE COMPUTER AGE

pp. 116 See Chamberlain, *Things Japanese*, p. 262.

pp. 116–19 See Schlossstein, *Japanese Foreign Direct Investment in the 1980s.*

p. 119 GM/Toyota: *NYT*, 4/29/83.

pp. 120–22 See U.S.-Japan Trade Study Group, *Japan: Obstacles and Opportunities.*

pp. 121–22 Personal interview with Ohmae Kenichi, Managing Director, McKinsey & Co., Tokyo, January 1983.

CHAPTER 14: EUROPE'S NOBLE ELITE

p. 123 See Chamberlain, *Things Japanese*, p. 263.

p. 124 See Chamberlain, *Things Japanese*, p. 261.

pp. 125–28 See Tsoukalis, *Japan and Western Europe*, especially Chapters 7, 8, and 9, for an account of the Japan-EEC trade disputes. See also Wilkinson, *Misunderstanding*, especially Chapter 3, "Open Markets and Double-Bolted Doors," and *WSJ*, 1/1/82, "Growing Trade Tensions Between Europe and Japan."

CHAPTER 15: THE CHICKEN WAR

pp. 129–33 See Talbot, *The Chicken War*, for an excellent review of the economic and political issues of this famous bilateral trade dispute. See also *NYT*, 2/21/83, "Trade War Feared over Bitter Issue of Food Exports," for a review of the most recent battle.

PART III: GREED VS. POWER: CONFLICTING STRATEGIES

CHAPTER 16: THERE JUST HAS TO BE A REASON

pp. 138–39 Mino quote: cited in Mino, "Nissan Reappraisals Cause Change in Tactics," *Business Japan*, December 1982, pp. 23–24.

CHAPTER 17: CONTRASTING IDEOLOGIES

pp. 147–149 Hayes and Abernathy, "Managing Our Way to Economic Decline," in Kantrow, *Survival Strategies for American Industry*. The entire volume contains an excellent collection of 33 articles from the *Harvard Business Review* dealing with America's position in an increasingly competitive international environment.

p. 150 Star performers: *In Search of Excellence*, p. 84.

p. 152 Productivity: see Sadler et al., *Comparative Productivity Dynamics*.

pp. 152–53 Bok report: *NYT*, 4/22/83.

pp. 153–54 Acquisition statistics: see Simic, ed., *Mergerstat Review*.

pp. 154–55 U.S. Steel/Marathon: *NYT*, 2/21/83.

p. 155 Johnson quote: see *In Search of Excellence*, p. 15.

pp. 156–58 Baldwin-United: *WSJ*, 3/28/83, 3/29/83, 3/30/83.

p. 158 Financial performance: see *In Search of Excellence*, p. 103.

p. 158 Yamamoto quote: cited in Gibney, *Miracle by Design*.

pp. 161–62 Market share strategies: see Yamamura, *Policy and Trade Issues*. See also *NYT*, 4/19/83, "Japan Places Markets Above Profits."

p. 162 Growth/Share Matrix: based on discussions with associates of a leading Boston-based consulting firm.

p. 163 Mutations: see *In Search of Excellence*, p. 114.

CHAPTER 18: DEAR SHAREHOLDER: MANAGING FROM A TO Z

pp. 165–68 A-types and Z-types: see Ouchi, *Theory Z*. Personal interview with Dr. William Ouchi, Princeton, February 1983.

pp. 170–71 Japan Storage Battery Co., Ltd., 1980 Annual Report.

p. 171 Toyota Motor Co., Ltd., 1980 Annual Report.

p. 171 Toshiba Corporation, 1980 Annual Report. See also *WSJ*, 3/27/83, "Japan vs. Japan: Only the Strong Survive."

p. 171 Hewlett-Packard, 1982 Annual Report.

p. 171 3-M Company, 1982 Annual Report.

p. 171 IBM, 1982 Annual Report.

CHAPTER 19: THE JAPANESE CHARACTER IS NOT ALL *KANJI*

p. 172 Rabinowitz quote: cited in *Law and the Social Process in Japan*, pp. 93–95.

pp. 172–73 Topsy-Turvydom: see Yamaguchi, *We Japanese*.

For a contemporary update of Topsy-Turvydom, we are indebted to Mitsubishi Heavy Industries. Their 1981 summer seminar produced the following caveats:

1. Any woman should obey her husband. This is a natural principle.

2. Any woman should find her pleasure in following her husband, because her husband deserves the homage of his family.

3. Any woman should take care of her husband without being asked, if she is wise.

4. Any woman should be a sexy entertainer for her husband in the bedroom if she does not want him to go to a Turkish bath.

5. Any woman should regard her husband as a kind of child at home, because he is exhausted from his work.

6. Any mother should be responsible for bringing their children up, because children were born not from the husband, but from her.

7. If a woman does not agree with the above, a nice guy will refuse to marry her.

So much for feminism and equal rights. As an old Japanese proverb put it, a good husband is hardworking and absent.

pp. 174 Misunderstanding: see George Packard, "A Crisis in Understanding," in Rosovsky, *Discord in the Pacific.*

p. 174–75 Form and substance: see Rabinowitz, *Law and the Social Process in Japan*, pp. 79–96.

pp. 176–77 Contrasting value systems: see Bellah, *Tokugawa Religion*, especially Chapters 1 and 2. This seminal work is a veritable treasurehouse of perceptive observations on the development of cultural values in pre-modern Japan.

p. 177 Self-discipline: see Benedict, *The Chrysanthemum and the Sword*, pp. 228–252. Researched during World War II and first published in 1946, it is still a classic.

pp. 178–79 Kunihiro: personal interviews, but see his "U.S.-Japan Communications," in Rosovsky, *Discord in the Pacific.*

pp. 179–80 The Baka Valve: see Seward, *Japanese in Action*, pp. 90–91.

pp. 181–83 Negotiating strategies: see Blaker, "Probe, Push and Panic," in Scalapino, *The Foreign Policy of Modern Japan*. See also *WSJ*, 1/25/82, "Many in Japan Are Writing Off the West."

p. 182 Nineteenth century: See Abbott, et al., "Black Ships and Balance Sheets."

p. 183 With thanks to Blaker's *Japanese International Negotiating Style*, p. 154.

CHAPTER 20: ZEN AND THE ART OF FLOATING CURRENCIES

p. 186 Bretton Woods and all that: see Hirsch, *Money International.*

p. 189 Exchange rates and bilateral deficits: see U.S. Department of Commerce, *Survey of Current Business*, and *IMF: International Financial Statistics* for the relevant years.

pp. 189–90 Yen/dollar swings: see Bergsten, "What to Do About the U.S.-Japan Economic Conflict," *Foreign Affairs*, Summer 1982. See also *NYT*, 4/11/83, "Weak Yen Hurts Trade Ties."

pp. 190–91 Personal interview with Rimmer deVries, March 1983. Also

NYT, 4/29/83 and 5/3/83. See also *NYT*, 5/8/83, "Have Currencies Floated Too Long?" for an excellent overview of the floating vs. fixed rate controversy.

CHAPTER 21: SO WHY IS EVERYTHING GOING WRONG?

pp. 193–95 See Yankelovich, *New Rules.*

pp. 195–97 Three agendas: personal interview with Mr. Stephen Zimney, YSW, New York, February 1983.

pp. 197–200 Productivity: see Denison, *Accounting for Slower Economic Growth.* Also, personal interview with Dr. Edward F. Denison, Washington, D.C., March 1983.

pp. 200–201 Japanese intelligence: see especially Lynn, "IQ in Japan," *Nature*, 5/20/82.

p. 201 Johnson quote: cited in *National Journal*, 2/26/83.

p. 202 Savings rates: see Rapp, "Industrial Structure."

p. 203 Education: see *NYT*, 3/29/83 and 5/5/83. See also *WSJ*, 3/23/83, "Concern Over High-Tech Competitiveness Spurs Attention to Science, Math Education"; and *NYT*, 3/27/83, "Brainpower: A New National Concern."

PART IV: INDUSTRIAL POLICY. (WHAT?)
INDUSTRIAL POLICY. (LOUDER, I CAN'T HEAR YOU!)
INDUSTRIAL POLICY!

CHAPTER 22: HOW ON EARTH DID THE JAPANESE DO IT?

p. 207 See Hearn, *Japan: An Interpretation*, p. 451.

p. 208 See Norman, *Origins of the Modern Japanese State*, pp. 224–225.

pp. 209–12 See Johnson, *MITI and the Japanese Miracle* for a superb review of Japanese industrial development policies, especially Chapter 3, "The Rise of Industrial Policy," and Chapter 4, "Economic General Staff," which supplied most of the material for these pages. See also Phil Trezise, "Politics, Government, and Economic Growth in Japan," in Patrick et al., *Asia's New Giant*, for a minority view. Phil Trezise, among others, contends that free-market forces are as powerful in Japan as they are in the United States and that MITI's power is vastly overrated.

p. 212 Productive virtue: see Kuttner, "The Free Trade Fallacy," *New Republic*, 3/28/83.

pp. 213–16 See Johnson, *MITI and the Japanese Miracle.*

pp. 216–17 MITI: see Magaziner and Hout, *Japanese Industrial Policy.*

pp. 219–20 See Naitoh, "American and Japanese Industrial Structures," in Tasca, *U.S.-Japanese Economic Relations: Cooperation, Competition and Confrontation.*

CHAPTER 23: GOOD OLD AMERICAN PLURALISM: FIVE EXPERTS AND SIX
DEFINITIONS OF INDUSTRIAL POLICY

p. 222 Industrial base: see Fallows, "American Industry: What Ails It, How to Save It," *Atlantic*, November 1980. See also *Business Week*, cover story of 6/30/80, and *National Journal*, 10/25/80.

p. 223 Industrial policy: see Diebold, *Industrial Policy as an International Issue.*

p. 224 Industrial policy: *National Journal*, 2/26/83. See also *Harper's Magazine*, February 1983, and Alic, *Industrial Policy: Where Do We Go from Here?*

pp. 224–27 Personal interview with Mr. John Alic, Office of Technology Assessment, Washington, D.C., March 1983.

p. 226 Motorcycle tariffs: see *NYT*, 4/2/83.

p. 227 MIT conference: see *High Technology*, June 1983.

p. 227 Winners and losers: see Fallows, "American Industry," in *Atlantic*, November 1980; and *National Journal*, 2/26/83.

pp. 228–29 Personal interviews with Ms. Eleanor Hadley, Washington, D.C., January and March 1983.

pp. 229–30 The RFC: see Rohatyn, "Reconstructing America." *New York Review of Books*, 3/5/81.

pp. 230–32 The FICB: see Weil, "Federal Industrial Coordination Board," *Law and Policy in International Business*.

p. 232 Industrial policy: see Magaziner and Reich, *Minding America's Business*, especially Part IV, "Toward a Rational Industrial Policy," pp. 329–380.

pp. 233–34 National Industrial Council: see Wheeler et al., *Japanese Industrial Development Policies in the 1980s*.

pp. 234–36 DOC/DOT: see U.S. General Services Administration, *The United States Government Manual, 1982/83*, pp. 128–149. Also, U.S. Department of Commerce, *Serving the Nation*, pp. 44–49, and *NYT* articles on DOC reorganization dated 4/27/83 and 5/5/83. Also, *WSJ*, 4/29/83, "Reagan Trade Policy Seems in Disarray," is a good overview. Reorganization is almost as old as red tape.

CHAPTER 24: FIRST-CLASS HAMBURGERS FROM A SECOND-CLASS INDUSTRIAL POWER

p. 237 Chamberlain quote, *Things Japanese*, p. 251.

pp. 238–39 Zero-sum games: see Thurow, *The Zero-Sum Society*, p. 101.

p. 240 Insidious unfairness: quoted in *National Journal*, 2/26/83.

p. 240 Olmer: U.S. Department of Commerce trip report, November 26–December 4, 1982.

pp. 241–42 See U.S. House of Representatives, Committee on Ways and Means, Subcommittee on Trade, *High-Technology and Japanese Industrial Policy*, pp. ix–x and p. 15. See also *Business Week*, 5/23/83, "Chip Wars: Japan's Stronger Semiconductor Threat"; *WSJ*, 5/11/83, "Japan, U.S. Gird for Micro-Chip War"; and *Fortune*, 5/16/83, "The Next Battle in Memory Chips." The 256K-RAM chip may well be the focal point of the next pitched battle in the high-tech trade war.

pp. 242–43 Targeting: see Semiconductor Industry Association, *The Effect of Government Targeting*, pp. 103–106. See also *WSJ*, 5/23/83, "U.S. Contends Tokyo's Industrial Policy Limits Sales of Foreign Goods in Japan."

pp. 244–46 Houdaille: see *WSJ*, 3/29/83 and 4/27/83. Also, personal interviews with Washington bureaucrats, unnamed, March 1983.

p. 246 Bruce-Briggs: *WSJ*, 2/24/83, "The Coming Overthrow of Free Trade." See also *NYT*, 4/13/83, "Is Free Trade a Useful Myth?"

pp. 246–47 Service industries: *National Journal*, 2/26/83.

pp. 248–50 PACs: see Drew, "Politics and Money."

p. 249 Rostenkowski quote: NYT, 11/18/83.

p. 250 Mondale: see *WSJ*, 5/11/83.

p. 251 Nitzan: see *National Journal*, 2/26/83.

pp. 251–52 Sputnik: see *NYT* for the specified dates.

p. 253 Shapiro: see *Foreign Policy*, Winter 1980/81.

p. 253 Military-industrial complex: see Taylor, *Shadows of the Rising Sun*, p. 281.

p. 256 "Do it, try it, fix it": see *In Search of Excellence*, p. 134.

p. 258 Free-trade theory: see Kuttner, *New Republic*, 3/28/83.

BIBLIOGRAPHY

Abbott, Kenneth W., et al. "Black Ships and Balance Sheets: The Japanese Market and U.S.-Japan Relations." *Northwestern Journal of International Law and Business*. Spring 1981.

Abegglen, James C., ed. *Business Strategies for Japan*. Tokyo: Sophia University, 1970.

Abegglen, James C. "The Trade Gap with Japan." *Foreign Affairs*. Fall 1978.

Abernathy, William J. *Testimony Before the Subcommittee on Industrial Growth and Productivity*, Senate Budget Committee, Washington, D.C., January 27, 1981.

Abernathy, William J., et al. "The New Industrial Competition." *Harvard Business Review*. September/October 1981.

Alic, John A. *Industrial Policy: Where Do We Go from Here?* Washington, D.C.: Office of Technology Assessment, 1982.

Alic, John A. *Government Attitudes Toward Programmable Automation*. Washington, D.C.: Office of Technology Assessment, 1983.

Alic, John A. *Manufacturing Management: Effects on Productivity and Quality*. Washington, D.C.: Office of Technology Assessment, 1983.

Allen, G. C. *How Japan Competes*. London: Institute of Economic Affairs, 1978.

Amaya, Naohiro. "Who's Being Unfair in U.S.-Japan Trade War?" *Japan Times*. November 9, 1980.

Amaya, Naohiro. *Nihon Kabushiki Kaisha: Nokosareta Sentaku (Japan, Inc.: Our Remaining Options)*. Tokyo: PHP Press, 1982.

Anderson, Alan M. "The Great Japanese IQ Increase." *Nature*. May 20, 1982.

Anderson, Martin. *Financial Restructuring of the World Auto Industry*. Cambridge: MIT, 1982.

Asahi, Isoshi. *The Secret of Japan's Trade Expansion*. Tokyo: International Association of Japan, 1934.

Atkinson, Thomas R. *U.S. and Japanese Business Ethics and Values Contrasted*. Speech delivered to the World Council on Religion and Peace, November 10, 1983.

Baldwin, Robert E. *Trade, Growth, and the Balance of Payments*. Amsterdam: North-Holland Publishing Co., 1965.

Baldwin, Robert E. *Economic Development and Growth*. New York: John Wiley & Sons, 1966.

Baldwin, Robert E. *Non-Tariff Distortions of International Trade*. Washington, D.C.: Brookings Institution, 1970.

Baldwin, Robert E. *International Trade and Finance*. Boston: Little, Brown & Co., 1974.

Baldwin, Robert E. *The Political Economy of Postwar U.S. Trade Policy.* New York: New York University, Center for the Study of Financial Institutions, 1976.

Baldwin, Robert E. *The Multilateral Trade Negotiations: Toward Greater Liberalization?* Washington, D.C.: American Enterprise Institute for Public Policy Research, 1979.

Behrman, J. N., et al. *International Economics.* New York: Reinhart & Conway, Inc., 1957.

Bell, Daniel. *The Cultural Contradictions of Capitalism.* New York: Basic Books, 1976.

Bellah, Robert N. *Tokugawa Religion: The Values of Pre-Industrial Japan.* Glencoe, Ill.: Free Press, 1957.

Benedict, Ruth. *The Chrysanthemum and the Sword.* New York: Houghton Mifflin Co., 1946.

Bergsten, C. Fred. *Toward a New International Economic Order.* Lexington, Mass.: D. C. Heath, 1975.

Bergsten, C. Fred. "What to Do About the U.S.-Japan Economic Conflict." *Foreign Affairs.* Summer 1982.

Bergsten, C. Fred. *The Japan Problem: What Is It and What Should the U.S. Do About It?* Statement before the Subcommittee on Trade, House Ways and Means Committee, Washington, D.C., March 10, 1983.

Bidwell, Percy W. *Tariff Policy of the United States.* London: Council on Foreign Relations, 1933.

Bidwell, Percy W. *The Invisible Tariff.* New York: Council on Foreign Relations, 1939.

Bidwell, Percy W. *What the Tariff Means to American Industries.* New York: Harper & Brothers, 1956.

Blaker, Michael. *The Japanese International Negotiating Style.* New York: Columbia University Press, 1977.

Bluestone, B. "The Deindustrialization of America." *Nation.* September 11, 1982.

Bronfenbrenner, Martin. *Japanese Productivity Experience.* Unpublished manuscript. 1982.

Bylinsky, Gene. "Japan's Ominous Chip Victory." *Fortune.* December 14, 1981.

Bylinsky, Gene. "The Race to the Automatic Factory." *Fortune.* February 21, 1983.

Carlson, Jack, et al. *The Economic Importance of Exports to the United States.* Washington, D.C.: Georgetown University, 1980.

Caves, Richard E. *Industrial Organization in Japan.* Washington, D.C.: Brookings Institution, 1976.

Chamberlain, Basil Hall. *Things Japanese.* Tokyo: Charles E. Tuttle, 1971. Reprint of the 1905 edition.

Christopher, Robert C. *The Japanese Mind.* New York: Linden Press, 1983.

Clapp, Priscilla, and Morton Halperin, eds. *U.S.-Japanese Relations: The 1970s.* Cambridge: Harvard University Press, 1974.

Corrigan, Richard, et al. "In Search of an Industrial Policy." *National Journal.* February 26, 1983.

Coyle, William T. *Japan's Rice Policy*. Washington, D.C.: U.S. Department of Agriculture, 1981.

Davidson, William H. *The Amazing Race: Winning the Technorivalry with Japan*. New York: John Wiley & Sons, 1983.

Della Femina, Jerry. *From Those Wonderful Folks Who Gave Us Pearl Harbor*. New York: Simon & Schuster, 1970.

Denison, Edward F. *Why Growth Rates Differ*. Washington, D.C.: Brookings Institution, 1967.

Denison, Edward F. *Accounting for Slower Economic Growth*. Washington, D.C.: Brookings Institution, 1979.

Denison, Edward F., et al. *How Japan's Economy Grew So Fast*. Washington, D.C.: Brookings Institution, 1976.

Denny, B. C. "The High-Technology Fix: Methods of Attracting Industry." *Science*. August 27, 1982.

Destler, I. M. *The Textile Wrangle: Conflict in Japanese-American Relations*. Ithaca, N.Y.: Cornell University Press, 1979.

Destler, I. M., et al. *Managing an Alliance: The Politics of U.S.-Japan Relations*. Washington, D.C.: Brookings Institution, 1976.

Destler, I. M., et al. *Coping with U.S.-Japanese Conflicts*. Lexington, Mass.: D. C. Heath & Co., 1982.

Diebold, William. *Dollars, Jobs, Trade and Aid*. New York: Foreign Policy Association, 1972.

Diebold, William. *Industrial Policy as an International Issue*. New York: McGraw-Hill, Inc. 1980.

Drew, Elizabeth. "Equations." *New Yorker*. May 7, 1979.

Drew, Elizabeth. "Politics and Money." *New Yorker*. 12/6/82 and 12/13/82.

Drucker, Peter, et al. "On Japan." *Foreign Affairs*. April 1978.

Etzioni, Amitai. "Reindustrialization of America." *Science*. August 22, 1980.

Etzioni, Amitai. *An Immodest Agenda: Rebuilding America Before the 21st Century*. New York: McGraw-Hill, 1982.

Fallows, James. "American Industry: What Ails It, How to Save It." *Atlantic*. November 1980.

Flynn, James R. "Now the Great Augmentation of the American IQ." *Nature*. February 24, 1983.

Fuller, Mark B., et al. *Note on the World Auto Industry in Transition*. Cambridge: Harvard Business School, 1981.

Gall, Norman. "Black Ships Are Coming?" *Forbes*. January 31, 1983.

General Agreement on Tariffs and Trade (GATT). *Text of the General Agreement: Basic Instruments and Selected Documents*. Geneva: 1969.

General Agreement on Tariffs and Trade (GATT). *Japan's Economic Expansion and Foreign Trade, 1955–1970*. Geneva: 1971.

Gibney, Frank. *Miracle by Design*. New York: Times Books, 1982.

Graham, Thomas R. "Global Trade: War and Peace." *Foreign Policy*. Spring 1983.

Green, Carl J. "The New Protectionism." *Northwestern Journal of International Law and Business*. Spring 1981.

Gregory, T. E. *Memorandum on Japanese Competition*. Tokyo: Unpublished memo. 1935.

Haavind, Robert. "The U.S. Is Losing the Technology Race." *High Technology*. June 1983.

Hadley, Eleanor. *Antritrust in Japan*. Princeton, N.J.: Princeton University Press, 1970.

Hadley, Eleanor. "Industrial Policy for Competitiveness." *Journal of Japanese Trade and Industry*. September 1982.

Halloran, Richard. *Japan: Images and Realities*. New York: Alfred A. Knopf, Inc., 1969.

Hasegawa, Keitaro. *Robotto Jidai no Yomikata (Living in the Robot Age)*. Tokyo: Yodensha, 1982.

Hearn, Lafcadio. *Japan: An Interpretation*. Tokyo: Charles E. Tuttle, 1970. Reprint of the 1903 edition.

Hemmendinger, Noel. *Non-Tariff Barriers of the United States*. Washington, D.C.: United States-Japan Trade Council, 1964.

Hirsch, Fred. *Money International*. London: Penguin Books, 1969.

Hoffmann, Stanley. "The American Style: Our Past and Our Principles." *Foreign Affairs*. January 1968.

Hollerman, L. *Japan and the U.S.: Political and Economic Adversaries*. Boulder, Colo.: Westview Press, Inc., 1980.

Imai, Masaaki. *Never Take Yes for an Answer*. Tokyo: Simul Press, 1975.

Institute of East Asian Studies. *U.S.-Japan Economic Relations: A Symposium*. Berkeley: University of California Press, 1980.

International Economic Policy Association. *American Foreign Economic Strategy for the Eighties*. Washington, D.C.: 1981.

International Monetary Fund. *International Financial Statistics*. Washington, D.C.: 1980–83, various monthly reports.

Jansen, Marius B., ed. *Changing Japanese Attitudes Toward Modernization*. Princeton, N.J.: Princeton University Press, 1965.

Japan Center for International Exchange. *Dialogue with America*. New York: Japan Society, Inc., 1981.

Japan Customs Association. *Keizai Masatsu to Nihon no Taio (Economic Friction and Japan's Response)*. Tokyo: 1982.

Japan Economic Foundation. *Journal of Japanese Trade and Industry*. All issues since inception, January 1982.

Japan Economic Institute. *Japan's Import Barriers: An Analysis of Divergent Bilateral Views*. Washington, D.C.: 1982.

Japan Economic Institute. Washington, D.C.: 1982 and 1983, various economic reports.

Japan-U.S. Economic Relations Group. *Report*. (Also known as *The Wisemen's Report*.) Washington, D.C.: 1981.

JETRO. *The Japanese Market in Figures*. Tokyo: 1980.

Johnson, Chalmers. *MITI and the Japanese Miracle: The Growth of Industrial Policy, 1925–1975*. Stanford, Calif: Stanford University Press, 1982.

Jones, Joseph M. *Tariff Retaliation: Repercussions of the Hawley-Smoot Bill.* Philadelphia, Penn.: University of Philadelphia doctoral dissertation, 1934.

Kahn, Herman, et al. *The Japanese Challenge.* New York: William Morrow & Co., Inc., 1980.

Kantrow, Alan M., ed. *Survival Strategies for American Industry.* New York: John Wiley & Sons, Inc., 1983.

Kaus, Robert M. "Can Creeping Socialism Cure Creaking Capitalism?" *Harper's Magazine.* February 1983.

Kindleberger, Charles P. *Foreign Trade and the National Economy.* New Haven, Conn.: Yale University Press, 1962.

Kindleberger, Charles P. *Power and Money: The Politics of International Economics and the Economics of International Politics.* New York: Basic Books, 1970.

Kindleberger, Charles P. *The World in Depression, 1929–1939.* Berkeley: University of California Press, 1973.

Kindleberger, Charles P. *Government and International Trade.* Princeton, N.J.: International Financial Seminar, 1978.

Kindleberger, Charles P. *International Economics.* Homewood, Ill.: Richard D. Irwin, Inc., 1978.

Kraft, Joseph. "Annals of Industry: The Downsizing Decision." *New Yorker.* May 5, 1980.

Kunihiro, Masao. *Nihon to Amerika (Japan and America).* Tokyo: Eikyo, 1982.

Kuttner, Bob. "The Free Trade Fallacy." *New Republic.* March 28, 1983.

Lappé, Frances Moore. *Diet for a Small Planet, rev. ed.* New York: Ballantine Books, Inc., 1975.

Lawrence, Robert Z. *Toward a Nation of Hamburger Stands? The Impact of International Trade on U.S. Industry, 1973–1982.* Unpublished manuscript. 1983.

Lewis, Hunter, and Donald Allison. *The Real World War: The Coming Battle for the New Global Economy and Why We Are in Danger of Losing.* New York: Coward, McCann, & Geoghegan, 1982.

Lloyd, Lewis. *Tariffs: The Case for Protection.* New York: Devin-Adair Co., Inc., 1955.

Lynn, Richard. "IQ in Japan and the United States Shows a Growing Disparity." *Nature.* May 20, 1982.

Magaziner, Ira C., and Thomas M. Hout. *Japanese Industrial Policy.* London: Policy Studies Institute, 1980.

Magaziner, Ira C., and Robert B. Reich. *Minding America's Business.* New York: Harcourt Brace Jovanovich, Inc., 1982.

Mass, N. J., et al. "Reindustrialization: Aiming for the Right Targets." *Technology Review.* August/September, 1981.

Ministry of International Trade and Industry (MITI). *Hachiju Nendai no Tsusan Seisaku Bijon (Vision of International Trade and Industry Policies for the 1980s).* Tokyo: 1980.

Ministry of International Trade and Industry (MITI). *Report of the Information Industry Committee, Industrial Structure Council.* Tokyo: 1981.

Mino, Hokaji. "Nissan Reappraisals Cause Change in Tactics." *Business Japan.* December 1982.

Miyoshi, Masao. *As We Saw Them: The First Japanese Embassy to the United States, 1860.* Berkeley: University of California Press, 1979.

Monroe, Wilbur F. *Toward a More Viable U.S.-Japan Trade Relationship.* Washington, D.C.: Japan Economic Institute, 1982.

Nakane, Chie. *Tate Shakai no Ningen Kankei (The Vertical Society).* Tokyo: Kodansha, 1967.

National Academy of Engineering. *The Competitive Status of the U.S. Auto Industry: A Study of the Influences of Technology in Determining International Industrial Competitive Advantage.* Washington, D.C.: National Academy Press, 1982.

Norman, E. Herbert. *Origins of the Modern Japanese State.* Edited and with an introduction by John W. Dower. New York: Random House, Inc., 1975. Reprint of the 1940 edition.

Ohara, Keishi. *Japanese Trade and Industry in the Meiji-Taisho Era.* Tokyo: Obunsha, 1957.

Ohmae, Kenichi. *The Mind of the Strategist.* New York: McGraw-Hill, Inc., 1982.

Okita, Saburo. *Economisto Gaiso no 252 Nichi (An Economist's 252 Days as Foreign Minister).* Tokyo: Toyo Keizai Shinyosha, 1980.

Okita, Saburo. *How Can Japan and the U.S. Reduce Economic Frictions?* Washington, D.C.: National Press Club speech, May 19, 1982.

Ouchi, William G. *Theory Z.* New York: Avon Books, 1981.

Patrick, Hugh, ed. *Japanese Industrialization and its Social Consequences.* Berkeley: University of California Press, 1974.

Patrick, Hugh, et al. *Asia's New Giant.* Washington, D.C., Brookings Institution, 1976.

Patrick, Hugh, et al. *The Political Economy of U.S.-Japan Trade in Steel.* New York: Symposium on U.S.-Japan Economic Relations, March 23–27, 1981.

Peirce, Neal R., et al. "Reindustrialization: Economic Panacea or Political Mirage?" *National Journal.* October 25, 1980.

Peters, Thomas J., and Robert H. Waterman, Jr. *In Search of Excellence: Lessons from America's Best-Run Companies.* New York: Harper & Row, Publishers, 1982.

Rabinowitz, Richard W. *Law and the Social Process in Japan.* Tokyo: Asiatic Society of Japan, 1964.

Rapp, William V. "Firm Size and Japan's Export Structure: A Microview of Japan's Changing Export Competitiveness Since Meiji," in *Japanese Industrialization and Its Social Consequences*, Hugh Patrick, ed. Berkeley: University of California Press, 1974.

Rapp, William V. "Industrial Structure and Japanese Trade Friction: U.S. Policy Responses." *Journal of International Affairs.* May 1983.

Rapp, William V. *Reevaluating Past Policy Approaches to U.S.-Japan Trade Problems.* Unpublished manuscript. 1983.

Reich, Robert B. "Industries in Distress." *New Republic.* May 9, 1981.

Reich, Robert B. "Beyond Reaganomics." *New Republic.* November 18, 1981.

Reich, Robert B. *The Next American Frontier.* New York: Times Books, 1983.

Rohatyn, Felix. "Reconstructing America." *New York Review of Books.* March 5, 1981.

Rohatyn, Felix. "Time for a Change." *New York Review of Books.* August 18, 1983.

Rosovsky, Henry, ed. *Discord in the Pacific.* Washington, D.C.: Columbia Books, 1972.

Rosovsky, Henry, et al. *Japanese Economic Growth.* Stanford: Stanford University Press, 1973.

Rukeyser, Louis. *What's Ahead for the Economy: The Challenge and the Chance.* New York: Simon & Schuster, 1983.

Sadler, George E., et al. *Comparative Productivity Dynamics: Japan and the United States.* Houston, Tex.: American Productivity Center, 1982.

Sanderson, Fred S. *Irritants in U.S.-Japanese Agricultural Relations: Can Food Fill the Trade Gap?* New York: Japan Society speech, April 2, 1982.

Sanderson, Fred S. *U.S.-Japanese Agricultural Trade Problems in Perspective.* Honolulu: National Council of Farmers Cooperatives speech, January 1983.

Sansom, George B. *Japan: A Short Cultural History.* London: Barrie & Jenkins Ltd., 1931.

Sansom, George B. *The Western World and Japan.* New York: Random House, Inc., 1973.

Sayle, Murray. "Explaining Japan to America—and Vice Versa." *Harper's Magazine.* November 1982.

Scalapino, Robert A., ed. *Foreign Policy of Modern Japan.* Berkeley: University of California Press, 1977.

Schlossstein, Steven. *Japanese Foreign Direct Investment in the 1980s.* New York: Japan Society presentation, January 22, 1981.

Schlossstein, Steven. *Kensei.* New York: Congdon & Weed, Inc., 1983.

Schrank, Robert. *Ten Thousand Working Days.* Cambridge: MIT Press, 1978.

Semiconductor Industry Association. *The Effect of Government Targeting on World Semiconductor Competition: A Case History of Japanese Industrial Strategy and Its Costs for America.* Cupertino, Calif.: 1983.

Semiconductor Industry Association. *Public Policies and Strategies for U.S. High Technology Industry.* Cupertino, Calif.: 1983.

Seward, Jack. *Japanese in Action.* Tokyo: John Weatherhill, Inc., 1968.

Shapiro, Isaac. "The Risen Sun: Japanese Gaullism?" *Foreign Policy.* Winter 1980–81.

Shaplen, Robert. "Letter from Tokyo." *New Yorker.* April 6, 1981.

Shimomura, Osamu. *Nihon Keizai no Setsudo (Moderation of the Japanese Economy).* Tokyo: Toyo Keizai Shinyosha, 1981.

Shinohara, Miyohei. *Patterns of Japanese Economic Development*. New Haven, Conn.: Yale University Press, 1979.

Shiroyama, Saburo. *Kanryo-tachi no Natsu (The Summer of the Bureaucrats)*. Tokyo: Shinseibunsha, 1980.

Shiroyama, Saburo. *Yusha wa Katarazu (Heroes Don't Talk)*. Tokyo: Shinseisha, 1982.

Simic, Tomislava, ed. *Mergerstat Review*. Chicago: W. T. Grimm & Co., 1981.

Smith, Adam. *The Money Game*. New York: Dell Publishing Co., Inc., 1969.

Smith, Adam. *Supermoney*. New York: Random House, Inc., 1973.

Smith, Adam. *Paper Money*. New York: Summit Books, 1981.

Smith, Adam. "Japan's Rearmament and Reaganomics." *Esquire*. December 1982.

Snider, Delbert A. *Introduction to International Economics*. Homewood, Ill.: Richard D. Irwin, Inc., 1975.

Steiner, Jesse F. *Behind the Japanese Mask*. New York: Macmillan Co., 1943.

Storry, G. Richard. *Japan and the Decline of the West in Asia, 1894–1943*. New York: St. Martin's Press, Inc., 1979.

Sun Tzu. *The Art of War*. (Translated and with an introduction by Samuel B. Griffith.) London: Oxford University Press, 1963.

Talbot, Ross B. *The Chicken War: An International Trade Conflict Between the U.S. and the EEC*. Ames: University of Iowa Press, 1978.

Tasca, Diane, ed. *U.S.-Japanese Economic Relations: Cooperation, Competition and Confrontation*. New York: Pergamon Press, Inc., 1980.

Taylor, Jared. *Shadows of the Rising Sun: A Critical View of the Japanese Miracle*. New York: William Morrow, 1983.

Thurow, Lester C. *The Zero-Sum Society*. New York: Basic Books, Inc., Publishers, 1980.

Toland, John. *The Rising Sun*. New York: Random House, Inc., 1970.

Trollope, Mrs. Anthony. *Domestic Manners of the Americans*. London: Whittaker, Treacher, 1832.

Tsoukalis, Loukas, et al. *Japan and Western Europe: Conflict and Cooperation*. London: Frances Pinter, 1982.

U.S. Congress, Joint Economic Committee. *1983 Economic Report of the President*. Washington, D.C.: 1983.

U.S. Congress, Office of Technology Assessment. *U.S. Industrial Competitiveness: A Comparison of Steel, Electronics and Automobiles*. Washington, D.C.: 1981.

U.S. Congress, Office of Technology Assessment. *International Competitiveness in Electronics*. Washington, D.C.: 1983.

U.S. Department of Commerce. *Highlights of U.S. Export and Import Trade (FT 990)*. Washington, D.C.: December 1980, 1981, 1982.

U.S. Department of Commerce. *Serving the Nation*. Washington, D.C.: 1981.

U.S. Department of Commerce. *Survey of Current Business*. Washington, D.C.: 1980–83, various monthly reports.

U.S. Department of Commerce. *Annual Report of the Secretary, FY 1982*. Washington, D.C.: 1982.

U.S. Department of Labor. *Hourly Compensation Costs for Production Workers in Motor Vehicles and Equipment Manufacturing, 14 Countries, 1975–1982.* Washington, D.C.: 1982.

U.S. General Services Administration. *The United States Government Manual, 1982/83.* Washington, D.C.: Office of the Federal Register, 1982.

U.S. House of Representatives. *Trade Act of 1974.* Washington, D.C.: 1975.

U.S. House of Representatives. *Trade Agreements Act of 1979.* Washington, D.C.: 1979.

U.S. House of Representatives. "The Export Trading Company Act of 1982." *Congressional Record.* July 27, 1982.

U.S. House of Representatives, Committee on Foreign Affairs. *United States-Japan Relations.* Hearings before the subcommittees on International Economic Policy and Trade and on Asian and Pacific Affairs. Washington, D.C.: 1982.

U.S. House of Representatives, Committee on Ways and Means, Subcommittee on Trade. *Task Force Report on United States-Japan Trade.* Washington, D.C.: 1979.

U.S. House of Representatives, Committee on Ways and Means, Subcommittee on Trade. *High Technology and Japanese Industrial Policy: A Strategy for U.S. Policymakers.* Washington, D.C.: 1980.

U.S. House of Representatives, Committee on Ways and Means, Subcommittee on Trade. *United States-Japan Trade Report.* Washington, D.C.: 1980.

U.S. International Trade Commission. *Rules of Practice and Procedure.* Washington, D.C.: 1983.

U.S. International Trade Commission. Various reports to the president on investigations under Section 201 of the Trade Act of 1974.

U.S.-Japan Trade Study Group. *Japan: Obstacles and Opportunities.* Tokyo: President, Inc., 1983.

U.S. Senate, Committee on Finance. *International Trade and Investment Act.* Washington, D.C.: March 14, 1983.

U.S. Senate, 98th Congress, 1st Session. *Department of Trade and Commerce Act of 1983.* Washington, D.C.: January 25, 1983.

U.S. Trade Representative. *A Preface to Trade.* Washington, D.C.: 1982.

Vogel, Ezra. *Japan as Number One.* Tokyo: Charles E. Tuttle, 1980.

Weil, Frank A. "U.S. Industrial Policy: A Case for and Outline of a Federal Industrial Coordination Board." *Law and Policy in International Business.* March 1983.

Wheeler, Jimmy W., et al. *Japanese Industrial Development Policies in the 1980s: Implications for U.S. Trade and Investment.* Croton-on-Hudson, N.Y.: Hudson Institute, 1982.

Wilkinson, Endymion. *Misunderstanding: Europe vs. Japan.* Tokyo: Chuokoronsha, 1981.

Williams, R. "Reindustrialization Past and Present." *Technology Review.* November/December, 1982.

Yamaguchi, H. S. K. *We Japanese.* Yokohama: Yamagata Press, 1934.

Yamamura, Kozo, ed. *Policy and Trade Issues of the Japanese Economy: American and Japanese Perspectives.* Seattle: University of Washington Press, 1982.

Yankelovich, Daniel. *New Rules: Searching for Self-fulfillment in a World Turned Upside Down.* New York: Random House, Inc., 1981.

Yankelovich, Skelly & White. *Meeting Japan's Challenge: The Need for Leadership.* New York: 1982.

Zenchu (Central Union of Agricultural Cooperatives). *Dai Jurokukai: Zenkoku Nogyo Kyodo Kumiai Taikai Gian (Report on the Sixteenth Conference of the National Agricultural Cooperatives).* Tokyo: October 1982.

Zenchu. *Naze Norinbutsu no Yunyu Jiyuka to Waku Kakudai ni Hantai suru ka (Why We Are Opposed to Agricultural Import Liberalization and Quota Expansion).* Tokyo: 1982.

Zenchu. *Nihon Nogyo no Tenbo to Nokyo no Nogyo Shinko Hosaku (Japan's Agricultural Perspective and Central Cooperative Promotion Plans).* Tokyo: 1982.

Zenchu. *Zenchu Position on the Japan Farm Product Import Liberalization Issue.* Tokyo: May 1982.

Zysman, John, et al. *Controlled Opening of the Japanese Market: Or, the Lyrics Change but the Malady Lingers On.* Berkeley: Roundtable on the International Economy, unpublished memorandum. 1982.

ACKNOWLEDGMENTS

The radio talk show host threw me a slider to kick off his program.

"In the wake of the IBM-Hitachi scandal," he began, "are we likely to see more cases of Japanese industrial espionage?"

We were sitting in a California station about to discuss bilateral economic and political issues between America and Japan, and the trick, he had told me only minutes before, was to open with a quick question, followed by a quick answer, then a switch to the sound studio for the show's introductory jingle. I had ten seconds to answer.

"In the *wake* of the IBM-Hitachi scandal?" I repeated, live, on the air. That took about five seconds.

The interviewer nodded silently. We both glanced at the studio clock. The sweep hand looked like a small guillotine, chopping off the seconds.

"Not likely," I said. I was frowning.

Then the jingle came, right on schedule, and we proceeded to walk systematically through the standard array of topics: the Japanese work ethic, their supposedly "closed" market, their unfair trading practices, their product superiority, their management style. None of this was rehearsed.

That first question bothered me, however, not so much because it was unexpected, but because it carried a hidden assumption. Namely, that we *were* likely to see more Japanese spies arrested in Silicon Valley, especially since high-tech competition between the two countries has become so intense and the stakes—industrial supremacy—are so high.

But that hidden assumption went even further: it suggested that the Japanese would be so stupid as to get *caught* next time. That's why, with a frown, I repeated the question, and why I followed with a two-word response.

People in broadcasting tell you that when you're on the air, ten seconds is like ten days. It's not true. If we had had ten days, I probably would have said something like, "Not likely. Why? Because if the IBM-Hitachi case, with all its attendant publicity, has taught the Japanese *anything*, it is that they must be extra diligent in the future, not that they have to cut it out. Which raises the obvious question: since they feel their educational systems and their product quality and their management techniques are so superior to ours anyway, why do they feel it is necessary to engage in industrial espionage at all?

"Well, Sun Tzu had the answer to that. Sun Tzu was a contemporary of Confucius who laid the groundwork for Chinese military strategy thousands of years ago. (And the Japanese have borrowed Chinese military strategy, although they may not admit it, just as they borrowed all those Chinese ideographs and Confucianism itself.) One thing Sun Tzu said was, know your enemy better than he knows you. An important corollary was, one spy in the enemy camp is worth 10,000 foot soldiers. So the Japanese will no doubt continue their covert activity, but they just won't allow themselves to get caught again."

This book has many debts, besides that to Sun Tzu, which I gratefully acknowledge.

First, to Bill Rapp, currently Commercial Counselor at the U.S. Embassy in Tokyo and a former colleague at Morgan, who over the years has shared countless thoughts and ideas regarding Japanese economic and commercial strategies, and to Dennis Helms, of Knipe & Helms in Princeton, who knows the merits of the simple declarative sentence and who gave invaluable advice on the manuscript, very special thanks. Both individuals served as helpful sounding boards, above and beyond the call of friendship.

Thanks also to Timothy Curran, previously Research Associate with the East Asian Institute at Columbia University in New York, and to Frank Weil, formerly affiliated with Ginsburg, Feldman, Weil & Bress in Washington and a past Assistant Secretary of Commerce for Industry and Trade, both of whom graciously read and commented on the first draft of the manuscript.

To the many friends in Tokyo, in New York, and in Washington—businessman and bureaucrat alike—who suggested yet another source, or arranged yet another meeting, or provided yet another introduction, I am most grateful. In Tokyo, Ishikawa Takenori, Nakagawa Katsuhiro, Yamada Taisei, John Christensen, Steve Lohr, and Jack Loughran deserve special mention, as do Tom Atkinson, Sandy Burton, Isayama Takeshi, and Mizutani Shiro in New York. In Washington, Mac Destler, Ed Lincoln, Wilbur Monroe, Nanya Katsuhide, and Susan Schwab provided valuable assistance.

To the research librarians and staff of Princeton University's Firestone Library—notably its Social Science Reference Center—and the Princeton and New York Public Libraries, special thanks for special help.

To my Apple-III 128K professional computer, on which the manuscript was entirely created, composed, edited, revised, and printed—without eating a single disk, without losing a single byte of memory, and without taking a single day off—well, how do you go about thanking a *machine*? Still, what the microprocessor has done for the writing profession has to be experienced to be believed.

To my editor, Peter Weed, thanks not only for suggesting the market could stomach *another* book on Japan, but also for smoothing out a choppy manuscript and sculpting a mature irreverence from a more impetuous beginning. Editors, if they are very good, are hard to find. Peter is one of the best. He rightfully deserves credit for making the book work, although the opinions and judgments expressed herein are entirely my own.

And, finally, to my precious daughter, Claire Verity, a quiet *domo* for coming into this world at just the right time.

Princeton, New Jersey
December 1983

INDEX